Killing for Britain

John Black

Published 2008 by Frontline Noir Publishing,
an imprint of Books Noir, Scotland

A CIP catalogue record for this book is available from
the British Library.

ISBN: 978 1 904684 99 2

Printed and bound in the UK

CONTENTS

FOREWORD

JOHN BLACK HAS written a very important book. *Killing for Britain* is another significant chapter in the as yet unfinished history of Northern Ireland's 'Dirty War'. Slowly, ever so slowly, the carefully constructed British cover up designed to conceal the actions and activities of the intelligence agencies is unravelling. Bit by bit the defensive wall is crumbling as more and more people gain the courage to speak out and reveal what really happened here in this small but troubled province. What was once a trickle of information has now become a steady stream! John Black's book will add to that flow.

There are those within the British Establishment who, come hell and high water, will never admit to what went on within the murky and extremely dangerous world of counter-terrorist operations. But, they would do well to remember the old adage – the truth has a habit of seeping out when least expected.

There are also those within the unionist community who, to the day they die, will dismiss as nonsense the very idea of state sanctioned murder. The suggestion that the state to which they espoused loyalty all their lives would ever operate in such a devious and ruthless fashion is abhorrent to them. The very idea members of their own community were recruited, trained and used as tools of the state to carry out acts of murder simply beggars belief. But, its time they wake up and faced reality – it did happen. Killing for Britian is yet further proof – if indeed more were needed – of what happened out the outset of more than 30 years of violence in Northern Ireland. The state was complicit in murder.

Loyalists and their paramilitary organisations were fertile recruiting areas for RUC Special Branch and Military Intelligence in the early years of the 'Troubles'. At that time Northern Ireland was in turmoil. Civil War appeared inevitable. The IRA were killing soldiers and members of the RUC on a regularly basis. Republican bombs were ripping the commercial heart out of major towns across the province. Nothing – it appeared - could be done to halt the campaign of carnage and destruction. The loyalist/unionist community was devoid of the proper leadership it so desperately needed at that time. Defence of family, friends and home became a priority. Revenge also became a major issue in the mindset of many within the loyalist community. It was a time to stand up and be counted and many young protestant joined the ranks of the UVF or UDA simply because they thought it was the right thing to do at the time. However, the loyalist paramilitaries lacked the required training, equipment and intelligence to enable them to take the war to the IRA. Enter the Military Reconnaissance Force (MRF) a specialist unit within the British Army's military intelligence network. Based at Palace barracks, Holywood the MRF came into being in mid 1971. As well as carrying out undercover operations in the early 1970's MRF soldiers also recruited members of loyalist and republican paramilitary organisations.

Killing for Britain is one mans personal account of what it was like to work for the MRF. John Black's book is an in-depth, chilling insight into what really happened in those early days more than thirty years ago. It literally lifts the lid on a previously hidden and suppressed chapter of Northern Ireland's bloody history. One of the most important features of Black's book is his exposition of the manner in which MRF 'securo-crats' callously decided who should live and who should die. As in later years London dictated operation policy to further its own political ends. A strategy so successful that it persisted for over 3 decades before eventually culminated in the signing of the Belfast Agreement in April 1998.

The MRF's objective was basic – by arming and training loyalist death squads to kill Catholics they hoped to pressurise the Provisional IRA into abandoning their military campaign. History has already delivered its verdict on that particular ill-conceived concept!

I shall not in this forward, try to summarise the absorbing and shocking episodes which form *Killing for Britain*. These are both complex and disturbing and my attempt to summarise them by compression would simply distort and spoil the book for the reader. I should, however, ask the reader to consider one particular theme which runs through the book – complicity. Respectable Ireland – North and South – businessmen, clerics, professional classes and politicians have throughout the history of the Troubles condemned the numerous atrocities carried out by loyalist and republican paramilitaries. Yet all parties, in one way or another, have helped prolong the very existence of these same organisations. The distinctly shabby role played by some senior British politicians who either condoned or turned a blind eye to breaches of law and order by the security forces in the early years of the Troubles must also be condemned.

Writing about Northern Ireland's 'Dirty War' also comes with price, as those of us who have already done so can testify. You need courage and support to take on the British Establishment which has its own predictable way of dealing with allegations and claims of state sponsored killing. It simply closes ranks, rides the storm, assesses the situation and fights a defensive rearguard action down the line. If a 'defensive wall' is breached, another stands immediately behind it ready to stall those who dare to attack the system. It is a process that has proven to be effective in the past. Because of that success it is a system that will be used again when the need arises. I have absolutely no doubt that same rear-guard defensive action will be applied in respect of the allegations contained in *Killing for Britain*.

John Black's account of what really happened over 30 years ago is a disturbing and startling account of the actions of the Military Reconnaissance Force. I trust the majority of those who take the time to read *Killing for Britain* will agree the truth about Northern Ireland's 'Dirty War' must be exposed. We are moving forward but the bloody history of the Troubles must be confronted and laid to rest otherwise it will simply return and haunt future generations in the years to come.

Chris Anderson October 2008

ACKNOWLEDGEMENTS

I WANT TO put on record my debt of gratitude to the various writers whose works I have referred to for background material and sundry facts. Notable among these are: *Those are Real Bullets, aren't They?* by Peter Pringle and Philip Jacobson; *The Dirty War* and *The Shankill Butchers* by Martin Dillon; *Faith and Duty* by Nicky Curtis; *Lost Lives* by David McKittrick, Seamus Kelters, Brian Feeney and Chris Thornton; and the Conflict Archive on the Internet project website, http://cain.ulst.ac.uk, created by Martin Melaugh. I have written this book to demonstrate how facts can be looked at in different ways. If nothing else I hope this exercise in non-fiction may alert a few more readers to the betrayal of trust committed during the 'Long War' by Governments, politicians, religious leaders and many others, both here and in America. I must also humbly thank a wonderful person and truly remarkable friend, Cecilie, without whom this work would never have reached the publisher in the first place. She was always there when I needed support in completing the script, when I was ready to pack in the whole project and dump it in the bin. Her contribution to correcting the grammatical mistakes and rewriting parts of the manuscript was invaluable. She took a rough piece of granite and gave me back a polished version. I must mention the help received from Bob Smith, my publisher, who advised and helped throughout the process. And a big thanks to Martin Ingram for pointing me in the right direction in the first place.

AUTHOR'S NOTE

EVERY SINGLE PIECE of information and incident described
in this book is based on actual events which took place at
the beginning of Northern Ireland's latest round of Troubles.
A key characteristic of this conflict was the need for absolute confidentiality on all sides, especially true in terms of the
Government, including all Intelligence Services, MI5, MI6 and
the Army's own Intelligence Agencies. Covert activities had
to be carried out with careful, necessary and devious methods. Surreptitious activities are like muddy water, especially in
Northern Ireland. You lie to your enemy and then you spy on
them. What you later learn is that the lie becomes the truth,
because it has been re-categorised as intelligence. Deniability is
a fundamental part of this subversive world.

After I started to write this account I read a lot of books
dealing with the Troubles. I did this to see if anyone else who
was involved in operations had already put these facts into the
public domain, before I myself tried to get these facts published. Unfortunately no one had so it was up to me to set the
record straight. It's time all those relatives who lost loved ones
knew the truth about how and why those people were singled
out and murdered.

In order to draw the IRA into a sectarian war, the Military
Reconnaissance Force (MRF) used Loyalist paramilitaries as
their weapons to incite a sectarian conflict, in order to weaken

the Provisionals' (Provos') support within the Catholic community. We knew that ordinary Catholics would be targeted but we were also led to believe that many of the people who were being targeted were either Republicans or at the very least supported them. Loyalists were just given the name, time and place where the target would be, then in, do the job and out again. Protected by the MRF's code of practice, an OOB (Out of Bounds call). At the time Loyalists never worried who the targets were, they just carried out the job; Catholics or Republicans, kill them all, let God sort them out, was the Loyalist motto.

John Black October 2008

For Cecilie, Janie and the many other very good friends who didn't want their names included in this dedication who brought some joy and happiness into a troubled, traumatised and deranged soul, helping to create a little peaceful island to which it could retreat when chaos and turmoil reigned in its mind and memories brought it close to madness. Thanks to one and all.

This book is a warning to those who say it couldn't happen again and a reminder that there are many who wish it could. Remember: out of chaos comes order, but to achieve order we must first have chaos.

Some commentators have described Loyalists as monsters and criminals. This book will show that, whatever they were, they were often acting on MRF orders. The MRF in turn claimed they were simply carrying out instructions that came ultimately from the British Government. In my view, we were not criminals – we were proxy soldiers.

PROLOGUE

THIS BOOK IS aimed at many people, especially any young person born since 1969 in Northern Ireland, who by the time they were 15 or 16 became involved in sectarian conflict and joined paramilitary organisations in the 1980s.

From the beginning of 1971 until the end of 1976 over 1,800 people were killed. As the total number of people who died in the 30 years of conflict is in the region of 3,600, half of them died in those killing years.

Most people know the Republican side of the story, especially in the United States where many people gave money and support to the IRA, and thought of them as freedom fighters, not terrorists. It wasn't until that ill-fated day, now referred to as 9/11, that they suddenly realised what the innocent Protestant and Catholic communities in Northern Ireland had suffered for 30 years. This book, I hope, will help them to comprehend the violent reaction Loyalists were forced to take, to try to halt the Provos' onslaught on a way of life and religious belief.

The book covers actions committed by normal young men who took up arms and became killers and bombers. I have attempted to describe what it was like back in the early 1970s when almost every news bulletin was about men, women and children being murdered. There were nocturnal gun battles and the bombing campaign reached its peak, disturbing people's sleep at night and their normal daily lives. By the 1980s, due to the experience gained by the Security Forces in the 1970s, they were able to bring the situation down to what became known as 'an acceptable level of violence'.

Many Republicans will have waited for this book for years. There has indeed been a direct link between British Military Intelligence and Loyalist Paramilitaries or Loyalist death squads, as Republicans liked to call them. It must have been obvious to most people that there was something odd going on, when so many people were being killed and very few were ever caught. Or in the case of Billy Wright, assassinated in prison, in front of prison warders and under very suspicious circumstances.

I was one of those men who took to the streets as a vigilante and the last thing on my mind was that I was going to murder someone while patrolling the streets. Of course it did come to that for some at a later stage, but only, in my view, when it came to the point of no return, when the Irish Republican Army (IRA) finally pushed Loyalists over the edge and revenge took over.

I want to point out that not all the men and women who joined Loyalist Paramilitaries were psychopathic killers, as some writers and journalists try to make out. We were normal human beings who thought our country was going to be forced to amalgamate with the Irish Republic. It was a time to stand up and be counted, as our country was being torn apart and the hearts of our towns and cities were being ripped asunder by the relentless thunder and assault of bombs. Our policemen and soldiers were being picked off and killed on a regular basis; they seemed powerless to do anything to stop the onslaught. Civil war was looming on the horizon. Some well known politicians and religious leaders were preaching doom and gloom.

Defending our families, homes and neighbourhoods became our priority. Unfortunately, the violence did attract natural born killers, on both sides of the divide. They were the men who were detrimental and damaging (to the genuine guys, whose only crime was loyalty), and their personalities and actions have very much overshadowed the rest. That is not to say that people like the Shankill Butchers (UVF) and C Company (UFF) didn't have the effect and desire they intended. They instilled fear and terror, amongst the Catholic community and probably amongst the Protestant community as well.

I have remained silent throughout the years, knowing my life would be in danger if I revealed what went on in the first years of the conflict and the part played by the Intelligence Agencies of Her Majesty's Government. Back in the 1970s no one ever thought what we were getting involved in would last as long as it did and cost so many lives. We all believed if the Catholic population were hit hard it would force the Provisionals to end their own campaign of violence. How wrong can people be? It took 30 years and 3,600 deaths before it eventually, and arguably, worked.

I made up my mind to write this book in the hope that it would deter anyone from joining any paramilitary organisation. If it succeeds in preventing at least one young person from doing so, it will have achieved its goal.

I will outline the role the British Government played in the above, through Military Intelligence, in training, arming and moulding squads of Loyalists, for their own purposes and to put pressure on the Provisional IRA (PIRA) to abandon their campaign of bloodshed and carnage. We were going to take the war to the Republican movement; all the British Army was doing was helping us to achieve what we were determined to do anyway and protecting us while doing it. Basically, the correct term to describe us would be auxiliary or proxy soldiers. We were to be used in circumstances that normal soldiers couldn't be involved in. (This was deemed a crime and many lost their freedom, sometimes many years after the operation was successfully carried out and their way in and out had been protected by OOBs at the time, without their knowledge. A prime example was the bomb attack on McGurk's Bar. After seven years, the driver of the car that night confessed to his part in the attack.)

This book also demonstrates that the Criminal Justice System was corrupt. Men caught, and who subsequently made statements admitting their part in a crime, were found not guilty and released, when pressure was put on judges to have the men set free. Not only were judges playing the game, agents of the Government were likewise manipulating the Director of Public Prosecutions and charges were being dropped. In one mysterious case, a judge wouldn't do what he was being asked; some years later, he and his wife were set up and blown to pieces by the PIRA while crossing the border on the way home from a holiday. I have my doubts. It looked very suspicious. Personally, I wouldn't look past Her Majesty's Intelligence Services as the culprits, possibly passing the information on to the IRA. They really were a law unto themselves.

There have been many revelations about the role of the Force Research Unit (FRU) in the late 1980s and early 1990s. I look at how it all began, with the undercover Army unit (the Military Reconnaissance Force) who did the groundwork for whichever name the subsequent units called themselves.

What you are about to read will shock you but it will give you some insight into what went through young minds as they watched their country being blown to pieces and friends being shot dead on the very streets where they once played together. Try to picture how you would react if chaos reigned all around you, in a situation where your own life, or those of your family and friends, was not a promise any more.

When I joined the Ulster Volunteer Force (UVF) in the early

1970s, I thought it was right and necessary. The country was in turmoil. It really did seem as if civil war was just around the corner. I joined in order to defend my homeland from the danger of being overrun by Republican terrorists. We went from a defensive position to an offensive one as the body count rose and the country descended into total anarchy.

Since the 9/11 atrocities, when America and indeed the world felt threatened, terror has now spread throughout the world and no one feels safe. This sums up how ordinary, decent, law-abiding citizens felt when they saw the fabric of their society being undermined and eroded before their very eyes. It was exactly the same thing, on a smaller scale. The hearts of our cities and towns were being systematically blown to Kingdom come. Many men took to the streets to protect their homes and family. But this was deemed illegal for some in Northern Ireland and many ended up in prison or dead, for trying to protect their country. It's all right for the authorities to kill, but when you try to defend and protect your homes and family, you are a criminal.

I know many people are going to say that a lot of innocent Catholics were killed. True, but this was considered a war situation, just like Afghanistan, Bosnia and the two Gulf Wars, when innocent civilians were killed by American and British bombs and put down as casualties of war. Sometimes, as in all wars, mistakes were made. That said, there were times when innocent Catholics were targeted just to instill fear and get revenge for some atrocity committed by the PIRA.

I know of times when such operations were sanctioned by London, to hit hard and try to cause maximum death and destruction in order to score points in the political arena. The Secret Services could not do it all by themselves, so they enlisted men and provided the arms, explosives and expertise to carry out their dirty work. They were very careful in their selection, picking dedicated, sincere men with no criminal records to become low-profile, highly trained operators. These men in turn trained other members of their teams. They covered their arses as much as possible so that nothing or at least very little could be traced back to them.

In the early 1970s they enlisted people who were hell-bent on revenge, people who had lost relatives or friends to some PIRA murderous attack. They preyed on the vulnerable, people who were distressed after burying their loved ones; brothers, sons, uncles, friends. Sitting in bars, after funerals, listening to conversations when people talked of revenge, they would hone in on any individuals who looked promising, then do a bit of research on who they were, check out any connections to the Paramilitaries and so on, and approach and offer help in achieving it.

On 2 December 2001, US Defence Secretary Donald Rumsfeld paid tribute to Britain's help and support of the US since 11 September 2001. I quote: 'In the war against global terrorism, Americans have no greater ally than Great Britain. That is because the British people know that the events of September 11 were more than acts of terror, they were an assault on the traditions of freedom and religious toleration that are the common patrimony of both our nations.'

Inspiring words. It's a pity Rumsfeld, Bush Junior and Blair were not in power in the early 1970s when the PIRA were doing exactly the same thing – killing innocent civilians – as Osama Bin Laden did in New York on that tragic day in 2001. It may have been on a smaller scale, but tell that to the people killed, maimed or injured in the Bloody Friday bombings or the La Mon House Hotel fire bombing, and many others, that this was not an attack on their freedom or religious toleration.

Adams and McGuinness are brilliant strategists. They knew

the British had had enough and wanted out of Ireland, just as they had given up most of the Empire. Once the Provisionals were able to bomb the commercial heart of London, John Major's Government contacted them regarding a negotiation. In this instance, I must give the Republicans their dues. They had worked it well. Johnny Adair's team was hammering them, but that one bombing in London meant they could negotiate with the British Government from strength.

As a journalist once said, 'When is a terrorist not a terrorist? When he works for Military Intelligence.'

Go back to the early days, 1972 to be exact. The events of Bloody Sunday shocked the world. As you will see later in the book, Lord Chief Justice, Lord Widgery's tribunal report, published in April of that year, largely exonerated the Army of any blame. This was another whitewash. What I am about to disclose was witnessed by me at that time, and it reveals a whole new dimension to the atrocity committed that day. The most recent Bloody Sunday inquiry ended in 2004. The Saville Tribunal lasted seven years. 433 days later, and hearing the evidence will have cost in the region of at least £200 million. It heard from 921 witnesses and 1,551 people provided written statements. In a newspaper report, Christopher Clarke's closing statement was as follows: 'Even after many days of evidence, the answer to even the first question, Who shot them?, is not, on the soldiers' evidence, in anyway clear.' Mr Clarke was also critical of the planning by military chiefs on the days before the march.

When you join a paramilitary organisation, no matter on which side, you do not join a democracy; you join a ruthless dictatorship where you do as you're told or suffer severe punishment and even death for not carrying out orders. The fact is, the more ruthless you are, the higher you rise in the ranks. You rule by fear. It is necessary because, when you are controlling men who have access to guns and are not afraid of using them, you could end up looking down the wrong end of the barrel. Unfortunately, sometimes this strategy backfired, and you became too big for your boots, went out of control, and thought no one could touch you.

You get too cocky and think everyone is afraid of you; basically, do whatever you want. There have been quite a few throughout the Troubles, Lenny Murphy, Jimmy Craig and Dominic McGlinchey, to name but a few, who were killed because people feared them. They became too dangerous, even to their own, and got to the stage where they became gangsters, lining their own pockets or colluding with the other side. When you get to that stage, you will inevitably get on the wrong side of someone just as ruthless, and get taken out.

As the Troubles progressed, the attitude and dedication to the defence of Ulster became a determination to fight and defeat what we saw as the Pan Nationalist Front. But then gangsterism and the quest of power became the priority of certain leaders of the Loyalist Paramilitary groups. The lure of big money from drugs and other illegal scams took over, which resulted in a bloody conflict in 2000. Men were killed and families were put out of their homes, including the ex-leader of the UVF, Gusty Spence, and resulted in the leader of the UFF, Johnny Adair, having his licence revoked and being returned to prison.

The people looked for their protectors only to find they were the oppressors. They went from saving them from a fate worse than death to killing and destroying lives with their drugs and wars.

In 2005 the UVF were back on the streets of Belfast, killing more Protestants, only now the Loyalist Volunteer Force was their target. I read in the *Sunday World* newspaper of 14 August that year, that the disgraced UVF man Jackie Mahood was Brigadier-in-Chief of the Loyalist Volunteer Force (LVF) and he was fed up with the drug dealing, racketeering and general criminality of the LVF. He was almost killed on a number of occasions by UVF attacks for his criminal deeds.

Regarding British Government and Security Services' dirty tricks, obviously, there is little hard evidence, but there is enough circumstantial evidence, within the records of the judicial system, to at least open people's minds and plant questions of doubt about why so many people could be murdered with very few convictions ever obtained? It has got to the point where a special task force of ex-detectives, the Historical Enquiries Team, has been set up to try to solve over 2,000 unsolved murders. As I said earlier, everything was done with the view that, if anyone tried to prove the intelligence connection, it could and would be emphatically denied.

Maybe, some day, the whole truth will come to light, but I doubt it. In all probability the integrity of successive Governments could be called into question. The answers would, more than likely, be highly embarrassing to all concerned. They sanctioned many covert activities and, indeed, one of the most controversial (and not so secret) incidents, the Bloody Sunday Massacre. My personal account is in chapter three.

As the UVF motto says, 'For God and Ulster': if there is such a person as God, may he forgive us, for all we have done in his name. I would like to make clear that all the emotions – good and bad – expressed in this book about the atrocities that were committed are mine alone. In no way do they relate to those of anyone involved in producing this book. While these feelings were genuine at the time, they do not reflect how I feel now. I feel a deep regret and despair at all those futile deaths. May your god go with you.

John Black October 2008

PUBLISHER'S NOTE

WHEN THIS TYPESCRIPT first landed on my desk, I was incredulous. During several years of publishing I have met many individuals involved in many organisations – Loyalist, Republican, British Military, Intelligence Services, RUC and others – so I receive many scripts of a controversial (sometimes even of a dubious) nature. This makes me sceptical when spectacular claims are made: life is too short to investigate outlandish claims and often I don't even finish a script that seems outrageous. However, I did finish *Killing for Britain*. I was impressed by the level of detail, and by the fact that there were clearly two stories being told – that of the Troubles from one man's perspective, and, more interestingly, that of one man's life being shaped by the Troubles.

Initially, I brushed off the incident of the author having been taken out in uniform by the British Army on Bloody Sunday as an exaggeration, but, after careful re-reading of the text, I realised it had to be either the truth, or a downright lie – there was no in-between regarding this claim.

In the course of my research I managed to confirm that the MRF did indeed take people to Palace Barracks in 1971/72 (and beyond) and train them in arms, espionage and counter interrogation techniques. So, with the concept of the British training Loyalists as well as Republican 'touts' to tackle the IRA firmly established, it was not a gigantic leap to consider the next logical step – the training of 'counter-gangs' (as the British had done in many colonial and post-colonial outposts from Kenya to Aden). In fact, it would have been exceptional had collusion not existed. Are we really to believe that Northern Ireland was the exception to the rule, and that for the first time the British decided not to, in the words of one military man, 'employ and destroy' (i.e. employ your friends to destroy your enemies)? Now that would have been incredible.

Firstly, consider the UVF in Portadown and elsewhere. Some of them were also members of the UDR, the locally recruited force of the British Army. In this basic sense, the British already had Loyalist 'terrorists' out on patrol in British uniform. So how much more of a leap is it really to consider the claims in this book?

One former soldier thought it credible that 'a handful' of Loyalists were taken to Palace Barracks to be 'indoctrinated' and 'made to feel like soldiers'. Another source suggested that there was at times almost an unofficial, parallel structure that seemed to be operating on orders 'from others'. He later confirmed that he meant MI6. This was in 1971 and 1972.

I came across tales of Loyalist and Republican 'touts' being taken variously to Wales, Scotland and English country estates for training in weapons, torture techniques etc. 'Basher' Bates, one of the infamous Shankill Butchers, was said to have been a British Army deserter. One source stated his unequivocal belief that Bates 'never deserted, but was sent to Belfast, with his local knowledge, with the intention of leading a counter gang'. Raymond Murray's book, *The SAS in Ireland* (Mercier Press, 2005) refers specifically to this possibility. 'Kevin Fulton', the British soldier from Newry who infiltrated the IRA for MI, told me he was recruited in a similar fashion in the late 1970s.

Far from being outrageous, the author's claims appear to tie in to an established pattern. You may have the same initial re-action I did, but once you acclimatise to the claims, consider this. What is in it for the author? If some of his claims might discredit the whole book, why did he not take the easy op-tion and leave them out? The book would work perfectly well without them.

Having met the author dozens of times over the last two years, I became convinced that he was telling the truth as he understands it. Liars and fantasists are of course able to fool people, and I don't claim to be a detective or psychologist – ultimately, one has to trust one's own experience and judge-ment. It is clear that John Black is a man determined to tell the truth for various reasons. Firstly, no one else has told the story; Black realised that the onus was on him to do so. Secondly, he suffered a stroke a few years ago and surviving it spurred him on to complete the text and get the truth out there. I am also convinced the major motivation was cathartic. Writing books can be a form of therapy, particularly when describing horrific events. I am certain this is the case here.

Bob Smith
Publisher

1968–70 THE EARLY YEARS

1968 The Beginning

ON SATURDAY, 24 August 1968, the first civil rights march was organised by the Campaign for Social Justice, the Northern Ireland Civil Rights Association and a number of other groups. The march was to set off from Coalisland and finish in Dungannon. Loyalists organised a counter demonstration in an attempt to get the march banned. In fact, the planned rally was banned – a tactic used throughout the Troubles. Despite the ban, the civil rights march took place and passed off without incident. The publicity encouraged other protesting groups to form branches of the Northern Ireland Civil Rights Association.

I had just turned 20, never voted, and enjoyed my work as a trainee manager in a large company near the docks. I was unaware of the differences between one side and the other. I recollect asking one old man in the firm, just coming up to our holidays (the Twelfth Fortnight as it was called, when most of Northern Ireland closed down), if he was going to watch the Orangemen walk on the Twelfth of July.

He looked at me as though I had two heads and replied, 'No, I don't think so.'

I wondered why the men beside us all started to laugh. Later, one of the men explained that old such and such had been an IRA man in the 1950s. I asked who or what was the IRA, that's how naïve I was. It was soon explained to me and he pointed out that, while there were some Catholics working down in the yard, if I checked, I would find there were no Catholics employed in the office. I checked what I'd been told. He was right. The manager was an Orangeman and had a policy of not employing Catholics in the office. A big man I worked with in despatch loved the Orange Order and held some office in the hierarchy of the Order. He always tried his best to get me to join. I never did.

While I watched the drama unfolding on the streets of Northern Ireland, I was also engrossed by what I was observing on television. I asked my parents to explain why these people were protesting and what their problems were. What did one-man, one-vote mean? What was the Special Powers Act? God help them, they tried their best to explain. I became obsessed with it all and wanted to know more and more, about what was going on in my country. It was all new to me and I wanted to increase my knowledge of past events in the history of Northern Ireland. I couldn't get enough information and kept asking men in work what they could tell me. I went to the library and got books on Irish history. I was fascinated to learn about how the state of Northern Ireland was formed, of the trials and tribulations endured by the people in order to stay within the United Kingdom and of the armed struggle by the IRA to achieve an all Irish Republic.

My mother had grown up in a street just next to the New Lodge Road. She told me of the time when there used to be an Orange Arch at the top of the New Lodge Road and the Catholics came up to the Eleventh Night bonfire, joined in the party and really enjoyed themselves. Then, on the Twelfth

Day, they went down to Royal Avenue in the centre of town and watched the parade. It all started to sink in and I began to understand why we were celebrating King William III, Prince of Orange's victory over King James II at the Boyne River. Although I knew there had been a famous battle and the gates of Londonderry had been closed by the Apprentice Boys, that was all I knew about it.

It's hard to believe but it wasn't until December 2005 that I knew the facts surrounding these two important events in Ireland's history. I'd only studied from the early twentieth century onwards about how the State of Northern Ireland was formed.

My father was born and bred in County Fermanagh near the border with the Irish Republic. As a young man, during World War II, he had to patrol along the border – it was thought the Republic would let the Germans land there and attack Great Britain through the back door. Even then the people of Ulster didn't trust the southern Government. Some of this suspicion possibly came from the time of World War I when Irish rebels seized the opportunity and took over the General Post Office building in the heart of Dublin, declaring an Irish Republic. Although the British Army crushed the uprising in a relatively short space of time the same treachery was expected again.

On Saturday, 5 October 1968, a huge march was arranged in the city of Londonderry by the Derry Housing Action Committee and the Northern Ireland Civil Rights Association. The Apprentice Boys of Londonderry announced their intention to hold an Annual March on the same day, route and time. As mentioned, this tactic was used frequently. It worked again and William Craig, then Home Affairs Minister, banned the proposed civil rights march from the areas of the city centre and Waterside, under the Public Order Act. At this time a new university opened in Coleraine, a largely Protestant town in the North of the Province. It was named The New University of Ulster – another bone of contention to all the people of Londonderry who thought, as they were the second city of Northern Ireland, they should have received the economic stimulus the university would have brought.

On Saturday, 5 October 1968 (considered by many people to be the start of the Troubles), the Civil Rights Association march was stopped by the RUC before it had properly begun. The marchers were to walk from Duke Street in the Waterside area of Londonderry to the Diamond in the centre of the city and included British Labour MPs, Gerry Fitt, then Republican Labour MP, several Stormont MPs and lots of media including a television crew from RTE. The march was broken up when the RUC baton-charged the crowd, leaving many people, including a number of MPs, injured. The attack was filmed and given worldwide coverage. The whole incident had a profound effect on people throughout the world and, particularly, on the Catholic population in Northern Ireland. However, it wasn't only the Catholics it affected. In myself and in a lot like me, it raised questions. Who were these people who were breaking the law? Why else would the police hammer them if they weren't doing something wrong?

I watched this news footage in amazement and apprehension. The following nights, as fierce rioting continued in Londonderry, I couldn't wait for the news to come on. By the third day it had started to die down, with only sporadic disturbances. It was the main topic of conversation amongst my mates at work. We had never seen anything like it before: crowds of people out on the streets, only 100 miles away, attacking the police with petrol bombs, bottles and stones; images of policemen getting carried away on stretchers with blood pouring from head wounds. The only trouble we had ever been in was kicking a football about the streets. Then, if you were caught, the Peelers would give you a slap round the ears and tell you not to get caught again. If you went and told your parents what had happened, you were likely to get another clip round the ear from them and told the same thing: don't get caught again.

To sit and watch your police force being subjected to what seemed barbaric attacks made you automatically assume the people doing this were criminals. On Wednesday 9 October, one of my mates rang me at work and told me Ian Paisley was holding a demonstration in town to block a march by the People's Democracy (PD) from the Queen's University and did I fancy going. I was so intrigued by the events going on that I said yes. It ended with a three-hour sit-down protest by the PD. I considered it all a bit of an anti-climax and went home. The march went ahead the following week without any protest.

At the end of October, Jack Lynch, then Taoiseach met with Harold Wilson, then British Prime Minister, in London. The Taoiseach wanted the ending of partition to resolve the un-rest in Northern Ireland. It was a red flag to a bull. People were talking about nothing else. They really thought Wilson would, at the very least, consider the proposal, if not go the whole way and actually try to implement it. Men were talk-ing about another Home Rule bill and how we would need somebody like Lord Carson to rise up, marshal the men into another Ulster Volunteer Force and defend our right to remain part of the United Kingdom. This was exciting stuff. I had read some books from the library on the subject. We all had a feeling it was going to repeat itself.

November 1968 brought more marches and protests, begin-ning on Saturday 2 November with a march in Londonderry by the 15 members of the Derry Citizens' Action Committee

(DCAC), following the same route of the banned 5 October march. Thousands of people walked behind them. The crowd was so large the police were unable to prevent it. A couple of days later, three leaders of the Northern Ireland Government, Prime Minister Terence O'Neill, Home Affairs Minister William Craig and Minister of Commerce Brian Faulkner, met in Downing Street with Harold Wilson and Home Secretary James Callaghan for talks concerning the situation in Northern Ireland.

Everyone feared the worst – that these men were going to be told to make arrangements for the termination of the Stormont Government and prepare to become part of the Republic of Ireland. You could feel the tension in the air as we awaited the outcome. After the conference, Harold Wilson stated there would be no change in the constitutional position of Northern Ireland without the consent of the Northern Ireland population. Everyone let out a sigh of relief. The following Saturday, Ian Paisley and Major Ronald Bunting led a march to the Diamond area of Londonderry. During the next week, William Craig banned all marches in Londonderry from 14 November to 14 December, with the exception of customary parades. This meant Loyalist institutions could walk as usual, but civil rights marchers couldn't.

This didn't have much effect as, on the Saturday after the ban was introduced, the DCAC defied it and marched to the Diamond in the city centre where around 15,000 people took part in a sit-down demonstration. We watched in horror at the television images, this mass of human beings all defying the law. It looked as if most of the inhabitants of Londonderry were out in force and I remember feeling intimidated. I'd never seen so many people together, except at football matches. I was gradually becoming engrossed with watching the news to find out if anything awe-inspiring was taking place.

Now, whenever I was with my mates, we would talk incessantly about the state of affairs. One of them worked with men from the Shankill, in Mackie's Foundry on the Springfield Road and he always knew a lot more than the rest of us. The Shankill Road was to become the centre of Loyalist resistance as the years passed.

December started with a march in Dungannon by the civil rights people. There was a violent clash with Loyalists, tension was palpable and fires of insecurity were being lit. I could sense nervousness in older people who had lived through previous periods of unrest. On Monday 9 December, Terence O'Neill made a television appeal to moderate opinion. It became known as the 'Ulster stands at the crossroads' speech and gained a lot of public support. The DCAC stopped the marches and protests for a month. A few days later, O'Neill sacked William Craig because he challenged the legality of Westminster intervention on devolved matters. The lead-up to Christmas was quiet, except the Peoples' Democracy (PD) announced on 20 December that its members would hold a protest march from Belfast to Londonderry, beginning on 1 January 1969. I deliberated on the year's events and thought it would fizzle out after the New Year started.

1969

Ignoring advice from the Civil Rights Association and some people in Londonderry, the PD began their march in Belfast on 1 January 1969, imitating the Selma–Montgomery march held by Martin Luther King some years before. Approximately 40 members started out on the first stage, Belfast–Antrim. Over the next four days 200 people would join. The marchers were confronted and attacked by Loyalist crowds. I watched and listened to the news constantly. The second stage, on day two, was Antrim–Maghera; the third stage, Maghera–Claudy. That night, a friend came round to see me. He told me about a bus leaving the Shankill to intercept 'these fuckers' and stop the march from reaching Londonderry, and that there would be loads of men there from all over the Province, including B Specials. I was burning to go but declined, saying it was too short notice, with work and other commitments. To be honest, I was a bit frightened, thinking if I were about 80 miles from home and something went wrong, how the hell would I get back home when I didn't know where I was. Plus, there seemed to be plenty police protecting the marchers.

By the fourth day I was glued to the radio at work and then the TV when I came home. I was engrossed in the footage of the attack at Burntollet Bridge, largely because I didn't understand why these things were happening. Around 200 Loyalists, armed with sticks, stones, iron bars and bottles, attacked the marchers. The police who accompanied them seemed to do very little to stop the onslaught.

The friend who had gone to stop the march told me the gory details when he returned. I could see he was on a high, ecstatic would be the best way to describe his mood. Telling us how they had waited out of sight until the marchers were close and then launched a fierce assault on them, chasing after them over the fields, with blood pouring out of some protesters. He said the police had stood and watched, doing absolutely nothing to prevent it.

The following Saturday, 11 January, more riots broke out in a number of places, particularly in Londonderry and Newry. Terence O'Neill set up an official inquiry into the disturbances in the Province. The Chairman was Lord Cameron, a Scottish judge who would look into the causes of the civil unrest. Suddenly there was a spate of resignations from the Stormont Government. Deputy Prime Minister and Minister of Commerce Brian Faulkner and William Morgan resigned in protest at O'Neill's politics and what they saw as a lack of strong Government. Meanwhile, Paisley and Bunting were stoking the fires of hell in order to throw O'Neill into them. It became farcical when, on Monday 3 February, the Northern Ireland Prime Minister announced the dissolution of the Stormont Parliament. An election would be held on Monday, 24 February 1969. During February, Ian Paisley led a huge parade from the Shankill Road to the Ulster Hall in the centre of Belfast, one of his 'O'Neill out!' rallies. Although I still hadn't much of a clue about the reasons behind all this protesting, my mates and I went on this march.

When we arrived there was a clamour for seats inside the hall. For some reason we followed a group down a side corridor and found ourselves on the stage behind Ian Paisley and others. Now I could understand how Hitler could command the thousands who came out to support him at his rallies. There was exhilaration, excitement and enthusiasm at just being a part of what was taking place. I hung onto every word of the speeches, cheered as loud as anybody else. And to be on the stage behind the Big Man – I felt good, euphoric even.

When the election took place it was the first time I had ever voted. I selected an anti-O'Neill candidate as my choice. When the votes were counted, it caused the break-up of the Unionist party.

The division into 'Official Unionists' and 'Unofficial Unionists' was the start of the slide into a political vacuum. Our enemies seized their chance to exploit the chink in the Unionists' armour. Out of 39 Unionist candidates returned, 27 were in support of O'Neill's policies, while 12 were against or undecided. Ian Paisley had stood against O'Neill in his North Antrim constituency and polled over 6,000 votes.

I remember watching Paisley as the number of votes cast was being announced. He misheard and muttered something about 60 votes, looking really dejected. O'Neill had made his thank-you speech and Paisley got up to speak. Somebody whispered to him, 'Bad luck, you nearly won.' He checked the results, discovering that more than 6,000 people had voted for him and he had only been defeated by a very small majority. You could see his spirits rise up and he launched into a passionate denunciation of O'Neill's policies, accusing him of selling out the Loyalist people. Of course, Terence O'Neill was re-elected as leader of the Unionist party and therefore became Prime Minister again.

At the end of March, new disturbances broke out when Ian Paisley and Ronald Bunting were jailed for organising an illegal demonstration in Armagh on 20 November 1968. The most significant event was on Sunday 30 March, when loud explosions had the people of Belfast out at their doors. A number of bombs had gone off at an electricity substation at Castlereagh, in the east of the city. These explosions caused a blackout in a large section of Belfast and did damage estimated at half a million pounds. It was automatically blamed on the IRA and people who had lived through other IRA campaigns were quick to say they were at their evil handiwork again. Many had never heard an explosion before that. Terrence O'Neill announced the mobilisation of 1,000 B Specials to guard public utilities.

Everyone talked about it for days afterwards. Then, just into April, a second bomb went off at Dunadry. The target this time was a water installation, on one of the main supply pipes to Belfast. Once again, everyone was up in arms and the blame dumped squarely at the feet of the IRA. To me it was quite exciting; more and more people were talking about a sustained attack by Republicans.

In mid-April, a by-election was held in Mid-Ulster. Bernadette Devlin, standing as a Unity candidate, was elected to the Westminster Parliament. Aged only 21 she became the youngest woman to be elected as a Member of Parliament. I'll never forget the photograph in the papers, showing her smashing paving stones during a riot, with what seemed to me hate etched into her features. I felt gutted. How could someone like her be elected as a MP? Surely there was something wrong?

The following Saturday, 20 April, a march by the Northern Ireland Civil Rights Association (NICRA) members in Londonderry was halted when Loyalists confronted them. After the clashes with Loyalists, there was serious rioting in the Bogside area of Londonderry. At some stage, Royal Ulster Constabulary (RUC) officers entered a Bogside house while chasing rioters who had run in there to escape being caught. Samuel Devenny, who wasn't involved in the disturbances, was severely beaten with batons, causing internal injuries and he suffered a heart attack. He never recovered from the beating and died on 17 July. Many believe he was the first to die in the course of these Troubles, although actually he died three days after Francis McCluskey, also beaten badly about the head with batons by the RUC in Dungiven.

I kept up-to-date on these events and tried to get my head round the images being broadcast. Men are more easily fascinated with violence, I think. Although I was becoming more and more aware of some of the problems and issues at stake, it was captivating to watch scenes of violent behaviour and aggression aimed at the police. My mates and I were spellbound and longed for the news bulletins. Normal life had been suspended while all this vehemence was taking place on the streets.

The next day, Sunday 20 April, there were two more explosions. The first one, at the Silent Valley reservoir in the Mourne Mountains in County Down, cut off water supplies to Belfast. The second bomb was at an electricity pylon at Kilmore, County Armagh. People were becoming concerned that the IRA had begun another offensive, which would lead to somebody being killed. British troops were being deployed to guard key installations across the Province. O'Neill was under pressure to do something to stop these outrages.

On 23 April, the Unionists voted by 28 to 22 to introduce a one- man, one-vote system, which had been one of the most powerful slogans of the civil rights movement. James Chichester-Clark resigned in protest at what he saw as the concessions given to these protesters. The day after saw another explosion at a water pipe between Lough Neagh and Belfast, followed quickly by a second one, at yet another pipe. Much of Belfast was left without water.

Towards the end of the month Terence O'Neill resigned because he couldn't regain the confidence of the Unionist party and, on 1 May, James Chichester-Clark succeeded him as leader of the Unionist party and became Northern Ireland Prime Minister. We expected fireworks. The first thing he did was to announce that he would see through the reforms initiated by his predecessor. Everyone was infuriated. It seemed there were definitely strings being pulled by Westminster. He then announced an amnesty for all offences associated with demonstrations since 5 October 1968. It led to the release of, among others, Ian Paisley and Ronald Bunting.

We could feel the tension. There was a strange kind of gut feeling amongst the general population, especially older members of the community, that this could be the start of something serious, akin to the Troubles in the 1930s. It had been a time of ruthless cold-blooded killings, vicious street turmoil and sectarian riots, particularly in Belfast.

The Reverend Ian Paisley addressed a crowd in Loughgall, where he was reported as saying, 'I am anti-Roman Catholic, but God being my judge, I love the poor dupes who are ground down under that system.'

The rioting had now spread across Northern Ireland to other Catholic areas, to relieve the pressure on Bogside and at the same time stretch police resources to the limit and beyond. The conflict deteriorated rapidly into sectarian hostility between Catholics and Protestants. Many people, mostly Catholics, were forced to leave their homes. Jack Lynch, the Taoiseach of the Republic, gave a televised speech, informing people that field hospitals were being set up in border areas to aid Catholics injured in Protestant and RUC attacks. Then he added, 'The present situation is the inevitable outcome of the policies pursued for decades by successive Stormont Governments. It is clear also that the Irish Government can no longer stand by and see innocent people injured and perhaps worse.'

We were terrified. Did he mean he was ready to send the Irish Army across the border and invade part of the United Kingdom? Did he honestly believe we would allow that to happen? More importantly would the British Government let that happen?

As the police were being overstretched and becoming less able to control the situations happening on the streets of a number of towns, the conflict became increasingly sectarian in nature, with crowds of Protestant and Catholics clashing in many places. Two of the worst districts where violence erupted were centred around the Shankill Road and Falls Road, and between the Shankill and Ardoyne areas at the other side. Police and B Specials were outnumbered and relieved that Protestants had come out in force to protect their districts from what was seen as a Catholic onslaught.

The Catholic crowds suddenly found they had bitten off more than they could chew, as more and more Protestants poured onto the streets, from different areas, including my own, and soon outnumbered them. As they were pushed back, the Protestant crowds began torching Catholic-owned houses. You could hear gunfire echoing around the streets – it was very frightening, as in all the noise you couldn't establish where it was coming from or, more importantly, where it was headed. I had never heard gunshots fired close to where I was before, and at times I was trying hard to fit into a doorway half my width.

Total anarchy and mayhem took over people's minds as the crowds grew each night and the rioting took on a will of its own. Herbert Roy died after the IRA fired on a Protestant crowd as it spilled out onto Divis Street, Lower Falls, from Dover Street. By this time, buildings on the Falls Road were being burned as Protestant crowds pushed deeper into 'enemy territory'. I could see from where the shots were being fired at us and it didn't take me long to put something solid between them and me. Hugh McCabe, a Catholic, was killed while on the roof of a block of flats in the Divis complex, when police started to use their heavy-calibre Browning machine-guns mounted on the top of their armoured cars.

The Stormont Government asked for British troops to be placed on the ground to help police restore order. This was granted and no one realised how long they would have to remain in the Province.

An uneasy calm descended over the Province and we all held our breath. My mind was reeling with thoughts of people who had died – although at this point I hadn't actually seen any bodies – and my thoughts would always return to the gunfire I had heard, which sent shivers up and down my spine. I witnessed mobs out of control, hell-bent on attacking people's homes and setting fire to them. It was very difficult to comprehend the scenes I had witnessed and taken part in.

On 29 August 1969 the British and Northern Ireland Governments met at Downing Street to discuss the situation. A joint communiqué set out a number of reforms related to the Government administration services. There would be an inquiry into the reasons the riots had taken place and Justice Scarman would chair it. Another inquiry known as the Hunt Committee would be put into action to look at the structure of the police and the B Specials. The Government seemed determined to force its will on us by appointing Ian Freeland, the General Officer Commanding of the British Army as Director of Operations, for all matters of security, removing control of security from the Stormont Government.

On 9 September, the Army started to erect a temporary peace-line between the two sides to prevent riots. It was completed the following day and it is still there. Now it's a permanent concrete wall, which I doubt will ever be pulled down.

The rest of September was fairly peaceful. I thought the turmoil was over, and we could get on with the rest of our lives in peace and harmony. October was to change that. On 10 September, the *Hunt Report* was published, going down like the proverbial wet balloon in Loyalist communities. The report recommended that the police should return to being an unarmed force. The B Specials should be disbanded and a new RUC reserve should be established. A local part-time force known as the Ulster Defence Regiment (UDR) would be recruited and under the control of the Army. At the request of Harold Wilson, Arthur Young was appointed as Chief Constable to oversee the reforms suggested in the *Hunt Report*. This was one of the first of the many concessions made to Republicans, as far as I could see.

It caused the Loyalist community to believe that it was a step closer to a United Ireland. The major battle that night was fought on the Shankill Road, where Loyalists took on the Army and police in fierce rioting and the UVF engaged the soldiers in a gun battle. The first policeman to be killed was Constable Victor Arbuckle who was shot dead at the bottom of the Shankill Road. The police and the Army had been hiding behind their armoured vehicles when a sniper opened fire at their legs, visible under their Land-Rovers. As far as I remember, the policeman was hit in an artery in his leg and bled to death. Soldiers were pinned down with constant sniper fire. I had no time to be afraid; this was a battle scene and the sound of guns firing now seemed to stimulate rather than terrify me. I was becoming familiar with the sound of guns. I had conquered any fear.

The situation continued through the night until dawn. The Army admitted it was one of the hardest and toughest resistances they had encountered anywhere in peacetime. It had taken them ten hours to finally bring things under control and they had advanced less than half a mile up the road. Two UVF men, George Dickie and Herbert Hawe, were killed along with Victor Arbuckle.

On 19 September, a bomb went off at a power station near Ballyshannon in County Donegal. It detonated prematurely as Thomas McDowell, a member of the UVF, was planting it. This act sent shockwaves around the Protestant community and changed the picture completely. It was no longer a straightforward case of the IRA being responsible for the series of bomb attacks around the Province; it meant there was a Loyalist conspiracy to create the impression that the IRA was responsible. Why? was the big question.

1969 Statistics

Deaths by status		Responsibility for deaths	
Protestant civilians	6	Republicans	5
Catholic civilians	9	Loyalists	3
RUC	1	Army	2
RUC/R	0	RUC/RUC/R	8
UDR/RIR	0	UDR/RIR	0
Army	0	Others	1
Republicans	2		
Loyalists	1		
Others	0		
Total	19		
Bombs	10		
Shootings	73		

1970

1969 was over and a New Year had just begun. It's hard to put into words how I was feeling. I had witnessed and become involved in violence, close-up. I had stood behind UVF snipers as they fired on Security Forces. I had been connected with events that were totally alien to me and it was very hard to erase those pictures from my mind.

I was always evaluating and debating these events with my mates and myself. I found it difficult to come to terms with what I had seen and to put a meaning to it all. Although I had read a bit about the history of the formation of Ulster, I still didn't fully understand the complexities of the situation.

Enrolling for the new Ulster Defence Regiment (UDR) began on this date. The regiment was supposed to replace the B Specials – a totally absurd situation, as many of the B Specials joined the UDR. So, the same men under a different name. As the Specials were all Protestant men who were loyal to the crown, it stands to reason they knew all about the IRA and would help Loyalist paramilitaries in the years to come by giving details of IRA men to them. In fact, many Protestants were connected to both the UDR and Loyalist paramilitaries; even my team had UDR members. I recall we were allowed in later years to go to special nights at Girdwood army camp in North Belfast for a drink and a laugh as long as a UDR soldier signed us in.

On Friday 3 April, Ian Freeland, the General Officer Commanding of the Army, announced a new get-tough policy. Anyone seen throwing a petrol bomb would be warned and, if they persisted in using them, they could be shot dead. If they were arrested, they could be jailed for ten years. A petrol bomb was considered a weapon and those using them were guilty of using a potential weapon that could result in death and injury to whom it was being thrown at. We agreed with that statement and waited to see if it would be put into force.

Later that same month, a dramatic event was to take place that spelled the beginning of the end of the Ulster Unionist Party's united front against the 'enemy'. Ian Paisley, standing as a Protestant Unionist, was elected for the seat in the Stormont Government. He took the seat vacated by the outgoing MP and a second man, William Beattie, was also elected as a Protestant Unionist. It demonstrated that many Protestant men and women were unhappy with the reforms the Northern Ireland Prime Minister, Chichester-Clark was trying to put into practice.

A dramatic event took place in the Republic in May and seemed to confirmed our worst fears. Jack Lynch, the Taoiseach, sacked Charles Haughey and Neil Blaney over allegations that they were involved in trying to procure arms for the IRA. At the end of the month, both men, along with two others, were charged with the offence of 'conspiracy to illegally import arms for the use of the IRA'.

This episode was swiftly followed by another horror story on Friday 26 May. In Londonderry, five people died as the result of the premature explosion of an incendiary device inside the home of IRA man, Thomas McCool. (Two other IRA men, Thomas Carlin and Joseph Coyle, also died. I thought they got what they deserved at the time.) The tragedy, for me, was the death of McCool's two young children. When the news broke into the public domain I was shocked that such a thing could happen. How could men even consider having their children around while such a device was being made? The rumour went that the men had been mixing the ingredients on a stone floor with a metal shovel. The shovel had caused a spark which then detonated the mixture.

Around this time, the two main areas of rioting were Ardoyne, North Belfast, and the Catholic enclave, Short Strand, at the bottom of Protestant East Belfast. We had gone up to the Crumlin Road that day when serious rioting broke out. Many people were out on the streets, from both sides, with no sign of the Army appearing. At the height of the battle I saw three hooded men making their way to the front of the Catholic crowd and taking up firing positions. I dived for cover. Three men, William Kincaid, Daniel Loughins and Alexander Gould, all died in a hail of bullets. Theirs were the first dead bodies I had seen. I beat a hasty retreat home as the Army arrived. We all went to the bar and had a sombre drink.

Later that same night, disturbances erupted in East Belfast. A gun battle between the UVF and the IRA took place inside the Catholic chapel at the bottom of Newtownards Road. Shootings went on for some time with the Security Forces unable to do anything – thankfully, I was drunk on the opposite side of town and wasn't near the trouble.

Twelve people had died in two days, three of them where I had been. I had watched as IRA gunmen took up firing positions. What was this madness that appeared to be taking over people's minds? Being involved in riots was exciting – us and them, having a go. But now guns had been thrown into the cauldron. It was making me nervous and now I was constantly watching for any signs that gunman were about to open fire.

The third of July is one of the dates that would have a huge impact on how people viewed the position of the Army, in terms of their role on the streets of Ulster. In the afternoon the Army took over the lower Falls Road district and carried out a widespread search for weapons and IRA suspects. They decided to impose a military curfew, for around 34 hours, restricting the movement of the residents.

Both wings of the IRA fought serious gun battles with the Army during this period. Although many guns and explosives were uncovered, it was the manner in which the search was conducted that became the issue for the Catholic population. After months of being attacked the soldiers used the curfew to vent their frustration. Houses were trashed, literally pulled apart piece by piece. I heard rumours that people were actually throwing weapons into the street before the Army would arrive to search their houses. The Army's hostile actions in this instance destroyed any goodwill Catholics had left for the Army. Four people died, including a man who was deliberately run over by an APC (armoured personnel carrier).

Everyone wondered what 1971 would bring.

1970 Statistics

Deaths by status		*Responsibility for deaths*	
Protestant civilians	8	Republicans	22
Catholic civilians	10	Loyalists	1
RUC	2	Army	5
RUC/R	0	RUC/RUC/R	0
UDR/RIR	0	UDR/RIR	0
Army	0	Others	1
Republicans	7		
Loyalists	0		
Others	2		
Total	29		
Bombs	170		
Shootings	213		

1971 SLIDE INTO CHAOS

THE STRAW THAT broke the camel's back came on a Saturday night, 6 February 1971. The Provisional IRA (PIRA) detonated a bomb in North Belfast. It was about a third of mile from my house, on the fringe of the Tiger's Bay district of North Belfast. My father and I, upon hearing the explosion, left the house to go and find the source, as it had sounded quite close. This was the usual reaction of people. First, in case somebody had been injured or trapped and needed help. Second, sheer curiosity: just to view the bomb site. It may sound ghoulish but a sort of morbid fascination had taken hold of people.

Word soon spreads when a bomb has exploded. We walked down to where the small device had detonated, outside a public bar just off York Street in North Belfast. No one had been hurt and superficial damage had been done to the outside of the building. After about half an hour, I met up with a few mates who had also come to see what had happened. We all decided to call it a night as it was getting quite late and started to walk home. As we approached Adam Street, off Duncairn Gardens, to turn in towards home, a crowd emerged from Lepper Street, about 120 feet away, which led directly onto the Republican New Lodge Road area.

All of a sudden, we came under attack. Stones, bricks and bottles rained down on us. There were 20 of us at most, facing 50-plus pouring out onto Duncairn Gardens. It was horrific:

windows were being broken; bottles were smashing all around us; bricks and stones bounced off the ground and walls. A metallic clang resounded in our ears as something hit a lamp-post. A sickening noise as a brick thudded somebody on the head. A couple of friends crumpled immediately with cracked skulls and a bottle glanced off my shoulder, before breaking behind me and cutting a young lad on his leg.

We had no time to think. We had to stand and fight, or run and leave the houses and families living in Adam Street at the mercy of the advancing crowd. A couple of us grabbed our friends who were half conscious by the scruff of the neck and dragged them behind a wall to safety. Meanwhile, the other people with us fought back, picking up whatever they could find to hurl back at the ever increasing crowd. The attackers seemed to have things well planned, with piles of rubble stockpiled close to the corner of Lepper Street, and Duncairn Gardens. They kept up their barrage, disappeared round the corner, then were back in a minute loaded up with more missiles to throw at us. All we could do was to try and pick up what was being thrown at us, and hurl it back as quickly as possible. Of course, this put us in danger, because the moment one of us stopped moving to pick something up, he became the focus for the crowd's attention – an easier target. Suddenly there were petrol bombs. They hit concrete and balls of flame mushroomed up, then splashed out and skittered along the street towards us. It felt like it was raining bricks.

One of the factors that saved us, at the initial onslaught, was the fact that there were more of them than us. When we threw missiles back, it was harder to miss, especially if you pitched like a baseball player, aiming at head height. If the person at the front saw the stone and ducked, then the poor bastard behind him got smashed in the head.

I saw a couple of women standing down Adam Street and yelled as loud as I could for them to start knocking doors and get the men out of their houses. We were at the point of being overwhelmed, and more and more petrol bombs were being thrown at us. Although it was a cold February night, the sweat was pouring from us. We couldn't stop. Our safety depended on us keeping up what little defence we could muster. Thankfully, my shouting worked, and more and more men came to swell our ranks.

Cars began pulling up full of men from different areas close by. Of course, the Republican side was also increasing every minute and a full-scale riot was now escalating. A lot of men were getting injured on both sides because of the sheer numbers involved. Men continued to fight with blood pouring from wounds. Cheers went up every so often, as someone was seen to get whacked and fall to the ground. This was the first major confrontation in the Tiger's Bay area.

After an hour of total mayhem, a dozen policemen eventually arrived on the scene. There was nothing they could do at this stage; they were unarmed, equipped only with small shields and batons. Having stopped above Lepper Street, all they could do was observe the chaos unfolding in front of them. They were hopelessly outnumbered; there must have been about 200 to 300 on each side by this time, determined to cause as many casualties to each other as possible. At this point, I think everything was being hurled at us, including bits of a kitchen sink.

As our numbers increased and some of the police had actually resorted to throwing stones, to help us, we pushed the Republicans back down Lepper Street. Whether this was a premeditated come-on, to lead us into a trap, as later events would show, I just do not know, but when we got to Lepper Street, the entire street lights were out and the place was in total darkness.

So, we confined our activities to keeping them hemmed in their own area. It was a game of cat-and-mouse. We would attack; they would retreat; they would attack; and we would retreat. By this time, the Loyalists had organised young lads to collect milk bottles, and petrol had been siphoned from some cars, so we had a few petrol bombs to throw back at them. Eventually, it returned to the original formation: us back at Adam Street and them at Lepper Street.

As the Protestants were concentrated below Lepper Street, batches of Catholic youths would load up and launch their assault. When they retreated, another lot would appear and keep up a constant barrage. There was the occasional lull, while everyone caught their breath, gathering debris and rubble, getting ready for the next round.

During one of these lulls a group of about 30 guys loaded up with as many stones as their arms and pockets could hold, then went up Copperfield Street and into Edlingham Street, then on down uncaairn Gardens, above Lepper Street. They sneaked up unnoticed and when the next group came out they concentrated on the main crowd below Lepper street. We caught them in the middle and as they were not expecting an attack from behind them. They didn't know what hit them. Four or five of them went down and the rest made a run for safety towards Leper Street. Others hobbled, nursing their wounds.

Sensing victory, the Protestant crowd surged forward. Some of the guys that had fallen were getting the shit kicked out of them. The Catholics then piled into the fray to try to rescue their comrades. Vicious hand-to-hand fighting took place while the police clubbed all around them, trying to save lives. Eventually, the two sides retreated to their own areas again; the Catholics to Lepper Street and us back to Adam Street.

Two army lorries came tearing down Duncairn Gardens, screeched to a halt and spewed out troops who began forming in ranks in front of the Loyalist crowd. We gave a large cheer. Here were our soldiers arriving to beat the living daylights out of the Republicans. The soldiers, from the 1st Battalion Royal Artillery, were not long in the Province and very green. They must have been apprehensive, seeing this huge crowd facing them and preparing to advance on us. Only 50 to 60 troops stood there, ready to do battle.

The police had contacted the officers commanding the soldiers, explained that we were friendly and indicated where the Republican crowd was located. These young inexperienced men lined up then marched into Lepper Street, thumping their small three-feet shields with their batons. This was supposed to incite terror in the rioters.

The crowd had fallen back, allowing the soldiers to advance up the street. We all moved up to watch what was going on. What a daunting experience it must have been for those soldiers as they advanced into a strange unlit street, not knowing what was ahead of them, stumbling and falling over the rubble strewn on the ground. The Republicans attacked. The soldiers didn't have a chance, there were so few against so many. A nail bomb was thrown, exploding in a shower of red and white hot pieces of metal. After holding out for about ten minutes, the pressure became too much and the troops retreated. We moved away from our observation point.

As the last of the soldiers approached the corner, a deafening explosion took place in Lepper Street. The PIRA had thrown a blast bomb at the retreating men. As they turned to protect themselves from the blast, they were hit by a burst of sustained automatic fire from a Thompson submachine-gun. A huge cheer went up from the Catholic crowd and I could see sparks from some of the bullets ricocheting off the road, not far from where we had been standing minutes before.

We were paralysed with anger. Here were our soldiers being shot at, by the people they had been sent to protect in the first place. The noise was unbelievable, our nerves were shattered and we were trembling all over. We were witnessing utter terror, unfolding before our eyes. Young soldiers crouched in doorways, shivering with fear and shock in this alien world, not knowing who was friend or foe. We tried to comfort them, reassuring them that they were amongst friends and had nothing to fear from us. Some of them stammered nervously about their mates having been hit in the burst of automatic fire.

A stunned silence descended, like a blanket of snow muffling every sound and quietening the crowd. No one knew what to do next. We crept up to the corner and peered round; it took a few seconds for our eyes to adjust to the darkness. We could see some soldiers lying on the ground not far from us. The Catholic crowd had retreated back up the street towards New Lodge Road. A shout came from one of the soldiers lying on the ground, 'Help me! Please, God, help me!' In a moment of madness a few of us dashed forward then grabbed him and dragged him to safety. He had been hit in the leg.

A Saracen Armoured Personnel Car (SAPC), with red crosses on its sides, came racing down Duncairn Gardens and was directed into Lepper Street. It drove in, with soldiers behind it using it as cover, and the medics began rescuing the wounded. As I watched them carrying one young soldier away on a stretcher, I could see he was in a very bad way. He had been hit in the lower back and I could see blood pouring out of him. Five soldiers had been hit in that burst of fire. More Army reinforcements arrived and the crowd slowly dispersed. Gunner

Robert Curtis died in hospital a few days later and became the first British soldier to die in these Troubles.

It emerged later that Republicans in Ardoyne, under pressure from soldiers during very heavy rioting there, had asked the New Lodge Republicans (NLR) to start trouble to relieve the strain. One IRA man, James Saunders, and one civilian, Bernard Watt, had been shot dead by soldiers in a gun battle and serious disturbances in the Oldpark and Ardoyne districts.

A ripple of shock went through the Protestant community, and that night's events were discussed for many weeks.

Just a few days into March, one of the most horrific incidents took place. The bodies of three off-duty Scottish soldiers, Dougal McCaughey, Joseph McCaig and John McCaig, from the Royal Highland Fusiliers, were found at Squires Hill, Ligoniel, on the outskirts of North Belfast. They had been out for the night in Belfast and then lured to their deaths by the PIRA (including female members), on the pretense of going to a party. As they stopped for a pee in a dark lane, they were cold-bloodedly murdered – two brothers and a mate gunned down without compassion or mercy. People were incensed by this atrocity: you could feel the revulsion and horror hanging in the air.

No matter how hard we tried, our thoughts kept returning to the scene of the murders. The only consolation was trying to believe that it happened quickly and the lads didn't know much about it. How could a drunken night out end so tragically? The Province was descending into total anarchy. Something had to be done about it and it was obvious that the Security Forces were not capable of doing anything to stop it. People had to be mobilised to defend their areas. Vigilante groups sprang up in Protestant areas. We took over derelict houses and shops, and turned them into bases where men could stay at night. From

there you could organise patrols, keep warm, and get some rest
or a cup of tea, to help you through the long cold nights. While
all this was going on, we still had to get up and go to work the
next day.

We armed ourselves with what ever came to hand – knives,
hammers, hatchets, pickaxe handles –indeed, anything that
could inflict severe damage to anyone who wanted to come
into your area to cause trouble. Everybody entering your territory was challenged and checked out. This was how some people met their deaths, especially in North Belfast, where there
are so many small ghetto areas. People would take a short cut
from one part through an opposing area to get home, to avoid
making a detour. They would be spotted, challenged and captured. If they were found to be from the wrong side they would
be brutally tortured for information, shot dead and dumped
up some side street to be discovered the next morning. Many
innocent men met their death, simply by being in the wrong
place at the wrong time.

I remember the time when a mate's brother (an alcoholic
and no danger to anyone, other than himself) got so drunk he
ended up on Springfield Road in West Belfast, having no idea
where he was. This road starts as Catholic, becomes Protestant
and then ends up Catholic again as it winds its way towards the
Black Mountain. He was picked up by a group of vigilantes,
taken to a romper room, as they became known (after a children's TV programme). He was petrified and too scared to talk,
as he had no idea who had captured him. He was slapped and
thumped a few times, and told in no uncertain terms what was
going to happen to him if he did not talk.

The poor guy had pissed and shit himself, when he spotted
one of the men wearing a Loyalist badge on his lapel. He took
a chance and said he was a Protestant from just off Limestone

Road. Unfortunately, Limestone Road is another part-Protestant, part-Catholic road so he got another couple of thumps and asked if he knew anyone who could vouch for him and confirm his identity. Terrified of giving any names he lapsed into silence again. The guy in charge became really angry with him and ordered him to be hooded, taken out and nutted (shot in the head). As the hood was pulled over his head he took a final chance and screamed the name of a man whom he knew lived on West Circular Road and who worked with his father. Fortunately, this person was well known to these men. The man was awoken and asked to come and identify the person being held. This he did, taking him away and giving him a lift home. My mate's brother was a very lucky man. Too many poor souls lost their lives in this way in those early years.

Once we were inside our base, talk always turned to speculation: 'What would happen if the IRA should come in to attack us with guns and bombs?' You would feel very silly trying to attack someone with a knife or hammer if they were firing a machine-gun or pistol at you. Our conclusion was to contact the UVF, who were the only Loyalist paramilitary group at the time (the UDA did not form until August/September 1971), and ask for guns to protect our areas. I offered to contact a mate who knew a lot of people from the Shankill, to see if they could approach the UVF about discussing the matter. Shankill Road was the main stronghold of Protestant and Loyalist stalwartness in Northern Ireland.

I met him the next day with four other mates and a general discussion took place on what was happening to our country and, more importantly, what we could do about it. The consensus was that we were in grave danger from the Republicans winning this war and the British Government capitulating to their demands.

Daily riots took place at interface junctions; people from both sides were being intimidated and forced to leave their homes. Some people even burned their own houses as they left, so that the other side could not use them. A notorious example occurred in Ardoyne, North Belfast, when Protestants had had enough of the attacks. They were forced to flee and they set fire to three streets of houses, Farrington Gardens, Haddington Gardens and Velsheda Park.

As my friends and I approached home one evening we heard a lot of shouting and the sound of breaking bottles coming from Edlingham Street: 'Fenian bastards! Orange bastards!' Another night of rioting had begun. It had become the norm. There were five main interface spots on Duncairn Gardens[a58] where the two sides would confront each other. North Queen Street junction, an alleyway called The Stumps, Adam Street/ Lepper Street, Edlingham Street and Halliday's Road. That night it was Edlingham Street's turn to bear the brunt of the attack. The Army eventually arrived and placed themselves between the two crowds. No lining up to march; they just took up positions at the corners, with their rifles trained on both groups. A couple of SAPCs were parked between the two factions to keep them apart. The officer in charge shouted through a megaphone, in his upper-class English accent, 'This is an illegal gathering! Disperse, or we will be compelled to open fire!'

The sound of the soldiers cocking their rifles was audible. A silence descended over the crowds. All of a sudden, from behind me, I heard the distinct noise of another gun being cocked. And the man in charge seemed to have heard it as well, as his next words were, 'Get that fucking light over there!' A spotlight was aimed at the Loyalist crowd. Everybody just stood their ground and cheered at the officer yelling instructions to his men. Another batch of soldiers arrived and we all dispersed.

It was a time when a lot of people stayed out late at night even when they weren't on vigilante duty. Standing at street corners or outside people's doors talking and listening to sporadic gunfire, or even a major gun battle raging somewhere in the city. There was always something going on somewhere. Men from other areas would come into yours, and stand and talk for hours about what was happening in our own and their districts.

The next night my mate told me he'd made contact with the fellow from the Shankill and he would see if he could contact someone from the UVF to speak to us. A couple of days later he called and told me to be at his house the following night at 7 p.m., and to come alone. Believe me, I was shitting myself. I was about to meet someone from an illegal organisation, who probably bombed or shot people. It was a different matter talking about it amongst your friends. Now it was actually going to happen. What if they disliked me, this wasn't a boy scout movement that would slap your hand and tell you to go away. The UVF was known to be a ruthless organisation, one which didn't take prisoners. Needless to say, my nerves were shattered all the next day, as I waited for the meeting time to come around.

I arrived early, about 6.30 p.m., to discuss with my friend what we would say and to make sure there were no problems. I was told that Jim (not his real name) would pick us up and take us to the meeting. Just before seven Jim arrived. We were introduced and we sat down. Jim said he would take us up to the Shankill to meet some leading UVF figures and not to be nervous; just to explain exactly what we needed and to ask for their help. Easy for him to say, the butterflies in my stomach were like huge bats trying to get out by now.

We then drove to the Berlin Arms Bar where Jim ushered us to an upstairs room. Some men were already there, waiting for us. My heart was in my mouth, thumping so loudly I was sure everyone in the room could hear it. Jim introduced the mate and myself but didn't mention his colleagues' names, for obvious reasons. The man who seemed to be in charge was in his mid-thirties with a small goatee beard, medium-built with piercing eyes. You felt when this man looked at you he could see your soul. There was no way you could lie to him or get away with any bullshit. He stared at us with those cold eyes and spoke with an air of confidence that comes with power. I was in awe of him. He oozed conviction and dedication to a cause. In all my time in the UVF and all the men I have known, I have met very few to equal him.

He questioned us about what we thought they could do to help and what our intentions were in the long term. I left most of the talking to my mate as I was terrified of saying the wrong thing. My mate, I'll call him Billy (not his real name), explained that we felt very exposed when on night-time vigilante duty. If the IRA decided to attack us, or, during one of the many riots taking place, ambush the young lads, there wasn't much we could do with what we had to hand. Basically, what we were looking for were a few guns to help defend our area from an ever increasing Republican threat. While Billy was talking I could feel this man's eyes on us all the time, scrutinising us and absorbing everything that was being said. When I eventually spoke, I sensed it was important to keep eye contact with him, believing that when people lie to you they have a tendency to drop their eyes or look away. The last thing I wanted him to think was that I was lying.

He asked us, 'Do you not think there's a UVF unit in Tiger's Bay?'

I replied, 'If there is, we don't know any of them and they don't seem to be very active in protecting our area.'

He then asked, 'If we are in a position to help, what would you be prepared to do for us, if the need ever arose?'

As the meeting had progressed our nervousness had abated, as these men appeared genuinely interested in helping us, so I explained: 'We are prepared to do anything to defend our country from the Republican plot to overthrow the Northern Ireland State and there is a real possibility that the British Government will capitulate to their demands. We feel that unless the Protestant people wake up to the reality of the situation, they will suddenly find themselves sold down the river as previous British Governments have tried to do.'

These were words of bravado, but I said them with utter sincerity, belief and conviction. It was a time to stand up and be counted. We also told them that about a dozen men, close friends, were behind us in our efforts to defend our area.

With that said, the meeting closed. We were told they would let us know through Jim what their decision was and we all shook hands. We thanked them for taking the time to talk to us and said we would appreciate anything they could do. Jim took us downstairs and bought us a drink, which I needed badly. He said the meeting had gone well and thought the decision would be favorable. After a few drinks he drove us home. We went straight to the Times Bar and got legless.

It was almost a week before Billy got back to me. We thought they weren't even going to bother giving us an answer but, on reflection, I'm sure we were checked out very thoroughly, from top to bottom, inside and out. The UVF was a closed secret group and didn't let just anyone in. Billy told me to be at his house at 8 o'clock that evening. Jim arrived just after eight, with another man we hadn't met before, and started to brief us about the outcome of our meeting the week before.

He informed us that the men we had met were impressed with what we had said and were prepared to offer our group some assistance in the defence of our district. They would provide two handguns, for which Billy and I would be responsible. There would only be minimal contact between them and us. In return, we would be required to provide safe houses and gather any intelligence needed for operations in our district for any of their men. This seemed fair enough. We said we would put it to our men and let them know.

We had done it; some weapons to defend ourselves, without actually becoming fully fledged UVF members. He also told us that, although the group with which we were becoming involved was affiliated to the UVF, it went under the name of USSF (Ulster Special Services Force), after a unit in the old UVF in World War I. This group operated all over the country with different UVF units. The pair left shortly afterwards and we breathed a sigh of relief.

The thought of being of use to one of the top units in the UVF intrigued us; even if it was only in a peripheral way, it made us feel a bit nervous and excited. We set up a meeting of our mates and friends for the following evening to get the ball rolling. One of them gave his parents a few quid to go for a drink and we took over his living room. The men who met that evening were all good trusted friends whom we had known for years.

After all, even though our primary aim was defensive, we were going to be in possession of illegal guns, which meant, if caught, you could face a long time in prison. None of us had ever been in trouble with the police before so it was a big step. After a general discussion, it was agreed by everyone that what we were being offered seemed like a good deal. It was agreed that Billy would be in charge and I would act as his 2IC (second in charge). Billy would keep one of the guns and I the other. We would alternate our nights on vigilante duty, so that one of us was always in control of the weapons.

One of the guys mentioned that a couple of friends from the Glengormly district would be willing to join us and do a stint a few nights each week. This was a residential area on the outskirts of North Belfast and not in any particular danger from Republican attack. (This situation was to change in later years as Catholics moved from ghetto areas to the outskirts.) One of them could organise the use of a small Orange Hall near Roughfort for meetings. It sounded all right and we agreed the more men we could muster on the streets the easier it would be to defend the area. It was also agreed that there would be no mention of weapons to any new member until we were sure of their trustworthiness, and under no circumstances was anyone to say whom we were connected with. The meeting broke up with the decision that Billy and I would contact Jim to make the arrangements and organise a rota for our nightly patrols. Also, we would meet the men from Glengormly and brief them on what was required.

Billy arranged to pick up the guns on the following Saturday afternoon from Jim's house. I would drive up to collect them and Jim would do lead car on the way home, in case of any Army or police VCP (Vehicle Check Point) on our route. Let me try and put this in perspective. Here we were, ordinary young men, never in trouble with the police before in our lives, never done anything to break the law, except maybe playing football in the streets and throwing a few stones or bottles in a riot, actually contemplating transporting illegal firearms across the city of Belfast on a weekend afternoon. Nervous wasn't the word for it, we were shit scared. The adrenaline was flowing; a buzz, heart pumping, stomach tingling, palms sweating and legs like jelly. When we arrived at our destination, what a relief. The feeling of euphoria surpassed everything I had ever done before. You'd think we'd just won a million pounds, such was the feeling of jubilation that we'd pulled it off – transporting two guns across town.

Things had moved quickly and we organised our rota for each evening patrol. Billy would be in charge one night, me the next. The men from Glengormly were brought in and we now had 16 men in our group, plus about two dozen other men from the area doing vigilante duties in our district. In those days we could tune into the police and Army radio frequency to keep up to date on events around the city. We took note of all stolen car registration numbers and kept watch in case they entered the area. It was a different feeling walking the streets with a gun stuck in your waistband; something about the weight of it gives you a feeling of security. We had the power, like God, to take somebody's life. We feared no one.

When a car was stopped, to be checked out, we knew we had the upper hand. If anyone gave you any hassle the mere act of opening your coat to show what was tucked in your belt was more than enough to subdue the most ardent objector. Many lovers got the surprise of their lives, parked in their car up a dark alleyway, caught in a passionate embrace, when all of a sudden the window would be knocked and a group of men would be standing there wanting to know what they were up to. I suspect it was done a lot of the time just to break the monotony of the long nights. Many sights were seen and married men caught, literally, with their trousers down; not to mention a few married women. It was always a good topic of conversation when you got back to base for your break.

The Provisionals' campaign of terror was escalating; their attacks on the Security Forces were increasing daily and the body count was rising. We used to take bets on how many explosions would take place the next day throughout the Province. We would listen to the nightly gunfire echoing round the streets as PIRA gunmen would take pot shots at the soldiers or confront them in a major battle. Late at night, when the city was quiet, the sound of gunfire could be heard for miles. It was unsettling, especially when it was nearby. Belfast city centre became a ghost town after six o'clock at night. No one ventured into town, bars closed early and people stayed in their own areas for safety.

Illegal clubs run by the paramilitaries sprang up everywhere. Old buildings were commandeered, done up and made into drinking dens. Some of these dens were actually very smart places: wall panelling, nice seats, clean glasses; others were more rough and ready, sawdust-on-the-floor. These clubs flourished and people with no other place to go would flock to them. The police didn't try to stop them and, of course, all the profits went straight into the organisation's coffers, to buy more arms and explosives. Some of them put on entertainment while armed guards watched the building in case of attack. Each district had its own, maybe two or more depending on how many groups operated there. The USSF took over a large room above a chemist's, at the corner of Brennen Street and Agnes Street, off the Shankill Road in Belfast, and we made this our local.

It was around this time I became friendly with two men who were to prove invaluable to my mates and me over the coming years. The first was an ex-policeman, who had served during the IRA's campaign in the 1950s. He had shown me a newspaper photograph of himself standing beside a lorry riddled with bullet holes. He had used a Bren gun on the lorry as IRA men tried to escape across the border after a police station raid. His arm was in a sling, due to an IRA bullet that had wounded him in the arm during the attack.

He was the security man in the firm where I worked. His name was George and he had an arsenal of legal guns: a couple of shotguns, a SLR .22 rifle, a single-bolt action .22 rifle, a Star .22 pistol, which he carried to work, a very powerful air rifle and a double-barrelled 410 shotgun pistol. He lived in a street close to the New Lodge Road and owned a small cottage in Islandmagee, near Ballylumford power station. We would go there at weekends and spend the days hunting and setting up firing ranges. At night we would adjourn to a wee pub nearby, the Mill Bay Inn. When I say wee, I mean wee. If a dozen people squeezed into it there was very little room to lift your drink to your mouth. The locals were always glad to see us arrive as the craic was brilliant. The owner of the pub was also glad to see us, as I'm sure his takings quadrupled when we hit the place.

The second man, with whom I became a close friend, was also through contact at work. He was a lorry driver, for a company in Ballymena, who came in once or twice a week. We got talking and I realised he was a Protestant. As I got to know him, it wasn't long before I knew he was loyal through and through. He asked if I knew anybody who would be interested in some gelignite. I asked him if he was joking. He shook his head, saying he was on the level.

I told him I just might know some men who would be very interested, adding a warning: 'Look, mate, please tell me you're genuine. I know these men and they don't like being messed around.'

He told me it was all above board so I left it at that and told him I would let him know the next time he was in.

After work I raced round to Billy's house to see if Jim had

dropped Billy's father off. I was relieved to find he hadn't and we went into the parlour to wait for him. When he pulled up Billy went out and asked him to come in as we had something to tell him. I explained what was on offer and Jim said, yes.

The next time I saw Harry, I told him these men were interested and we agreed the pick-up details. Harry suggested he set up a range, have a few weapons there, clay pigeon shoot and make a day of it. The very thought of it made me eager to be there. We arranged to meet on the Saturday at noon in a bar in Broughshane, a village close to Ballymena.

Billy contacted Jim and when he arrived at his house, I filled him in on the details of the meeting place. It was decided that we would drive to the bar and they would follow close behind us. When we made contact, they would follow at a safe distance until we had checked the place out, then come in behind us five minutes later. What a day we all had, magic. Harry and his family made us all feel at home and provided good food and drink for us all. The men from the Shankill arrived in a van with a special secret compartment cut into the floor. Arrangements were made for regular deliveries of the explosives between Harry and the men.

It was the first time I had tried clay pigeon shooting. I loved it. As well as shotguns there were .22 rifles, .22 pistols, a .38 revolver and an old .303 rifle, which still worked. Harry brought out a couple of bottles of poteen and made it up with hot water and brown sugar, so it looked like a hot whiskey. This was the first time I had drunk the firewater. I remember Harry testing each bottle, by pouring a small taste onto a tablespoon, before heating it and then setting it alight, just like cooks do with brandy. As long as it burns with a nice blue flame it was good. If it didn't it was impure and drinking it could make you blind, we were told.

Mind you, as we drove home, I thought I must have drunk some of the bad stuff, as it seemed to me we were driving through a fog. I'm glad it wasn't me at the wheel. The men from the Shankill had left early and we had stayed on until quite late, enjoying the craic. I will never forget the hospitality of those country folk and their ability to find something funny about almost anything.

The men from the USSF sent word down to thank us for such a valuable contact and how much they had enjoyed the day. The next time we were in the club we didn't put our hands in our pockets. Needless to say, we were carried home that night. I'm sure it was the only club in Belfast where you could buy a halfen of poteen across the bar.

On Tuesday 6 April, Harold Wilson, then leader of the Labour Party, claimed during a debate at Westminster on Northern Ireland that a draft bill for the imposition of direct rule existed. This sent shockwaves through the Province. We were in danger of losing our sovereign parliament and with it the right to remain part of the United Kingdom. It was the subject of much debate, nightly, for weeks on end, as we patrolled our district. Were we heading for another 1912 stand-off, to protect our right to remain part of the United Kingdom? It certainly looked like it.

On 15 May, an IRA gunman was shot dead by the British Army during a gun battle in Academy Street, not far from Belfast city centre. It was widely thought that William Reid was the person responsible for shooting Gunner Robert Curtis. The Thompson submachine-gun, used in the killing of Gunner Curtis, jammed that night and the soldiers killed him.

Soldiers were being picked off one by one, like ducks at a fairground shooting gallery, by increasingly accurate IRA snipers. Each area seemed to have at least one highly trained man with a rifle. It appeared to us that there was no defence against this kind of attack and, as the British Army Commanding Officer had said, the IRA could not be defeated by conventional means. (The general in charge of all land forces, Harry Tuzo, had issued a statement saying it would be impossible for the Army to win the war against the PIRA by conventional means.)

On 16 September, a number of Unionists resigned over the proposed tripartite talks involving Northern Ireland, Britain and the Republic of Ireland. Even moderate Unionists seemed to believe we were being sold down the proverbial river. There was a black cloud hanging over us. At a meeting with the men who had supplied us with the guns, I remember asking them, 'What's happening to stop this carnage going on all over the place? Is there anything that can be done to give these bastards a taste of their own medicine?' I couldn't believe what I was saying but enough was enough. We were told to bide our time, that there were things being put into place and the time would come when every man would be called to stand up and be counted. I left feeling good; there were men working on plans for an all-out offensive against not only the Republicans but the entire Catholic community. Feeling more positive, we went to the Times for a drink and called a meeting for the following evening.

We had been there about 90 minutes when I noticed a guy standing at the bar seemingly watching and listening to us. Leaving the table to go to the toilet, I gave this man the once-over as I passed him. He was in his late twenties, looked fit, black hair not too short, well dressed in casual clothes, about five eleven and fairly well built. When I returned from the toilet he'd gone. When I asked the girl behind the bar, whom I knew well, if she knew anything about him, she replied that his name was Mike, he was originally from Belfast, lived in London and was over here as a rep for some medical supplies company. He had been in a few times, didn't ask any questions, kept himself to himself, had a few shandies and left. He never said where he stayed and seemed a decent well mannered person. We never thought any more about it and headed home.

On 29 September, Alexander Andrews and Earnest Bates, both Protestants, were killed in a bomb attack on the Four Step Inn, Shankill Road, Belfast – a bomb attack in the very heart of the Loyalist community directed at innocent civilians having a quiet drink in a public bar. Although they never claimed it, everyone knew who the perpetrators were: the IRA.

Once again we were in the Times having a drink and I was fairly well oiled towards the end of the night. I remember, briefly, seeing that fellow Mike standing at the bar watching, but he wasn't there long and I dismissed it as a coincidence.

The PIRA was not content with attacking the Security Forces and the State of Northern Ireland; it had now turned its attention to ordinary decent people, because of their religion and their belief that Ulster should remain part of the United Kingdom. Up to that point, in my view, the Loyalists were mostly in a defensive role, letting the forces of the Crown deal with the deteriorating security situation. The Protestants had put up with a lot since the start in 1969 and, as mentioned, plans were being drawn up to go on the offensive. The Provos didn't appear to realise the violent backlash that was going to be released against the Catholic community.

The following Saturday night we were in the Times again, having a drink and discussing the bomb attack on the Wednesday and the killing of the soldier the day before, when I noticed Mike standing at the bar. Once again, I got the impression he was very interested in our conversation and told the lads to put a lid on it. While I was at the bar buying a round of drinks, I made a point of engaging him in conversation. He told me he was originally from Shore Road in North Belfast and that he'd left to live in England when he was 17. He was over here as a rep for a medical supplies company in London. He seemed all right and I invited him to join our company as it wasn't much fun standing alone at the bar. He agreed to join us, bought a round of drinks and we carried them to the table.

The topic of conversation soon returned to the Troubles and we asked him his views on what was going on here in his hometown. He told us the Troubles hadn't started when he had left but he'd followed it closely on the news and felt sickened by what was happening. He felt the British Government should be doing more to stop the Nationalists from achieving their aim and stop pussyfooting around, hit the IRA hard. It was time the Protestant majority stood up and let the world, especially the Republicans, know they weren't going to surrender without a fight.

Of course the drink was flowing and we enjoyed his words of war. They made a lot of sense to us. Enough was enough; if we were going to go down, then let it be with a fight. We bemoaned the fact that it was very hard to do anything without the armaments to do so. He agreed and said if the PIRA could achieve it, then surely the Loyalist paramilitaries could do the same.

Closing time came and Mike ordered a taxi. We all agreed to meet another night and continue our discussion. The taxi came and we all shook his hand. He had seemed genuine but, in those days, trust had to be earned and everyone was viewed with suspicion. Although I admit we were still a bit naïve; if someone expressed the same views as we held, we were inclined to say what we felt without thinking.

I applied to the RUC for a shotgun licence. I thought it

would be handy to have a legal weapon in my house as things were going from bad to worse. I asked Harry if he could get me a couple of letters from farmers, giving me permission to shoot on their land (one of the requirements needed to obtain a legal licence). He did, and I purchased a (licensed) shotgun.

The thirty-first of October 1971 was to prove the most significant day of my life – a day that tipped me over the edge into the abyss. The PIRA set off a bomb at the Post Office Tower, in the heart of London. This attack took the entire nation and the Government by surprise, proving that the Provos could strike anywhere at will. I was told later that Ted Heath, the British Prime Minister, ordered senior officers of the Army, Military Intelligence, MI5 and MI6 to his office where he instructed them in no uncertain terms to use whatever means necessary to put this insurrection down. From that date onwards, the handling of the conflict was taken over by these organisations.

On the same day, a young friend of mine, Thomas Kells, was found dead at Flowbog Road, Dundrod. His death marked my breaking point. Tom and I had been in the same Boy's Brigade Company together. He had been involved in the rioting and, being a big lad, stood out and was known to the Republicans. He had been picked up, tortured and shot. They had even gouged his Loyalist tattoos off his arms.

After Thomas's funeral we felt angry, frustrated and utterly helpless. We headed to the Orange Hall near Roughfort for a meeting. The main topic of discussion was: Where do we go from here? The Troubles were escalating; the Security Forces were unable to contain it. In fact they were being sent out onto the streets for the PIRA to pick them off at will. Try to imagine what those young men must have felt, seeing a friend killed in front of their eyes. Maybe holding him in their arms trying to comfort him, his life's blood flowing down a drain, the gurgle as he breathes his last breath. Or he might be lying a short distance away, screaming for help, and you're too terrified to move in case a sniper is waiting for you to make a move. People tend to forget the trauma those brave young men had to endure on the killing fields of Northern Ireland.

As we talked about the deteriorating situation, we weighed up what the politicians were drumming into our heads. Paisley and Craig were painting pictures of sell-outs, deals being done behind backs, the reforms of appeasement to Republicans. Don't get me wrong, there was a lot of truth in what they were saying, and we followed their rallies everywhere; but they hadn't the courage to carry their convictions to the bitter end, leaving young men who accepted their principles and put their words of war into practice rotting in prison or graveyards, disowned. In later years, the Loyalist paramilitaries would have nothing to do with Paisley and shunned him when he tried to drum up support for different causes. He is still a master of words and has phenomenal support in the Province, as election results show, but in those early years when the Protestant anger and frustration spilled into horrific acts of violence, he reneged.

We decided that Billy and I should approach Jim, and set up another meeting with the USSF and ask their advice about taking a more offensive role. We numbered about 23 men at that time, most from the Glengormly district on the outskirts of North Belfast. The meeting broke up and those of us who lived around Tiger's Bay headed to The Times for a drink.

We had been there a few hours when a strange thing happened. I was at the bar when all of a sudden that fellow Mike appeared at my side. He asked if he could have a word with me outside for a minute, he was in a hurry. I agreed. Going back to the table, I told a couple of mates to go out first and keep an eye out. Giving them a minute to get into place I followed them out onto York Road. I could see Mike standing beside a car about 20 metres away. As I approached, he put out his hand, shook mine, and said he was very sorry to hear about the loss of my friend Thomas. He said, 'Look, I know you've had a few drinks so just listen. I might be able to help you with a problem you have and I'll be in contact with you early next week. Don't be saying anything to anyone about it and I'll explain all when I see you. It could be to both our advantage.'

I started to say something, but he stopped me and said, 'Look, I'll see you next week and all will become clearer. I just wanted to let you know that I can understand your grief, as I have lost a few friends as well.'

With these words he opened his car door and started to climb in when he said, 'By the way, it was a good idea to send those couple of lads out, to keep a watch on you. See you next week.'

I was curious. Firstly, how did he know that big Tom Kells was a friend of mine and, secondly, what 'problem' of mine was he talking about. How could he help? I had a feeling of apprehension about the incident and it had the effect of sobering me up a bit. What was his game? I confided in Billy later that night about what had taken place, and he advised me to be careful and not to arrange to meet him alone.

As we made our way home there was a small riot going on in Edlingham Street, involving about 30 or 40 on each side. We went down to my house, picked up the revolver. Pulling the hood of my Parka over my head to protect my identity, I walked to the front of the crowd and fired three rounds at the Catholic crowd. Needless to say, I never hit anyone. I would probably have missed the proverbial side of a barn from the inside. But, it worked and the taigs ran for their lives. We rushed away amid cheers from the Protestant crowd. Getting home we felt elated, nervous, and I admit the cheering ringing in our ears made us feel good. It wasn't much, but with the drink in us, it felt we had struck a blow for freedom and for Ulster. I know now that it was a load of nonsense, but at that time we just savoured the moment.

1971 CONTACT

I WAS SITTING in work the following week when one of the clerks came to tell me that somebody wanted me in despatch. I thought it might be Harry. Walking out, my heart skipped two or three beats and my stomach churned when I saw Mike standing there. I felt a sense of dread.

Mike seemed cheerful, no outward sign of hostility; in fact, very relaxed. 'Hi, any chance of a quick word? It's important.'

I replied, remembering Billy's words the other week, 'I'm fairly busy at the moment, maybe later in the Times over a drink?'

He persisted. 'It'll only take a few minutes. I have a proposal for you that you might like to consider, no strings attached. If you're not interested, just walk away, but if it appeals to you it could work to both our advantage.'

I thought about it for a second and decided I had nothing to lose. He'd had to come through the security barrier to get into the yard and it was fairly busy so I knew nothing could really happen here. As he moved towards his car, I asked Big George to keep an eye on me. I felt a little safer.

Climbing into the car, Mike said, 'I assume you have another guardian angel,' and nodded towards the security hut. 'I like that, it shows common sense, which you're going to need if you embark on the action you are contemplating.'

'I don't know what you're talking about,' was my quick

response. 'I think this conversation is over,' I said, and made to open the door.

He grabbed my arm, 'Hold on a minute, hear me out. We're on the same side. Just give me time to explain.'

'Right go ahead but make it quick,' I told him, staring into his eyes to try and judge if he was genuine or not.

Just then there was a knock at the window. I nearly jumped out of my skin and turned to see George standing there, his huge frame filling the car window. As I wound the window down, he leaned over, the pistol clearly visible in his waistband. 'Any problem here, big lad?' He had seen Mike grabbing my arm.

'Not at the moment, thanks, but keep your eye on us.' I wound the window back up. 'You've got ten minutes.'

'OK. I'm connected to Military Intelligence and I've been observing you and your mates for a couple of months since that night we had a drink in the Times Bar. I was interested in your views on what's going on here, and, more importantly, what should be done to try and stop it. I know you meet in that small Orange Hall and had it wired to listen to your conversations. I know that your group are now contemplating going from a defensive role to an offensive one . . .'

I interrupted him, 'Before you go any further, if this is going the way I think it's going, you can stop right there.'

'Why, what way do you think it's going?' he asked.

'If you think for one moment you're going to recruit me as an informer, forget it. I would rather shoot you and take my chances, than go down that road. I'm more interested in fighting for my country's survival than becoming a traitor.'

'On the contrary. I could feel the sincerity in the things you and your mates were saying, that's why I'm here talking to you. You're just the sort of people we are looking to recruit, for a different kind of offensive, against the common enemy. I have tape recordings of your meetings to ensure that what I'm going to tell you will go no further than this car.

'Our Prime Minister, in his infinite wisdom, has ordered us to start training Loyalists in the art of counter espionage. After all, the PIRA are enemies of us both. In the aftermath of the attack in London he's ordered that the war be taken to them. Obviously, this can't be done in the open because of the propaganda war. It has to be done covertly. That's why we're looking for people like you – no criminal record, unknown to the police and prepared to strike back at Republicans. We're enlisting men from all over the Province to co-ordinate attacks, to convince the Catholic people that support for the Provos will only bring death and destruction to their own community. We need to show them this is a war they can't win, by whatever means possible.

'You'll be trained in firearms and explosives handling, and supplied with top-grade intelligence reports and targets. When you go on an operation, let me know, and we'll put out an OOB (Out of Bounds) code to the Security Forces. That means, as far as they're concerned, an intelligence operation is taking place. They'll leave that area for one hour. No one else will know your name but me. I'll give you a phone number and when you call, just ask for Mike. If I'm not there, you'll be told when I'm expected back. No one will ask any questions. If it's urgent, you'll have a code name or number – CO16. Just leave that and I'll contact you as soon as I can.

'Mr Heath and the top brass have given the green light for this, and as I said we can't be seen to have any part of it.'

I sat there mute, trying to make sense of it all. As I understood it, the British Government was advocating a war of attrition against the Provos and the wearing away of their Catholic support, as well as grinding down morale within their ranks. If they strike, then we strike harder, not only at them but the Catholic community as well. It sounded incredible. I asked, 'Will it work?'

'It's got to work, because as one of our top officers pointed out, it isn't a battle that the military can win by conventional means, it's given the Provos the incentive to intensify their campaign.'

I said, 'It sounds OK but I would have to see the other men and see what their thoughts were.'

He agreed but gave me this bit of advice which I have never forgotten: 'I know you have 20-odd men with you but the more people that know about things the easier it is for informers and Security Forces to find out. Put it this way, suppose the two of us decide to kill someone today and we go out and do it. As long as we're not caught red-handed and we leave no forensic evidence and, most importantly, don't tell anyone else, then we can never be caught. Pick another very trustworthy man, and operate within the unit. Never reveal your activities to the others and you'll be secure.'

We stared at each other – potential terrorist and intelligence officer – meeting at a common frontier of cynical comprehension. He gave me the phone number, and told me to ask for him and just say yes or no. If we were interested, then he would set up another meeting with me.

I got out of the car and nodded to George to open the barrier. I was in shock. George came over and asked if I was OK, I looked very pale. I felt nervous, confused and shaky. I muttered something to George about being all right and headed to the toilets.

As I sat there reflecting, I shivered uncontrollably. My mind was in turmoil. Was I capable of becoming a terrorist and all that it entailed: murder, bombing, indeed, any crime at all? Could I carry out these deeds to put these Republican bastards down? The men and I had discussed all sorts of revenge attacks, knowing full well we may never actually carry them out. Words of bravado from a group of men with no criminal experience, but they sounded good and made you feel brave. Then I thought of Big Tom Kells lying in his grave, tortured and murdered in cold blood, and all the young soldiers, policemen and other Protestants killed in the last nine months. If the British Government sanctioned it, felt it was essential, then somebody had to do it. Why not us? Fight fire with fire. Give them as good as we got.

My life would never be the same again.

I went home that evening a nervous wreck. We had a couple of guns and had fired some shots in a drunken escapade, but this was different. Was this guy for real or just a trick to recruit informers? If it was the latter, why involve two men? I had warned Mike that I would never inform on anyone. I had to cover my arse quickly.

I headed to Billy's house straight away and described the encounter with Mike.

He was astounded. 'Are you having me on? Does he think he's James fucking Bond?'

I confirmed that I thought Mike wasn't kidding at all, that he was very convincing. We decided to ask Jim for his advice. Maybe it was all a bit far-fetched: Government backing, counter insurgency groups, recruitment by Military Intelligence, actual missions. I left the house with mixed feelings and my body tingling with adrenaline. I found it difficult to sleep that night.

On Saturday, Billy and I met with Jim and a man I hadn't met before, and recounted our story. When we had finished, they looked at each other, then back at me, astonishment etched on their faces. The stranger asked, 'Do you honestly believe this man Mike is playing with the full deck?'

I confirmed that I thought he was genuine and repeated Mike's words: 'The Prime Minister, in his infinite wisdom, has ordered the war to be taken to the enemy and given the green light for Loyalists to be trained and armed to counteract the threat of the PIRA.'

The cards were on the table; it was up to these men whether we picked them up or folded. After a brief conversation with the stranger, Jim described their thoughts: 'The top men discussed this before we came down here and they've left us to make a decision, as to what you should do next. We feel you could be putting yourself at a terrible risk, but it's up to you. If you're prepared to take the chance, it's your neck on the block if anything goes wrong. You could be looking at a prison sentence or death. If you do decide to find out what's at stake, tell us what you think of the proposal. Whatever it is, see if it can be put to the test, without any danger to you or anybody else. If it's true, it will open a Pandora's box for us all.'

I replied that I knew nothing about any other activities so if it was a set-up I could hardly divulge any information to Mike. If it was true, the advantages outweighed the disadvantages. I said I would ask Mike if Billy could come along to the next meeting; if it was genuine, that shouldn't be a problem, and if there were any difficulty, I would walk away. We left it at that and shook hands. Jim wished us luck. I was going to need it.

Billy said, 'Right. There's no time like the present. Let's ring him now!'

We headed down to a public phonebox, nerves on edge. I was debating with myself, whether to call the whole thing off and walk away. Now, of course, I wish I had. But curiosity had got the better of me. As I dialled the number, adrenaline was pumping round my body. I was hooked on the buzz. I held the phone so Billy could hear too.

A man's voice answered on the second ring, just a straight-forward 'Hello'.

'Could I speak to Mike?'

'Hold on a second.' I was asking myself, maybe they're trying to trace the call. I'd seen too many movies.

Mike's voice came on the line, startling me. 'Mike here, what can I do for you?'

I froze. I didn't know what to say. Do I ask if it's a secure line? Do I give my name? Did he recognise my voice? I would have to stop watching fucking spy movies, I thought.

His voice brought me out of my dilemma, 'Hello, Mike here, can I help you?'

'Yeah, it's me. The answer is yes.'

'That's great, when can we meet?'

We agreed to meet outside the Times Bar at 2 p.m. the following day. (No Sunday opening back then.)

I decided to ask the 64,000-dollar question. 'Before you go, I need to ask you, can the man that's going to be involved, be with me tomorrow?'

There was no hesitation. 'No problem, I'll see you there.'

When I came off the phone, I realised I was sweating. I felt the cool wetness after the conversation was finished.

Billy said, 'There's no going back now. Tomorrow we'll know what's in store for us.'

I always found the waiting the hardest. The hours between the phone call and two o'clock the following day dragged. Sleep was non-existent, tossing and turning. Christ, I was anxious. The thought hit me again, only harder this time, to just forget all about it and walk away. It was the easy way out, the cow-ard's way. Then I reminded myself, this isn't about me; it's about protecting the Protestant community from terror. It could be me or any of my family, caught in an explosion, maimed or killed. Perhaps the Government and the Army knew best, and the only way to defeat a terrorist onslaught was to fight fire with more fire. I hoped they did.

At 1.45 p.m. Billy and I headed to the bar, had a look around, all the time trying to look nonchalant. No police or soldiers were hiding up entries, in fact the road was very quiet. Just after two, as we were on the verge of leaving, we heard the car. Each time I'd met Mike he was driving a different brand of car and I couldn't resist passing comment, 'You must have plenty of cars to use.'

'Yeah,' he answered, 'quite a few.' He acknowledged Billy, saying that he'd thought it would be him coming along, then continued, 'I was glad you said yes, because we're getting pressure put on us to come up with the goods fast.'

Billy cut him off, 'Before you say any more, drive to Belfast Castle first.'

We arrived roughly ten minutes later; not another word had been said. Mike pulled into one of the parking bays in the Castle's grounds.

Billy said, 'You don't mind walking while you speak to us?'

'Not at all,' Mike answered and got out of the car.

Billy said, 'Do you mind a body search, just in case of wires? You know a lot in relation to us, but we know fuck all about you.' It was Billy's turn to be paranoid, but better safe than sorry. My heart was pounding, and I was sure the other two could hear it.

Mike agreed and turned to face the car, putting his hands on the roof. It crossed my mind that if anybody had been watching, they would have been intrigued by the antics of the three of us. Billy gave him a quick once-over and removed a Browning

9mm from a holster under his left armpit. 'Do you mind if I hold on to this until we finish this conversation?'

'Not a problem.'

'He's clean now,' Billy nodded to me. We walked up one of the paths and sat down on a bench.

I opened the discussion, 'Right, Mike, go ahead. Persuade us we're making the correct decision here.' With his gun removed by Billy now, I was beginning to feel a bit more relaxed.

We listened intently as Mike talked. 'Lads, I'm very impressed by the way you've handled yourselves today. Other men we've enlisted were very cautious at first, but you went beyond that. You were vigilant and guarded. One mistake, you never checked the gun. It's empty.'

Billy reached into his pocket and confirmed it true, then handed it back to Mike.

'I'm not that stupid either,' he smiled. We all burst out laughing. I didn't think there would have been any laughter that day. We were warming to this guy.

'The main proposal on the table is we train men like you, in all aspects of guerrilla warfare, to go up against the Provisional IRA. We'll arm you with whatever you need to carry the war to them and also to attack the Catholic population, to drain support away from them. I know it sounds crazy, but with the Provos escalating their terror campaign and attacking civilian targets, it's felt a war of attrition against them is necessary, probably the only way to defeat the bastards. It's not a war that can be won by conventional means. But you don't tell that to the cunts who're shooting and bombing the shit out of you. This strategy can't be made public. The idea is four-man squads. If you're not caught in the act, you don't leave any forensic evidence behind, and you tell no one, you won't be caught.

'We'll do everything in our power to ensure you get in and

out without any hassle from the Security Forces. You let us know the area you're targeting and we'll put out an OOB call. The Security Forces will leave that district for one hour. They'll be under the impression that an intelligence operation is in place. I'll be your only contact with our unit, which is the Military Recognisance Force (MRF). Not very many people know of our existence and if anyone tries to make our presence public, it will be vehemently denied. We'll be covering our arses every step of the way. If you're apprehended, we might be able to pull a few strings, but it's a very big IF. If you're caught, it's very important no one mentions their connection with us and under no circumstances plead guilty, no matter how bad it looks. Our unit is in this for one purpose and one purpose only, to fight a very dirty war by whatever means possible. And I mean anything and everything. Any questions so far?'

We had been mesmerised. Looking at each other, I left it to Billy to ask the questions.

'It sounds the message all right; you seem to have covered all possibilities. Where do you train us, and, more importantly, how do we get there? We can't be seen driving into some Army base or climbing in and out of Land-Rovers. It would look a bit suspicious'

He answered, 'OK, you'll have realised you're neither the first nor the last to be recruited, so here's how it works. You'll drive over to a pre-arranged spot in East Belfast where a VCP will have been set up by some of our guys. You park about 200 yards from it and get out and walk towards it. Each week will be a different place. I'll give you a pass, which you'll show when you're asked for proof of identity. You'll be put against the side of the Land-Rover and searched. They will then proceed to arrest you and put you into the back of the jeep. Once you're secure, you'll be given balaclavas which you'll wear at all times, until you're driven back, close to where you parked in the first place. You'll remove the balaclava before exiting the Land-Rover. Your names will never be mentioned. You won't know any of the others taking part and they won't know you.

'It has to be cloak-and-dagger stuff for everybody concerned. We're in sole charge of the operations. You let me know the area you intend to strike and I put out the OOB. I'll tell you if another squad is going to do something else in the same area that night so you can cancel your action until another time. It wouldn't be safe if you or another team carried out an attack half an hour or so before the second one and they run into any Security Forces responding to the first attack. So, we'll co-ordinate all hits to safeguard you. The only nigger in the woodpile is if another team not under our control does something before you go in, then it could become difficult.'

Billy said, 'You could always send a legitimate car in first to do a reconnaissance of the area, before the armed team went in. Or issue us with radios to listen for any activity?'

Mike looked at him, 'They're not bad ideas. I'll let you know which one of them we'll use.'

Billy commented, 'You seem to know what you're talking about and it sounds workable, but will it succeed?'

'Believe me, this strategy has been studied in depth. It's based on one used in Kenya, where Brigadier Frank Kitson trained counter gangs to fight the Mau Mau. Although we have a different kind of war here, with some modifications it can be applied. Kitson's in the Province now, commanding 39 Infantry Brigade.' (What he didn't tell us and I only found out after reading Martin Dillon's book, *The Dirty War*, was that the MRF was attached to 39 Infantry Brigade. Now that I know the facts surrounding Brigadier Frank Kitson and his role in the MRF, it makes sense that he would be the man overseeing the whole operation. It was probably Kitson that gave us a lecture early in 1972.)

He continued: 'The whole idea is to terrorise the terrorists. There are a number of different strategies being applied; this is just one of them. There will be groups gathering intelligence, others working with informers and counter insurgency gangs. They want the Provos hit from all sides, to put them under so much pressure that they'll call their war off. We need to win the propaganda war as well as the military one. Different forms of interrogation techniques will be introduced, to break the men down when we capture them. This will revolutionise the way this conflict is being fought. These are some of the tactics that will be used, but a more in-depth lecture will be given at your first training session. Any questions?'

It was very hard to digest, sitting on a log bench close to Belfast Castle, overlooking the city. I made up my mind.

'It all sounds like something out of a book, like James Bond stuff, but, speaking for myself, at the moment, you can count me in. We'd been considering going down that road anyway, but we'd no idea how to go about it. You've convinced me it's authentic, so why not? In for a penny, in for a pound. It has to work or this conflict could go on for years.' How prophetic that statement turned out to be. Billy nodded his agreement and we shook hands. Mike told us to head to Connsbrook Avenue, off the Holywood Road, for two o'clock the following Saturday, where we would be picked up. Before he left us, he handed a small card to Billy, with MRF printed on it, and told him to show it to the soldiers at the VCP.

Our nerves were shattered. It was all right saying this and that, big brave words, but when you had time to reflect, doubts crept in. Now we knew what was expected of us, the reality sank in. We thought the Provos must have men with nerves of steel, to enable them to carry out their ruthless acts, seemingly without any qualms or moral principles.

I smoked in those days and I was getting through 40 a day, steadily getting worse by the hour. We were shaking like leaves in a gale. Would our conscience allow us to do it? The conclusion we came to was that it takes a faith in something that's right, in order to kill somebody. How else can you justify your actions, unless you think positively and have a belief in your cause, to put it in front of everything else? It has to take precedence over all aspects of your life, above and beyond your normal feelings; greater than your love of everything decent and, unfortunately, the love of your family.

Only single men should be involved with this level of responsibility and sense of duty. How could a man with a wife and children dedicate his life to something like this, alongside the moral obligation of taking care of his family? It should not be expected of them. They could help in the background, but front-line stuff should be left to single men.

Now, after all these years and the countless break-ups of marriages that I have witnessed, the significance of that perception Billy and I discussed at length comes back to haunt me: the hurt and suffering to all concerned, the torment men go through when imprisoned while their wives struggle to cope with their absence, caring for and protecting their children alone, in a hard and cruel society. It drove men to the brink of suicide. Not only being apart from the family, but the uncertainty of a future played on their minds to the point of distraction.

Mothers suffer terribly if their sons are incarcerated, as indeed my own would in later years. A mother will never abandon her child, but wives feel let down and betrayed when a man puts something in front of her and the kids. While they may understand the reasons behind it, the uncertainty of any sort of future plays a big part in their decision to terminate the relationship or not. It is only human nature. While everything possible to make life bearable for prisoners' families was done by various welfare groups, a lot of times it wasn't enough.

We thought about all the members of our team and decided it would be better to keep this to ourselves. We could pick men for each operation without any of the others knowing. It could also work by choosing four men and organising the mission and send them on the job, without them knowing their way in and out safely was guaranteed.

The days and hours dragged. I spent my time watching the clock. I was a nervous wreck; a man on death row would have been less on edge.

Saturday came. Billy and I headed into East Belfast. It was too late to pull out now, without looking like a coward in front of my mate. The roadblock in Connsbrook Avenue was already set up. After parking the car, we strolled up to it casually, as if we hadn't a care in the world. The soldiers stopped us and asked for identification. Billy pulled out the card. The soldier who seemed to be in charge went to the back of the Land-Rover and lifted the radio handset, as if he was doing a check on our ID, but he didn't actually say anything. A few minutes later we were told to stand with our hands on the side of one of the Land-Rovers, where they gave us a body search. We were then 'arrested' and bundled roughly into the back of separate vehicles, one in each.

The lieutenant in my vehicle apologised for the handling at the roadblock, explaining that if they hadn't handled us in the same way as everyone else, it would look suspicious to an onlooker. He handed me a balaclava. We knew we were headed for Palace Barracks as Mike had told us at our meeting.

We disembarked and spotted small groups of men standing inside the compound, all wearing balaclavas. The compound was enclosed with a solid wooden fence. We couldn't see out and no one could see in. Mike was waiting for us. He came over and shook our hands, welcoming us to the camp. There were other military personnel present; I assumed they were MRF who had recruited the other men. I had anticipated being a quivering lump of human jelly by then, but when I saw the other men scattered around the compound, it actually had a calming effect. I could feel a weight lifting off my shoulders. After a brief interlude the compound gate opened to admit another two Land-Rovers and the last team jumped out.

A voice barked, 'Men! Can we have you inside now?' We headed into a building where rows of seats faced a blackboard and desk. The first thing that leapt into my mind was, 'Fuck me, we're back at school.' It looked just like a classroom. I certainly wasn't expecting that. Everyone sat down and a soldier took his place behind a desk facing us, his pips indicated the rank of captain. The officer started with a meticulous review of the information Mike had given us that day at the castle. He covered how we would be accountable to the Official Secrets Act and all that that entailed. Under no circumstances could anything be made public. They would do everything possible to ensure no one would be apprehended. If we followed their instructions to the letter, about how not to leave forensic evidence and take precautions, it would be impossible for any of us to be caught. Most importantly, and he stressed this emphatically, no matter how tempted we were to shoot our mouths off to our mates about any operation, doing that was a sure way of it getting back to the police and arrest would quickly follow.

He described the Out of Bounds instructions and how they would be implemented. He told us that today's meeting was just a preliminary get-together, in order to establish a code of conduct, both here, during weapon instruction and on the firing ranges, so that everyone knew what to do and what was expected of us. We would be given tuition in field crafts and coaching, on methods to control our nerves. We would need to operate on our own initiative and contact would be minimal, except when we needed an OOB put in place. Our liaison officers would deliver weapons to each squad in the coming weeks and we would be given suggestions on where and how to store them.

As I sat absorbing the man's words, I felt increasingly elated. I wondered if any of the other guys felt the same. Everyone sat in silence, waiting for the next set of instructions he was about to divulge. I find it hard to describe that feeling: sitting amongst 20 to 30 men, all with balaclavas concealing their identity, committing themselves to an objective of death and destruction against the enemies of the State of Northern Ireland and their supporters. And, what's more, with the help and support of Military Intelligence and the British Government.

I realise how chilling it must sound. It was, but with a backdrop of total anarchy and pandemonium to our everyday lives. The PIRA were on a killing spree; towns and cities were being destroyed with their bombs; policemen and soldiers were being murdered; innocent civilians were being shot. The Security Forces were unable to contain the violence and increasingly bore the brunt of the violence. Somebody within the Republican movement must have realised that men within the million Protestants living in Northern Ireland wouldn't stand by with indifference and allow them to destroy our homeland. We believed their leaders must accept full responsibility for all Catholics targeted and killed in retaliation, for their acts of terror and violence against a vast majority of Godfearing, decent and peaceful people from both sides of the community.

We were respectable citizens, hard-working men looking

forward to a future, now provoked into protecting our way of life. I'm sure everyone in that room felt the same as I did. We would not go down without a fight.

I knew the Loyalist paramilitaries were getting ready for offensive action. We were all going to be an integral part of Ulster's fight to remove the threat the Republicans posed to our right to remain part of the United Kingdom. This group was only Belfast's contribution to the counter offensive at that time. Recruiting was still ongoing. Mike told me later they were enlisting men from both the UVF and UDA. Also, there were groups throughout the six counties, being trained like us in readiness for the commencement of hostilities. We were told it would take roughly eight weeks before we would be ready to carry out our objectives. Of course, the Captain joked, if the Provos surrendered between now and then, we would not be required. Everyone burst out laughing. Until then the mood had been sombre, but that off-the-cuff remark relaxed us and I could feel the tension in the room dissipate. I remember looking at these loyal men sitting in the room and thinking, 20 to 30 men isn't going to make a hell of an impact on the Provos' campaign. Then, I realised, although we were the only two in the group present, we had the backing of another 22 men. If the other men here had the same or more men in their squads, then possibly 150 to 200 men would be available. We were going to be a considerable force to contend with.

This network could be used for a lot of operations within your squad. The other squad members wouldn't know their backs were covered by an OOB when they went on an operation. It was a perfect system. We could pass the information on to the men who helped us from the Shankill and they could just tell Billy area and time. He would then contact Mike and the men would be in and out, no problem.

After about 90 minutes' listening to the Captain, we were given a chance to stretch our legs and cool down. It was stifling wearing the balaclavas. We filed out into the compound and lit up. It was then I felt the sweat trickling down my back as I hit the air. During the break, I told Billy my ideas about using these tactics for a number of teams. He agreed; it didn't matter who was doing the job, as long as it was done. No one need know a thing about this side of the operation, apart from our USSF contact.

Fifteen minutes passed and the compound gates opened to admit some Land-Rovers. We thought it was time to go home. Mike came over to us and seemed to be in good spirits. 'Right, lads, you'll be taken to a shooting range now where you'll be given instructions on a number of weapons and allowed to have a test fire on them. We want to see how well you use them, so we know what we are up against and the amount of practice each one of you needs.'

When we arrived at the firing range, just a short drive to Kinneger Army Camp, we were split into four squads. There were four wooden tables with the same weapons laid out on each of them. Each table had a Browning 9mm semi-automatic pistol, a .22 Star pistol, a Sterling submachine-gun and a SLR rifle. It looked impressive. There were a couple of instructors standing beside each table. I could see Mike and the other soldiers who were at the compound in the background, observing our tutoring in weapon handling. My heart was pounding and my palms were sweating.

The tutors were brilliant. They made us feel at ease, laughing and joking with us. They showed us how to keep the guns safe so no one would accidentally shoot himself or one of his team. They were covering the basics, letting us see how each weapon handles and come to grips with the power of the weapons. I confess, I felt exhilarated. It was like waking up after having a wet dream, fucking magic.

They showed us how to strip the guns down, clean them and then demonstrated how to fire each one. Then we all got our chance. It's almost impossible to describe the feeling I got with each round I fired. Mind-blowing, astonishing, out of this world – these words don't come close. Coupled with an awareness of the sheer power in your hands, the power over life and death, it felt like something akin to God. The Sterling machinegun surprised me by how quickly it emptied its magazine and the accuracy of the SLR was exceptional. The weight of the Browning compared to the lighter Star was noticeable. All in all, the experience was absolutely terrific. If the situation and the reason we were there, training to murder people, hadn't been so serious I could only describe it as an awe-inspiring episode in my life.

When everyone had finished shooting we were transported back to Palace Barracks. After another intensive session on the objectives of our actions – how we were out to destroy, discredit and eliminate the Provisionals' campaign of violence – we were told that an operation had been authorised to place a bomb, within the next two weeks, in a Catholic bar and blame it on the PIRA; in other words, an own goal. ('Own goal' was to become a common phrase in the years ahead.) One of us would be selected to organise a team, and this operation would be a test, to gauge the Provos' level of support in the Catholic community. No paramilitary organisation would claim responsibility for it, in order to keep up the pretense that it was an own goal.

This was thought-provoking stuff. I could sense it was also a test for us, to gauge our reaction so soon after our initiation. One of the groups was going to be involved in planting a bomb, aimed at killing people inside a public bar. The high I was on after the firing range suddenly became a low. It's one thing talking about actions, but when it becomes the reality . . . It's as well I had a mask on, so no one could see my pallor.

Arrangements were made for pick-ups for the following Saturday at noon and we were returned close to where our car was parked. Just before we'd left, Mike had come over and said he would see us during the week. With those words, I was almost reduced to a quivering wreck. Had he chosen us?

By that stage, I was contemplating disappearing across the water. When we returned to Billy's house, his mother made us a cup of tea. We felt a bit stronger, but we had a lot to discuss and were better doing it somewhere where no one could hear our conversation. I hadn't spoken much during the drive back, I was so deep in thought. It felt strange sitting in the parlour, sipping tea, after the afternoon's events. We were trying to speak coherently about it all, but we were so keyed-up we weren't really succeeding. I didn't know until later that Billy felt the same way. Some terrorists we were. I'm sure the Provos would be quaking in their boots if they knew we were on their case.

Anyway, we talked for another hour, and then went for a large drink.

The next week dragged by. I smoked like a trooper, one after the other, just waiting for Mike to appear. On the Wednesday, we had a meeting with the rest of our squad of men and told them the UVF was going on the offensive in the New Year. We would be taking part in the conflict and if anyone wanted out, now was the time to walk away; nobody would think any less of them if they did. Not every person would be capable of doing the things that would be required, if we were going to beat these Republican bastards. The men would have to be aware that taking a decision now might put you in jail, or even get you killed. Anyone who needed a bit of time to think it over, should feel free and take a week or so before letting us know. Once we started to operate, we would be under UVF leadership and rules, and then no one could leave. It wasn't a democracy; failure to obey an order would lead to punishment, anything from a beating or kneecapping to death. Lads, it's time to stand up and be counted. Everyone looked at each other and no one moved towards the door.

Billy said, 'Well, as no one's made a beeline for the door, I'll assume you all want to stay. If you're frightened somebody will say something to you for leaving and you're afraid you'd lose face, come to me afterwards and it can be said in private. This is the time to do it, because if we have to force anyone into doing something, they will become a risk and drastic action might have to be taken to safeguard the rest of the team.'

Not one man left. We were in business.

On 25 November, Harold Wilson, leader of the Labour Party, stuck his foot in his mouth again. He proposed that Britain should work towards a withdrawal from Northern Ireland, with the consent of the Protestants, after a period of 15 years. As part of the deal, The Republic of Ireland would rejoin the British Commonwealth. In our view, he talked the biggest load of shit any of us had ever heard. The only reaction to that proposal was one of contempt. He was to get worse when he came back to power a few years later. No wonder the Intelligence Services conspired to have him removed from office (if rumours are to be believed). The man was a jackass.

Mike called that night, to find out what we thought about the previous Saturday's experience. We told him we had been impressed with the professional way it had been managed, but they were taking a risk. Somebody might jump ship and blabber to the police, or the media. He told us not to worry.

Everything was under strict control. Every possible scenario had been carefully assessed long before we had put this into effect. We had a laugh at Mr Wilson's expense, then Mike stated that it wasn't going to be our team involved in the operation on the bar. He indicated it would be in North Belfast and to be prepared for a backlash from the Provos. I relaxed. We weren't going to be tested yet.

On Saturday we went back to Palace Barracks. There wasn't so much apprehension this week, thank God. We were shown how to make homemade explosives: the quantities of each chemical to be mixed; how to mix them without causing any sparks; how to assemble pipe bombs and gas cylinder bombs. While they would supply gelignite and other types of explosive, special booby-trap bombs, we were to supplement the high explosives with homemade ones. It would look very suspicious if every bomb was made of commercial explosives as the police knew there were some materials being smuggled to Loyalists from quarries.

We were given a choice of which gun each of us would like to know more about. Everyone who picked the Browning was taken to one area, and everyone who chose the Star was taken somewhere else, and so on. Each group was given a complete run-down on the weapon of their choice: how to strip it down; how to clean it; the velocity of the bullet when it leaves the barrel; the history behind the making of it. Everything was covered. An extraordinary day for all of us. The climax was the detonation of three different types of small bombs. Before leaving, the Captain told us the mission against the bar was scheduled for next Saturday in North Belfast. Some weapons would be distributed to those areas that might come under attack from the Provos when they discovered it wasn't one of their own bombs. Arrangements were made for the following

Saturday's pick-up time and place. After we were dropped off, we headed home.

This may sound cold-hearted but we couldn't wait until Saturday came around. I knew now we were part of a very ambitious strategy, and this was the first time it would be put to the test. We lived in anticipation the whole week. Billy had arranged for Jim to call on Sunday. We would give him all the facts then. He arrived with the stranger who had been present the last time. We went into every detail over and over again, and answered all their questions as best we could. They asked how it could be tested without any danger to whoever was going to test it. That's when Billy told them about the bomb attack being planned for the following Saturday. I told them it was the ideal way to prove if the whole operation was genuine or not, without any of us being at risk. They agreed wholeheartedly and said they would report back to the senior men and call next Sunday to confirm if the bombing had taken place.

On 2 December, a 17-year-old Protestant girl, Vivian Gibney, died of her injuries, after being shot during an IRA sniper attack on a RUC foot patrol at Cliftonville Circus, Belfast. We were so enraged by this murder we could barely wait for Saturday to come. Payback time was rapidly approaching. That night Mike delivered four weapons (two Sterling submachine-guns and two Star pistols), extra magazines and boxes of ammunition to Billy's house. We were armed and ready if the Provos tried any retaliation after the bomb went off.

We went to our usual rendezvous point that Saturday. Back at Kinnager Camp, each one of us chose a different weapon from the previous week's choice and was given comprehensive training. A lot of time was spent on the firing ranges with extensive instruction on how to aim and fire. Back at Palace Barracks, we were put through a session of fieldcraft. I loved firing a SLR (Self Loading Rifle); it was highly accurate. Mike came over towards the end of the day and said he might call over later to see us. It was strange. Nothing had been said about today's operation.

Back home, we checked our guns. Although they were new, we practised stripping and putting them back together again. We were like children with new toys. The banter was good between us and lifted the nervousness. I had no appetite. As I mentioned earlier the waiting always got to me. I wanted it to happen now and get it over with. The rest of our team started to arrive, and we told them to expect a bit of aggro in and around the Tiger's Bay area, and they were needed in case it got hot and heavy.

I wondered if all this preparation was to be in vain. It could be a bar in Ardoyne or Oldpark, which was a mile or two from where we normally did our vigilante patrols. If it was in one of those areas, it was unlikely that anything would spark off in the New Lodge Road district. Billy reminded me that weapons would be distributed to those areas that might come under attack after the bomb was detonated. If Mike had delivered weapons to us, it stood to reason that it must be one of the bars in the New Lodge Road district that was going to be hit. Simple logic, wasn't it?

Around 8 p.m. teams were organised to start their vigilante patrols and told to watch the interface areas on the Duncairn Gardens. Mike arrived. There were four groups and each of the handguns was given to the man in charge of each squad. The Sterlings were left in a safe house, in readiness. Mike joined us on our rounds, hinting that it wouldn't be long before something happened.

We arrived at a spot directly facing Lepper Street. There were a number of young lads standing at some of the street corners. I was hoping they fancied a riot tonight and would come down to attack us. It wouldn't be stones we would be firing back at them this time. As we watched them, out of the blue, a bright flash lit up the sky, followed by a loud explosion. A huge cheer went up from everyone in the streets around the New Lodge, thinking it was a Provo bomb. Mike shouted, 'Let's give them something else to think about!' and run to the corner of Lepper Street, pulling his 9mm out as he went. We followed close behind, pulling out our guns as we ran. When he reached the corner he fired a few rounds up the street. Not wanting to be outdone, we did the same, before we all ran into Adam Street.

McGurk's Bar, on North Queen Street, was destroyed. The building had collapsed and people were trapped under the rubble. Although there were rumours later that it had been another bar close by that had been the original target, the effect was the same. We carried on down to the junction of North Queen Street and Duncairn Gardens where we could see the smoke and dust hanging in the air where the bar had been. Crowds started to gather on both sides of the divide, as police, soldiers, the Fire Brigade and ambulances raced to the scene. We could hear people screaming, loud-pitched wails, as women realised it was a bar on their side this time and not a PIRA target.

It wasn't long before rioting started. The Protestant crowd was jeering and contemptuous; they were also under the impression it had been an own goal. Reports were coming in fast and furious, that a number of people were dead and some were trapped. There must have been a newsflash on the television. The crowd grew as the rioting intensified. The police and Army were caught in the middle. They had pushed the crowds back into their own areas and we could see the blue flashing lights of the emergency services close to the demolished pub. A lot of the Catholic crowd had drifted down to the bombsite, in an effort to help dig survivors or bodies from the debris. Every time an ambulance pulled away, a huge cheer when up from the Loyalist crowd.

It was a release of months and months of frustration. Protestants had been, it felt to us, constantly subjected to acts of violence for so long that when they thought this was a bombing which had gone wrong they felt elated. It might sound cold, but the feeling of revenge and counter offensive, was at the forefront of the majority of people's thoughts. We were actually celebrating and revelling in the success of the operation. Each time a news report came on the television or radio, the body count rose. Things had settled down a little when a group of women came out of Meadow Street and walked to the centre of the road. Needless to say, they became the target of the crowd's abuse. Suddenly, the women parted and an IRA man stepped out from their midst and emptied a machine-gun magazine, probably a Thompson, at the police and soldiers and us behind them.

It's one way to clear the streets pretty quickly. A couple of soldiers and a policeman were hit and fell to the ground as our crowd ran and dived for cover. I was turning when I felt my right calf muscle go numb. I staggered for a few yards then Billy and Mike grabbed me by the arms and carried me hobbling further up the road. I could hear bullets ricocheting all around; fully expecting one to hit you. Stopping in a doorway a short distance away, Mike pulled up my trouser-leg. No blood. Giving the muscle a rub, he reckoned I must have twisted it as I turned. There is nothing more exhilarating than to be shot at, without result. Escaping a near-death situation.

A couple of our guys came running over and told us there was a lot of aggro at the top of Tiger's Bay. Apparently, the taigs from Atlantic Avenue had attacked. Quickly, we headed up that way. Billy hung back with me as I limped along. When we arrived about five minutes after the rest of the squad, the riot was in full swing. There was a small alleyway, about eight feet wide, leading from Hallidays Road, in the Bay, to Newington Street, in the Catholic district of Atlantic Avenue. The place was black with people; all trying hard to throw as much as they could over a small six-foot fence in the middle. Streetlights were put out of action and the place was in total darkness. Men were running back and forth, gathering stones and returning to throw them across the fence. I stood at the corner, poking my head round now and again. My leg was aching so I wasn't much use to anybody.

I handed the gun to one of the men in case it was needed. After about half an hour, a volley of shots rang out from the Catholic side, scattering the Loyalists every which way. The next thing I knew, three men ran out and fired a volley of shots back up the alleyway at them, running towards me when they'd finished. I recognised Big George's physique and shouted jokingly, 'For fuck's sake, lads, you'll get into trouble for doing things like that!'

The next minute two Police Land-Rovers flew into Hallidays Road from the Limestone Road and stopped about 50 metres from where we were all standing. Half a dozen peelers jumped out and came towards us. As the first one came up to us he asked what was going on. I told him not to go round the corner as shots were being fired down the alleyway.

'Is that right?' he said, putting his head round the corner. By this time the crowd was just milling about; nobody wanting to be caught out in the open, now there were guns on either side. Just then, typical of the Prods, a fight broke out between a couple of drunks outside the Park Bar. The cops rushed down to break up the fight and we headed to a nearby house of one of our men. Time for a cup of tea.

I was rubbing the calf muscle of my right leg when I noticed a hole in my trouser leg. Turning it round I discovered a second hole. A trickle of blood was running down my leg. Lifting my trouser leg higher I could see where a bullet had grazed my calf, like a burn. My mate's wife cleaned and bandaged the wound. I was the first casualty in our squad. We sat there waiting for news. The last we heard was 12 dead and they were still digging. We called it a night.

Lying in bed that night, I tried hard to get off to sleep, but it was impossible. The events of the evening kept playing over and over again in my mind. I was buzzing. The flash of light and then the noise were etched in my brain. I napped fitfully throughout the rest of the night; awaking with the noise of the explosion ringing in my ears; sweating profusely; remembering the screams of those women chilled me. I thought about the people still digging in the wreckage of the bar, looking for survivors or more bodies.

At that stage, I believed in God. I prayed that the Provisional IRA would see the sorrow and suffering caused by that bomb amongst their community and call off their campaign of violence. After all, they were supposed to be the protectors of Catholics. Could they become aware that through their actions more Catholics were going to die horrible deaths? What sort of men were they, if they could let that happen? Could they not ask themselves, is this going to achieve our aim? If Loyalist paramilitaries were capable, equipped, organised and prepared to reap death and destruction against them and ordinary innocent Catholics, surely it would bring them to their senses. Only time would tell. They must realise that more Catholics would be targeted, Republican or not, if they continued their violence.

The plan had worked perfectly. The media blasted the Provos for an own goal. The Army Technical Officers (bomb disposal experts) put the scene of the explosion inside the bar. They even said, due to some of the injuries caused, that some of the people killed had possibly been leaning over the bomb, as if they were assembling or priming it. It's incredible that the theory stood the test of time. It wasn't until seven years later that the man who drove the bomb team to and from the bar that night, being interviewed by the police about a completely different matter, suddenly confessed to driving the car that night in December 1971.

Sure enough, Jim and his mate arrived at Billy's the next day. The first thing they said: 'The men up the road are very impressed, to say the least. They want you to keep them informed, through us, of everything you're told. They'll want to speak to you in about four weeks' time, so you can give them a complete rundown on a timetable of events, and possibly give a demonstration of any training you receive. But the word at the minute is, go for it, and if last night is anything to go by, it looks like an answer to all our prayers.'

My answer wasn't long in coming. The Monday following the attack on McGurk's Bar, 6 December, the Provos planted a bomb in Belfast's city centre. The resulting explosion, beside the Salvation Army Citadel, caused a wall to collapse on top of a 61-year-old Protestant, Mary Thompson, killing her.

It was one week after the McGurk's Bar massacre when the Provos attempted a revenge attack on the Protestant community. We were training in Palace Barracks at the time and heard the faint rumble of the explosion as it came across Belfast Lough. Reports filtered through to us that an explosion had taken place in a furniture shop on the Shankill Road. There were a number of casualties and, perhaps, people buried in the rubble. Some men, obviously from the Road, asked if they could leave. They were told that transport was already on the way. A few minutes later they were gone. The Captain came in and informed us that two small children had been killed. The Provisionals had given their answer, during the week, with their attacks and now again today. They had thrown down the gauntlet. The question was, were we going to pick it up? A resounding YES! went up from everyone in the room. It felt like a movie, the goodies all gathered together and big John Wayne at the front with his rallying speech and everybody rushing out to death or glory.

One of the men asked if the training could take place on Saturdays and Sundays, in order to get at these bastards sooner rather than later. The Captain confirmed that if that was what everyone wanted, he didn't see any reason why not. No one objected and we were told they would put it in place for next week.

The sight of those two small children being lifted from the debris and, a few days later, their tiny white coffins being carried at their funerals, it could do nothing else but bring a lump to your throat. Grown men cried inconsolably. I could never tolerate the death of children, no matter which side they were from. The killing of a child seems to bring with it the death of hope and the death of the future for mankind. I admit, I cried as well.

After the funeral I drove alone out to the Hightown Road at the back of the Cavehill, the hill that looms over North Belfast. I got out of the car and started walking. It was dusk, the sun had gone, and darkness was slowly creeping from the east. I felt oppressed by a heavy mood of melancholy. I wished God worked in ways that we could comprehend. Why should babies and children suffer like that?

It is difficult at such painful moments to believe that evil does not govern the world. Sitting on the top of the Cavehill that evening, looking at the sky, there was only a spray of wet stars on the black carpet of space, with a sliver of moon, white as exposed bone. I looked out over the lights of the city as darkness gathered over Belfast, a marketplace for bloodshed. I don't know how long I sat there, but I was blue with cold when I left

To strike at the heartland of Loyalism and kill two innocent children didn't just throw a gauntlet down; it declared war and swelled the ranks of the Loyalist paramilitaries. This was a turning point.

Saturday 18 and Sunday 19 December saw us back at Palace Barracks. The training was stepped up a couple of gears. We were taken to an assault course; they wanted us fit and toned. You can control your breathing and nervous system easier than a couch potato. I had thought I was reasonably fit with training and playing football. That was soon put out of my head. Every part of me was sore, even parts of me that I didn't know I had. I would have to stop smoking, it really was killing me. I imagined my lungs were about to be disgorged out my mouth, with each rasping cough that tore through me. I looked around and I'm glad I wasn't the only one, bent over, looking like coughing milk bottles. I was panting like an asthmatic in a wind tunnel. While we tried to recover and catch our breath, we were taken back to the compound. As we slowly returned to normal, the first thing I reached for was a cigarette.

The Captain gave us another morale-boosting talk. He explained that discussions were being held as to where and when we would be ready to begin operations. Certain targets were being looked at. Plans were being put together to co-ordinate strikes and people were being taught how to win the propaganda war. This was as important as winning militarily. He made it obvious that we wouldn't be rushed into operating until everyone was equipped, organised and capable of what would be required of them. The way the Provos had reacted to our warning shot across their boughs meant that we would definitely be needed to wreak havoc.

He went on to wish us all a Merry Christmas and Happy New Year, announcing that training would restart on 2 January. One of the men quipped, 'That's alright, the fight against terrorism is put on hold for Christmas. We hope the IRA have been told that as well.' Everyone in the room roared with laughter. A comradeship had grown between us all. Some bottles of spirits and mixers were brought in and we were told to help ourselves. Nobody needed any encouragement. It can be quite difficult to drink while wearing a balaclava, but, believe me, we managed. After a few drinks, we were feeling relaxed and slapping each other's backs, shaking hands and wishing everyone all the best for Christmas and the New Year, before heading back to our respective areas. None of us knew what things that New Year would bring, but I think we all hoped peace would be one of them.

There were four more deaths that Saturday. We greeted three of them with the spirit of the season: joy, delight and elation. That response sounds horrific but I was changing, slowly, from an ordinary decent man into someone I was beginning not to recognise. I wasn't alone. Thinking back, we were all Jekyll and Hydes, without a potion to blame. Part of me wanted to draw back, to immerse myself once again in the ebb and flow of day-to-day life. I wanted to unburden myself of what I felt, to restore myself to some semblance of a normal existence, but I felt frozen, suspended, by what was happening in our country. The three dead PIRA men were James Sheridan, John Bateson and Martin Lee. They were transporting a bomb in a car when it exploded prematurely on King Street, Magherafelt, County Londonderry. An own goal, only this time it really was. Perhaps you can understand why we were over the moon at these three deaths. These men had been on their way to possibly kill more innocent children and got their just reward. Maybe there was a God after all.

Edward Heath visited Northern Ireland on 23 December. He expressed the determination and commitment of the British Government to eradicate and end the violence, aware that the good people of the Province were suffering. We listened closely to those words of war from the top man, and knew the counter measures being put into place would be used in the New Year. After all, he was the one who had sanctioned them.

1971 Statistics

Deaths by status		Responsibility for deaths	
Protestant civilians	27	Republicans	107
Catholic civilians	65	Loyalists	22
RUC	11	Army	45
RUC/R	0	RUC/RUC/R	1
UDR/RIR	5	UDR/RIR	0
Army	44	Others	5
Republicans	23		
Loyalists	3		
Others	2		
Total	180		
Bombs	1,515		
Shootings	1,756		

1972 BLOODY SUNDAY

'By way of deception, thou shalt do war.'
motto of Mossad, Israel's Secret Service.

THE YEAR 1972 opened with an anti-internment rally in Belfast on Sunday, 2 January. Was this going to be the start of another year of marches, riots, violence, bombings and killings? In 1971 the total body count had risen to 180, almost *seven times* more than that of the year before. Surely the top men in the Republican movement would have stepped back during the Christmas festival and seen the unmistakable and pointless waste of life? In 1971 they killed quite a lot of Catholics in unsuccessful shootings and bombings. The bombing on McGurk's bar killed 15 more. They knew it was a Loyalist bomb that had been planted to cause maximum death and destruction, while the rest of the people thought it was an own goal.

I have done a quick calculation on how many Catholics were killed as a result of Republican violence. I have included IRA men shot by the British Army and innocent Catholics caught in crossfire, own goals and as a result of a feud between the two Republican groups. It comes to a grand total of 63. This figure does not include any Catholics murdered by Loyalists, who killed as a direct result of the Provos' murderous campaign. In my view, the blame of everybody killed lies squarely at the leadership of the Republican movement's door.

I, and thousands of other law-abiding men, would never have contemplated such drastic measures if we hadn't felt threatened by the insurgency and anarchy going on around us.

That same Sunday we were all back at Palace Barracks for training. We were given a lecture on forensic science and instructed on how not to leave any evidence connecting us to the crime. I don't know who the lecturer was, but he wasn't in uniform; he was in a suit and tie. With his wayward hairstyle, I would have described him as a mad professor type.

When going on a job, these were our instructions: always wear a boiler suit or similar, and a balaclava or hood; when you return from whatever you have done, put all of your clothes straight into the washing machine and wash them immediately; take a shower or bath; scrub under your nails and any exposed bits of skin, like around your eyes and mouth; also wash under your foreskin in case it's a bit cheesy. That final comment raised a laugh, and relieved the seriousness of the situation.

During the lecture, a number of men entered the room. We were informed that one of them was the man who had devised our operation. The Captain asked the Senior Officer to say a few words, and the latter took centre stage.

He spoke. 'You have been chosen for a very controversial conspiracy. If word got out that it even existed, the shit would truly hit a hell of a big fan. The Provisional IRA is our enemy and, therefore, we must all work in a manner that is as unified, organised and, above all, as ruthless, than them. I have found in other violent confrontations, in other parts of the world, this type of war cannot be won by conventional means. The only solution is to implement a counter operation, which counteracts the violence of the enemy by heaping more violence on them.

'Obviously, Army personnel can't be deployed in this sort

of action. That is why we have chosen men like you, to create trepidation and pandemonium amongst them and their support base, the Catholic community. We will be recruiting informers within their ranks. New interrogation methods are being introduced to break them when in custody. Our assemblage will be hitting them from all sides and from the inside, as well. A team is also being set up to combat their propaganda machine, which is second to none. I know one operation has been successful. The men at the top thought that might have been enough to tip the scales in our favour, and support would have dropped away, however, since then we have seen the Provos' answer to that, with their attack on a furniture shop on the Shankill Road, which killed two babies. We have to face a very big decision here. Do we try to out-manoeuvre them in terms of atrocities, or do we walk away and hope they come to their senses and call it off?

'The question is, if we do call a halt, will they take it as a sign of weakness and step up their assault on the very foundation of your heritage and birthright by trying to bomb, shoot, intimidate and coerce a million Protestants into a United Ireland. Our answer is "No fucking way". We will match whatever they do and, if need be, outdo them. This has to be a fight to the bitter end and pray to God it will be a short one. I understand from your trainers you're eager to get started. I ask for you to be patient. The time to start will be decided when all the sections are in place and ready to go at the same time.

'Recruiting informers will take a bit longer than everything else and we're trying hard to push at least one of them up the ranks of the Provos' command structure. All this will take time so don't be impetuous. Relax. You will get your chance and, hopefully, when the whole shebang goes into operation, it should end the war in under a year. I want to say that I'm relieved and reassured that there are men of Ulster, not only you, but other men within the ranks of the UVF/UDA, who are prepared to strike hard in the defence of your religious freedom and way of life.

'I want you men to recognise the genius of it. Every Military Intelligence adventure botched or otherwise will eventually come under public scrutiny. Not so us. Because we're on no one's radar. We don't have either a bureaucracy or constraints. When you work in an ad hoc fashion, with groups around the country, when you don't shy away from extremely aggressive intervention, then all you need is a very small number of highly trained operatives. You succeed by directing events, coordinating the desired outcome. Joseph Stalin once put it quite aptly: 'You can't make an omelette without breaking some eggs.' Leave it to the politicians to colour inside the lines, because those lines will be the ones that we have drawn. The historians will never know, and, the truth is, it's better that way.'

He then bid us all a happy and successful New Year and departed with his colleagues.

It's a marvellous feeling, when someone important speaks to you like that. It gets the adrenaline flowing through the veins. I used to get the same kick when I listened to Paisley preaching in the early years. He had the acumen and ability to persuade. He could get into your thoughts and compel you to act, before we were beaten into an all Ireland Republic. Lord Carson was his hero and he should have been man enough to follow Carson's lead. Thousands would have backed him to the hilt. If you listen to his stirring speeches now, from all those years ago, you can see why many of us followed his words of war and defiance.

The very next day the Provos gave their answer. On Monday, 3 January 1972, they detonated a bomb in Callender Street in

Belfast's city centre, injuring over 60 people. This was not a military target, but a blatant attack on civilians and commercial premises. They were setting the precedent for the rest of the year. The Republicans were going to show us all, no matter what; they were going to continue the crusade to the bitter end.

In the previous chapters I have described and commented on individual murders. My aim was to demonstrate what was taking place around young Protestant men and women during the run-up to the point when enough became enough. We were led to believe that unless we were prepared to fight fire with fire, Northern Ireland would be abolished and we would be plunged into the nightmare of the Catholic-controlled Republic. I have mentioned Ian Paisley as one of the main culprits. The second most prolific leader, who actually went so far as to tell us in a speech that 'there could come a time when we would have to liquidate the enemy ourselves', was William Craig.

William Craig, a former Minister for Home Affairs who created the Ulster Vanguard Party, held a huge rally that day in Ormeau Park, where he made that particular speech. The newly formed UDA gave a show of strength and paraded thousands of men in support of him. He went even further on Thursday 19 October that year while addressing a meeting of the right-wing Members of Parliament at Westminster. He said he could mobilise 80,000 men to oppose the British Government. He continued: 'We are prepared to come out and shoot and kill. I am prepared to come out and shoot and kill. I am prepared to kill and those behind me will have my full support.'

We all thought here's another Lord Carson and were eager to follow him. In the end, however, he was like Paisley. He hadn't the strength of character to carry his words of war to the bitter end.

Once again the Loyalist people were let down by politicians.

Mike would come over on different nights to visit Billy and me, especially if some operation was taking place in Belfast. He would know what time an OOB was to be in position. Many nights we sat in his car listening to the radio reports of the action unfolding. I enjoyed this routine. It meant we were kept up-to-date with most of the activities taking place. It was spine-tingling to know something was going down. It felt as though you were part of a militia, all working together towards one goal, the annihilation of the IRA.

On Saturday 8 January, there was a test of the OOB system in North Belfast, when a team went to kill a Catholic. No one claimed the murder and it was put down as a result of an armed robbery. But it was a MRF team flexing its muscles. The second one and no one was any the wiser. Although it was a very soft target, the idea was to instill fear into Catholics who lived in Protestant areas, let them know that they would be the most vulnerable and at risk in retaliatory attacks.

Our training was stepped up another gear; a lot of time was spent on the assault course and gym, to bring us up to an appropriate state of fitness. When I was fitter and stronger, I had more confidence in my own ability and could control my nervousness a lot easier, through a technique of controlled breathing we had been taught. We could now strip and assemble the four weapons almost blindfold.

Keeping a very low profile was drilled into us. It was absolutely critical to the success of the operation, not to mention the risk of informants passing details on to the police. Careless talk was the surest way of getting caught.

Reading books on the Troubles now, I can detect men who must have been recruited by MRF, or whatever they were called at that particular time, and later went out of control, were set up and then eliminated, probably by the MRF. As we now know, the Military Reconnaissance Force changed its name on a number of occasions when they were in danger of being exposed. Force Research Unit and 14 Intelligence Company were two of their names. Anyone investigating them was told it had been disbanded and personnel weren't available for questioning. It didn't disappear; the name simply changed and they carried on with their secret dirty war.

On Saturday 22 January, an anti-internment march was held at Magilligan Strand, County Londonderry. Several thousand people took part in the illegal march towards Magilligan Prison, which was being used as an internment camp. As they approached, soldiers from the Royal Green Jackets, backed by members of the Parachute Regiment, were waiting to stop the crowd. The soldiers blocked the way with barbed wire, closing the beach. The crowd made a run towards the end of the wire, intending to go into the water to bypass the blockade and the soldiers.

As it was a Saturday, we were in Palace Barracks listening to the battle reports coming in. The Army started firing rubber bullets and CS gas at close range into the crowd. I remember the Captain saying, 'If the bastards want aggro today they'll surely get it!' We knew the Paras were based in Palace Barracks, having seen them as we were taken into the camp.

Ferocious hand-to-hand fighting went on for a while, amidst the bullets and gas. A number of witnesses claimed that some of the paratroopers had gone berserk, severely beaten protesters, then had to be physically restrained by their officers.

Before we left for the day, Mike spoke to Billy and me, telling us that orders had been sent down from the top (I presumed he meant the Prime Minister) that they were to use whatever force and tactics were necessary to put these trou-blemakers down. He implied that MRF personnel had been coercing men from the Parachute Regiment, stationed with them in Palace Barracks, to take a more hard-line stance, against rabble-rousers. It appeared to be true, judging from the news reports. They were taking no prisoners. Of course, at that time, we loved it. Our attitude then was 'Get into the bastards at every opportunity, as hard as you can.' A lot of British soldiers had been killed. I knew it was not the bulk of the protesters who had committed acts of violence, but too much had hap-pened and the soldiers' pent-up frustration was spilling out. It had only been a question of when, not if, the dam would burst. The flood of violence had started and it was going to be very difficult to stop.

The following day at the camp, we were enthralled by the stories told by the Paras to our trainers, the previous night in the NAAFI. They revelled in their notoriety. We got the im-pression the Paras were the hard men of all the regiments sta-tioned in Northern Ireland – top dogs and willing to prove it. Maybe this prime minister would put an end to the violence. No more softly, softly approach; meet the Provos head on and not only beat them but destroy their will to carry on. We built up our hopes it would succeed, possibly before we would be deployed. Although it felt positive to be doing all this training with the backing of the Government, I still had doubts that I could actually carry out what was expected of me. I used to wonder if anyone else there felt the same way. It wasn't some-thing you could express, in case you were labelled a coward. It was a dread I tried to face in private. While, on one level, my confidence was increasing each week, the doubt was still there, nagging and eating away at my conscious thoughts; at work, in the bar, while trying to sleep.

I picked up the nerve to tell Mike of my misgivings and the reservations building up inside me. I collared him on his own on the Monday night, after we'd left Billy's house and he was giving me a lift home. He was very reassuring and told me not to worry about it. I wouldn't be a normal person if I didn't feel that way. Did I think that every man or woman who joined the Army was a natural born killer? No, I didn't think so. I remembered those young soldiers trying to make themselves as small as possible in shop doorways, trembling with fear.

He went on to say, 'As long as you believe in what you have to do and your cause is a just one, then you will be able to accept and justify any action you take to advance that cause. It's like soldiers going into battle in any conflict, they have to kill or be killed. It's the same here. If you don't defend your right to remain part of the United Kingdom from people trying to take it from you, then your enemies win, by lack of resistance on your part. Simply walk in and take what they want. What about the cry of your forefathers, 'No surrender'. They didn't hand it over, did they? Go back throughout Ireland's history. It's always been a struggle to survive, but survive they did. And now we're all part of that survival process. It's just another chapter from the book about the ongoing fight, against the same enemy, which has always been there. So, don't be worrying about it. You'll be fine when the time comes.'

I felt more positive after my conversation with Mike. He had the ability to alleviate my uncertainties. He gave me the encouragement and determination to persevere with the training, until the time came to use it effectively. I would evaluate each murder carried out by the PIRA, to see if their campaign was flagging or escalating. Then I would make my decision in my own mind, as to what I was capable of doing.

Events were soon to happen that would change the whole

concept of the Troubles and seal our fate for decades to come. Mike had called over to tell us that the Northern Ireland Civil Rights Association had told the RUC of their intention to hold a peaceful march in protest against internment on the following Sunday, 30 January, in Londonderry. It had originally been planned for Sunday 16 January. They had asked if the demonstration could take place without military interference. The RUC had agreed to recommend this course of action to the Commander of Land Forces in Northern Ireland. Mike put us in the picture; it had been discussed at British Cabinet level and an arrest operation was to be put into place. General Ford had put the Commander of First Battalion, Parachute Regiment, Lieutenant Colonel Derek Wilford, in charge of the operation. Edward Heath confirmed months later that British Government ministers were aware of the plan.

What we were told was that the bastards mustn't have got the message, the previous Saturday, that there wasn't going to be any leniency towards them any more and if these people thought they could march illegally, then they would have to suffer the consequences. As the Paras stationed at Palace Barracks were going to take part, it would give them the opportunity to get the message across again, only harder this time. They would incite some of the Paras, tell them that the boy scouts could do a better job of arresting rioters than they had done the week before. As he left, he said there might be something different for us at the weekend, so to be prepared.

Paisley's DUP got in on the act. They announced their intention to hold a religious gathering at the same place on the same day and at the same time as the civil rights people.

The Friday before the demonstration, the organisers emphasised the need for a peaceful march, in order to avoid a repeat of the previous week's violence. One of the main leaders of the civil rights movement was John Hume, a Social and Democratic Labour Party MP at Stormont. He believed in the reunification of Ireland, but done with the consent of the people, Protestants and Catholics, in the North and not with the gun. Michael Canavan, a professional businessman, was another. And Ivan Cooper, a Protestant and member of the young Unionist Party in the early 1960s, who had left to join the Derry Labour Party. They attracted support from moderate Catholics in Londonderry, as they appeared to be rational, responsible, liberal-thinking and focused on peaceful protest.

Also part of the campaign was Bernadette Devlin, MP for Mid-Ulster, who had received a six-month sentence for her part in the Battle of the Bogside in 1968. Eamonn McCann was a young Socialist campaigner. He and John Hume were trying to bring the Protestant and Catholic working class together by raising the problems of jobs and housing that affected both communities. Their intentions were good; unfortunately, the extremists from both sides put an end to that.

I'm sure everyone knows the catastrophic deeds that took place on Sunday, 30 January, 1972. What I am about to reveal is momentous and crucial to understanding what actually happened and, more importantly, why the day turned so gruesome.

Of course, every death that occurred throughout the Troubles is nauseating. But it's much more so when they are innocent civilians. The majority of the dead were just ordinary people in the wrong place at the wrong time.

I am ashamed to admit that when we heard the news of the number of dead we took a morbid pleasure in it. It is barbaric and mortifying, but I'm not going to tell lies now. All of us enjoyed the satisfaction of the retribution dished out to the IRA and Catholics that fateful day. That was why members of Military Intelligence, on direct orders from Her Majesty's Government, were training us. The feeling was similar to the jubilation felt after the successful operation at McGurk's Bar. I defy anyone, Loyalist or Republican, to say they didn't feel elated returning from a successful mission. It's only with hindsight and years of reflection that I realise how wrong it was.

Of course, no one knew at the time the detrimental and devastating effect that day would have on the rest of our lives. The consequences were fundamentally opposite to those that were intended. Instead of destroying once and for all the dwindling support for the Provos it drove hordes of young men straight into their ranks. The IRA must have thought it was Christmas come late, with volunteers queuing up to enlist across Ireland, North and South. What we thought was a victory turned out to be the main catalyst to the commencement of hostilities. Many of us, who thought it might have been avoided, were trapped in a battle of hatred, compelled to inflict the most devastation and destruction to the opposite side.

Although the Provisionals started their campaign to get the British out of Ireland, they must have realised it would turn into a sectarian conflict. They accused the British of inciting the Protestants to bring about sectarian turmoil. I know that was absolute rubbish, as I will prove in this book. Loyalists had already decided to embark on offensive action, before accepting help to achieve it. They weren't just going to sit on their hands and let the IRA destroy their British way of life. They might not have been as successful or able to function as easily, but they were ready to take them on, come what may.

On Saturday 29 January, we were picked up at noon as usual and taken down to Palace Barracks. The trainers seemed to be in excellent spirits, laughing and carrying on with us all. The craic was good with the entire group joining in. A lot of it was about the previous weekend's fracas and the demonstration in Londonderry the next day. After half an hour we were taken into a lecture room. There was somebody new there, talking to a couple of trainers. His pips indicated he was a Major.

You could have heard a pin drop as he stepped up to the front to address us. My first thought was, something important is going to happen. We had never seen anyone higher than a Captain, except for the Senior Officer who gave us his pep talk.

He spoke calmly and politely, with a refined English accent. 'OK, lads, I would like to take this opportunity to commend you all on having the courage and loyalty to participate in covert actions against the common enemy. I realise it is a very big step you are taking and I understand the suspicions and fears you must all be going through. You're probably asking yourselves, is your decision to embark on this course of action right or wrong? Well, I can give you my word of honour that you will all play a major part in the defence of Ulster and the defeat of PIRA. So, your choice to engage the antagonists is an emphatic endorsement of your cause. I salute you all. Your trainers tell me that there have been a couple of operations already carried out successfully. Good show. They also tell me you are wondering and eager to know when you'll get the green light to begin full operations. Well, that's why I am here today, to explain what your part in the overall stratagem is, in order to defeat these Republican bastards. I'm sure you're wondering why I've come here today with these fighting words? The men at the top are becoming aggrieved and angry at the security situation within the Province, especially Londonderry. The Chief of Defence Staff is putting a great deal of pressure on General Ford to come up with a strategy, to bring all areas in the country back under the civil law.'

I assumed he meant getting rid of no-go areas in Republican districts.

He continued: 'At meetings I've attended recently, regarding the state of law and order in the Province and especially Londonderry, it has become increasingly embarrassing to the Security Forces and indeed the Government. With regard to this civil rights march in Londonderry tomorrow, the Joint Security Committee, at a meeting in Stormont, felt that the demonstration taking place would be an illegal parade and must be treated as such, under the ban imposed by the Unionist Prime Minister, Brian Faulkner.

Three alternatives to deal with the insurrection had been put on the table. One, to keep up the containment of the Bogside and Creggan, keep up the softly, softly approach, and hope it will fizzle out. Two, get tough with Republicans, whether they are Provisional IRA men, sympathisers or troublemakers. This would require a large military force to implement. Three, to follow the second, when the area is secure, keep a permanent military presence within the Bogside and Creggan districts. In other words, take them over. This would still need a large military presence kept on the ground to maintain law and order within those two areas.

'At the end of last year, General Ford opted for scenario number one, containment. After touring Londonderry recently, speaking to officers on the ground, local businessmen and seeing the systematic destruction of the city centre by the IRA, he has suggested a much tougher stance. In effect, he has put forward a proposal that ringleaders should be shot, as a way of scaling down the daily rioting within the no-go areas. This would mean shooting unarmed civilians. Which would be as welcome to the Catholic community, the Irish Republic and the Americans as a fart in a space suit.

'For obvious reasons this cannot be a direct order from a senior officer, because of the political consequences and media condemnation that would arise. Up to the present time, in Londonderry, hundreds of soldiers have been injured and no one has been arrested. Since the first soldier killed in Londonderry, on 11 August 1971, another six have been murdered and many wounded. Our company has been given instructions to put into place a strategy which will be effective in demonstrating the Government's hard-line stance against lawbreakers.

'It has been decided that tomorrow would be an excellent time to implement these strict tactics, if the march degenerates into a serious breach of the peace. We think the Derry Young Hooligans and the IRA will use the protest to seek revenge for last week's violence by soldiers on Magellan sands.

'The IRA is becoming a more threatening, organised and ruthless company, and it poses a significant threat to peace and stability in Londonderry and indeed the whole Province. Earlier this month a major gun battle erupted between them and soldiers in the Creggan. Quite a number of combat uniforms were recently stolen from city-centre cleaners. They could be used for an operation, with their men dressed as soldiers. There is virtually no law and order on the west bank of the River Foyle.

'We are expecting anywhere between 10,000 and 15,000 people from all over the Province, the Irish Republic and the mainland, to take part tomorrow. General Ford has decided to use members of the Parachute Regiment, stationed here at Palace Barracks, in a detention operation. The paratroopers are very experienced in putting down serious disorder in Belfast, and the General thinks they will be ideal for the operation on Sunday. The Republican propaganda set-up and the media made a lot of waves about brutality last week and will be monitoring closely the measures we use to stop the march. It must be prevented from reaching the city centre at all costs.

'The code name for this operation is Forecast and it's been cleared from the top. GEN47 committee, the Cabinet and the Prime Minister have all sanctioned the modus operandi to prevent the crowd reaching the city centre and the arrest of rioters. This opportunity presents the ideal time for the Security Forces to implement these extreme measures and show we mean business. They want a lot of publicity for these arrests and the subsequent court appearances that follow.

'It is make or break time. A number of senior people calculate that whatever takes place during the protest, and how it's dealt with, will define long-term future strategy, of the hostilities, by the Security Forces, terrorists and yourselves. We are hoping to provoke a confrontation with the IRA and give them an example of what to expect in any future attacks. If, after tomorrow, they want to continue with their war, all the preparations being put into place at the moment will be given the green light. We would like to take any one of you who is willing to Londonderry in the morning to observe the operation in action. Please raise your hands if you want to accompany us.'

I glanced around the room and everyone had a hand in the air.

He joked with us saying, 'I'm sorry there didn't seem too many of you interested or keen in going.'

Everyone burst into a fit of laughter.

'Okay, I appreciate your enthusiasm. If each of you will see your contact man, he will fill you in on the arrangements for the morning.

As we listened intently to his encouraging and fighting words, we could feel the adrenaline pump around our bodies. The surge was exhilarating. No workout in a gym could it.

Billy confirmed later that he had the same feeling. I was glad when they give us a break and we all piled out for fresh air and not so fresh air, a smoke.

Mike came over to Billy and I, saying, 'I told you there could be something different this week.'

'Aye Mike, fucking magic,' Billy remonstrated. 'Any more of your wee surprises, you're holding back and not telling us about?'

He then took us to a room were we spent the night. A remark by Mike took us by surprise, while we were passing another compound, he said that's where the Fred's are trained.

Billy asked, 'who the fuck are Fred's.'

Mike replied, 'they are informers, who we train how to get information on republicans without drawing attention to themselves.'

After taking our sizes, he brought us combat uniforms. We were kitted out with full battle gear, helmet, flak jackets and camouflage paint for our faces.

Mike explained some things to us before leaving.

'MRF have priority on anything we require or deem essential to achieve our goal. If a senior officer has an idea that can't be given as a direct order, then he can pass it on to us. He can put a request to our top men and if we can find a way to proceed with that suggestion or proposal, we have the power to implement it. As you heard the Major say earlier, what General Ford recommended couldn't be ordered – but he thinks it would discourage these full time rioters. So we have been putting the final touches to the solution and tomorrow. It will be used if there's any aggro at all. We have spoken to Charlie and friends. The solution will be carried out at the demonstration tomorrow provided the bastards want a riot. The Prime Minister doesn't want a political bomb going off in his trousers.'

'Who the fuck is Charlie?' asked Billy.

'Now that would be telling. Look, this is highly confidential, so I can't say who Charlie is, but if you put your mind to it, you might be able to work it out. All I'm prepared to say is the answer to the problem will be solved one way or the other. Okay,' he replied.

Sleep was impossible, tossing and turning until it was time to get up.

Author's note

I should make clear at this stage that I had written the previous section of the book before reading *Those Are Real Bullets, Aren't They?* by Peter Pringle and Phillip Jacobson. I added this particular section to show the similarity between the oration given by the Major and the facts presented in that book. In order to create a true and unbiased evaluation from both sides, I have blended my experiences with factual information, previously unknown to me, revealed in the Saville Inquiry and Pringle and Jacobson's account. Apparently, these three choices we were told about appeared in a memo sent by General Ford, in almost the same words, to British Defence Chiefs. Major-General Ford concluded his memo with 'the potential political fallout of an invasion precluded its implementation'. Like Sir Michael Carver, Chief of Defence Staff, he thought many civilians would be killed. Much will be made of the slaughter of innocents. Military incursions with lots of soldiers into the Catholic enclave would produce marginal returns and drive the community further into the ranks of the IRA. Aggressive patrolling increased the risk that troops would have to shoot into crowds.

In fact, he opted for number one – to continue the policy of containing the no-go area – even though it meant tacit acceptance of the open revolt. This memo was sent in the middle of December 1971. Ford had become convinced the local IRA was becoming a significant threat. They were carrying out a sustained bombing campaign by their ability to elude soldiers and roadblocks, clambering through derelict buildings to avoid capture. Indeed, it was believed that shoppers shielded and assisted the bombers whenever possible.

A few weeks later, in the first week of January, Major-General Ford paid a visit to Londonderry for a second opinion. He was shocked when he learned that the no-go area was going to be extended by two blocks in the near future. It would mean the main shopping centre in Londonderry would become extinct in a few months. At a meeting with local businessmen and shopkeepers he was informed of Rossville Flats, a complex in the Bogside, with 5,000 inhabitants, where no soldier had ever set foot.

Ford sent a strongly worded report to General Harry Tuzo (GOC and overall commander in Northern Ireland). He had taken a much tougher stance than before. In that report to Harry Tuzo, Ford described the Derry Young Hooligans as the fundamental problem.

On 7 January, Ford made a controversial comment: 'I am coming to the conclusion that the minimum force necessary, to achieve a restoration of law and order, is to shoot ringleaders among the Derry Young Hooligans.'

As the march on 30 January had the potential of being a flashpoint, if a full-scale confrontation ensued it could be used by the Army to gauge the reaction to a military invasion of the Bogside.

Sir Michael Carver, Chief of Defence Staff, agreed that

suppressing the Catholic enclaves would require a major military operation incurring many casualties, most of whom would be civilians. In the end such action would inflame the unrest in the whole of Northern Ireland and infuriate the Irish Republic without producing a lasting solution in Londonderry.

I would like to make an observation of my own. When General Ford returned to Londonderry at the beginning of January, for a second opinion, why did he suddenly change his mind? He advocated the shooting of unarmed civilians. That was the first time a senior officer had suggested that unarmed civilians could be shot, under certain circumstances. Did he not realise that it was exactly the same as sending the Army to invade the no-go area, where unarmed civilians were likely to be shot as well?

No matter what the circumstances, as we were to witness throughout the Troubles, the Republicans' propaganda machine was second to none and would turn such incidences to their advantage. I remember an incident in the New Lodge district of Belfast. Danny O'Haggen was shot dead for throwing a petrol bomb at troops. According to Republican witnesses, the man was out at four o'clock in the morning trying to get a bottle of milk and doing no harm. Like all aspects of the Troubles, depending on which side you belonged, you believed one version or the other.

To put forward a proposal to shoot and probably kill unarmed civilians was going to achieve the same result as a full-scale invasion. Whether they were involved in rioting and seen as ringleaders or not, the fallout would last for decades. Ford's prognosis on his options was correct. Because Ford and Sir Michael Carver felt this course of action would inflame the whole Catholic population in Northern Ireland, the Irish Republic and indeed the rest of the world (especially America),

Ford knew it could not be authorised by senior officers. His choice of the operation name turned out to be prophetic, Operation Forecast. My point is that, as it could not be seen to be approved, another method had to be found; enter the MRF and the Parachute Regiment.

This course of action would involve sealing off the Bogside with the heaviest troop concentration ever seen in Londonderry. Army snipers with telescopic sights would ring the Catholic enclave; paratroopers armed with SLRs were poised to carry out arrest operations and engage IRA gunmen or bombers if they came under attack. As the military preparations for containing the march got underway, the mood in the Army's Lisburn headquarters was hardening. The assault troops of the Parachute Regiment would be on hand to implement the new sterner measures Ford was suggesting, not ordering. An important fact to be noted is that General Ford personally stated he wanted the Paras used in the arrest operation, as they were the most experienced troops for the job. The reason he gave for his decision? They were the roughest, toughest troops in his command and the only unit available with enough experience in Northern Ireland.

That was not the case. Soldiers from the Royal Anglican Regiment had served in Londonderry for 19 months. The men of the second Battalion, Royal Green Jackets, had been there for more than six months. Both these Infantry Regiments had an abundance of hard-earned experience on the streets of Londonderry. They were familiar with the layout of the Bogside and Creggan. Other officers from 39 Brigade units, described the Paras as 'little better than thugs in uniform'. Yet those troops from the other regiments were delegated to man static Army barriers.

Ford had decided against issuing orders for opening fire

because soldiers were bound in all circumstances to abide by the Yellow Card rules. He also wanted SLR rifles adapted to fire a .22 high-velocity round, instead of the more lethal 7.62 normally used, to ensure that only people directly fired on would be in danger. The larger bullet would endanger people behind the target, due to its high speed of 2,750 feet per second. It could punch a hole in an iron railway line at close range. As one paratrooper put it, a gunman is not going to stop a bullet. He revealed that 30 of these adapted rifles were already in 8th Brigade for zeroing and familiarisation training. If you read the warning on a box of .22 high-velocity bullets, it says 'Dangerous up to a mile'; I have seen these bullets go through a car and out the other side.

If the whole operation was planned to go the way it did, why were none of these weapons issued and used, instead of the normal SLRs? You are forced to conclude that there were plans for mass murder to be committed that day. Were the instructions passed on to the Paras through MRF? I understand that a Major 236 was in command of the support company who were to lead the assault. Was this the same Major who gave us the pep talk?

A lieutenant had informed his platoon that they were going to Londonderry to carry out internal security duties the following day. According to a radio operator with the platoon, they were all in high spirits when the lieutenant said, 'Let's teach these buggers a lesson. We want some kills tomorrow.' This was a tantamount to an order, i.e. an exoneration of all responsibility. Who gave the lieutenant the go-ahead to issue those instructions? I'm positive he didn't do it himself.

When Mike spoke about Charlie, we assumed he meant a paratrooper called Charlie was going to implement the solution for them. It is only now, after 30 years of guessing and reading

Pringle and Jacobson's book, that I finally know who Charlie and company were. Mike and the Major had been right; this line of attack had been approved at the highest level.

These are my comments on facts detailed in the book, before Sunday 30 January. I will now return to my own account of events. Then I will analyse and expand on those facts, unknown until now.

• • •

The noise of the Parachute Regiment's armoured cars and lorries revving and moving out before dawn woke us. Breakfast finished, we dressed in full combat gear and waited for Mike to show us how to apply our face camouflage. He then issued us with some further instructions: if things got out of hand, we were allowed to fire over the heads of rioters to create confusion and fear. By 7.30 a.m. we were ready to go. I was on cloud nine. At 7.55 a.m. we loaded up, each man being given a SLR as he entered the Land-Rover. At 8 a.m. the convoy moved out. There were 15 vehicles in all as we headed to Londonderry. During the journey we passed through a few checkpoints. Mike told us there would be a lot more of them and anybody suspected of coming to the march would be subjected to rigorous interrogation before being allowed through. They would get the same treatment at every checkpoint they encounter. That'll sicken the bastards.

I hadn't been to Londonderry since I was about nine or ten. My parents had taken my younger brother and me on a touring holiday. My father was originally from a small place called Crum in County Fermanagh. We had stayed with his relations in Fermanagh and then went on up to Londonderry. I had photos of me sitting on top of Roaring Meg, a huge cannon used to defend the city. I had recollections of a lovely city with walls, city-centre shops and picturesque views overlooking Lough Foyle.

What a shock was in store for me. As we drove through the city centre the damage caused by bombs was incredible. Burnt-out shops and boarded-up bars. Empty shells where someone's business had been levelled. We could not believe our eyes. We arrived at a place where a number of Army vehicles were parked and dismounted, glad to stretch our legs. Mike and the other guys in charge of each Land-Rover went over to a couple of senior officers then studied a map spread out on the bonnet of a Land-Rover. We could see them pointing and discussing where they wanted our groups. After ten minutes the men came back and picked their squads. The drivers stayed with the vehicles.

Mike led us up to the ramparts. I had sung about them many, many times, but it was only my second visit to them and the first time I appreciated the historical significance of them. The view was really something. It felt good being there, wearing combat uniforms, flak jackets and carrying a loaded SLR; our faces done in camouflage paint, helmet on and a respirator on our belts. No one gave us a second look. We were just part of the overall operation. Oddly, I felt no nerves. I was relaxed and comfortable. Excited and energised, yes, but definitely not anxious.

We were in position before 12 o'clock. The march was supposed to start at between 2 and 3 p.m. I noticed Mike and two other MRF men had telescopic sights on their rifles. One of them carried a .303 rifle instead of a SLR. I asked him why. He told me it was a more accurate weapon and he preferred it. The other soldier had a radio. Mike came over and asked us to go with him for a walk round the walls. The feeling was indescribable; I felt like King Dick, keyed up and ready for action. We had done plenty rifle training, but here I was walking in public with a loaded weapon and no one was paying much attention to us.

It was like a surreal sightseeing tour, with Mike pointing out different places of interest. You could see right across the Bogside into the Creggan. I couldn't comprehend the dereliction of William Street. Nothing was identifiable any more. The buildings were empty shells, boarded up and covered with graffiti. Belfast had had its fair share of bombs but this was beyond belief. Mike showed us Free Derry Corner (it breaks my heart to write that); Aggro Corner, where a lot of rioting went on daily. Today would be no different. I could see why the big wigs were pissed off with the security situation and needed a solution to remedy it.

Mike indicated where the barriers had been set up to prevent the crowd entering the city centre, explaining that the marchers would come down William Street to try to reach the city centre. Latest reports from sources indicated that the march organisers had changed their route and would turn up Rossville Street, instead of proceeding to the Guild Hall. They would stop at Free Derry Corner where speeches would be made. Mike told us that the Derry Young Hooligans were expected to ignore the stewards and aim for the city centre. He seemed to be well informed with the most up-todate information.

We were shown the Observation Posts where marksmen kept a vigilant watch on anyone moving about in the Bogside. The walls were very high, enabling you to see almost any suspicious movement. Two helicopters overhead kept a close watch on events on the ground. About 1.30 p.m. we returned to where the other two soldiers had remained.

Mike said, 'Part of the strategy is to cause pandemonium and enough noise to confuse the rioters so they won't know where to run for safety. Therefore, when the shooting starts, you can open fire at anything you want, except the crowd. If all of you were allowed to fire at these people, there might be more killed than is intended. As I said, the idea is to cause as much pandemonium and noise as possible.'

I picked up those important words: 'There might be more killed than is intended.' They were going to kill people. Simple fact, people were destined to die that day but they didn't want too many.

We waited patiently. Two p.m. came and went, and there was still no notification that the demonstration had left Bishop's Field. We all sat down with our backs to the wall and had a smoke. Coming up to 2.30 p.m., there was still no movement and we sat down for yet another smoke. We had just stubbed out our cigarettes when I looked up and saw a very senior officer and entourage up at the wall studying the Bogside and Creggan.

I said to Mike, 'Look lively, there's somebody important further up the wall.'

Mike looked round and headed towards the group, where he stood talking to the boss man for a few minutes. Now and again they would glance in our direction. I could see the senior officer nodding a few times. Then Mike came back down to join us.

Billy said, 'I take it that's the head buck cat?'

Mike replied, 'That's him. General Robert Ford, the man who suggested today's tactics. He's only here as an observer. Brigadier Pat MacLellan is overall commander, in charge of things.'

Something very strange then took place. It had just been broadcast that the marchers were starting to leave Bishop's Field. The next piece of information shocked Billy and me, standing watching over the wall. Headquarters in Lisburn decided at that moment, when tensions were high, to announce the death of Major Robin Alers-Hankey, of the Royal Green Jackets. Mike told us that he had been shot three months ago here in the Bogside. On reflection, I suspect this was done deliberately, to inflame an already fraught situation and make sure that what was planned went ahead with increased conviction and resolve to teach the bastards a lesson.

It was impossible to estimate how many were in the crowd. Numbers were coming over the radio, each time more than the last. No one seemed to have any idea how many were actually taking part. After coming down William Street, the coal lorry turned into Rossville Street, but the crowd of youths rushed on down towards the barrier, yelling things I couldn't quite make out at the time (later confirmed as 'What about the Guildhall? We're going to the Guildhall!'). There seemed to be hundreds of people charging down as the stewards tried unsuccessfully to divert the crowd up Rossville Street. They had no chance. Everyone was ignoring them. In the end, they gave up trying. It reminded me of a football crowd all trying to get out of a stadium at the same time.

I watched as they arrived at the barrier in William Street, one of the most frightening experiences you could ever find yourself in; at the front of a crowd with people behind you trying to push forwards. You have nowhere to go except into a barbed wire fence. How many times before and since then have people died through sheer weight of numbers pushing from behind at football games. I was at Wembley Stadium to watch England play Northern Ireland. The ground was packed to capacity. After the game was finished, being in the crowd leaving the ground was a nightmare. Everyone was trying to squeeze through narrow gateways. The crush was intense; you could lift your feet literally off the ground and be carried along, without knowing what lay ahead of you. If there were steps or something to trip over, you went down, never to get up again.

Watching that mass of people in William Street, all doing their best to push forward, I knew someone was going to get hurt or killed. Antagonism was growing, stress too. The crowd were directing obscene remarks and abuse at the young squaddies. Pushing and pushing. Fear on both sides, strained faces. The awful anticipation of the inevitable. There would be no backing down now. There were faces to save, scores to settle. Temporary containment. The soldiers stood with their backs to the APCs, shields up, batons drawn, armed detachments lay in reserve wearing respirators and full combat webbing.

There comes a critical point at which a protest switches from peace to violence. It could be an abusive word from a soldier, or the escalating chant of the mob. A small stone thrown. A volley of rubber bullets fired. You could see it getting close now, a momentum ready to sweep up and overcome the crowd. The Army squad looked nervous; mobs had a life and direction of their own. They could be spontaneous or planned, ordered or disordered, but you could sense the mood, know violence was close, just waiting for a spark to ignite it.

The soldiers were getting a lot of verbal abuse, close enough to shower them with spittle. How those men could stand there and control themselves without reacting says a lot for their discipline. From our vantage point the scene was sickening. Only a small number of troops seemed to be manning the barrier. We could see the paratroopers and the water cannon out of sight round the corner.

A policeman shouted something through a loudhailer, but with the noise of the crowd I don't think anyone heard what he said. That seemed to be the trigger. The air was suddenly filled with all kinds of missiles. The policeman got his cap knocked off, and stones and bricks were bouncing off helmets and shields. The officers went for cover, but the brave soldiers stood their ground. I could see the boss man standing with others behind the barrier, further back, near his Land-Rover. The Royal Green Jackets, who were manning the barrier, had had enough and ordered in the water cannon. It rumbled round the corner, and we could hear the powerful engine roaring as it approached the barrier. Then the purple water jets shot out, drenching the mob. I could see one man sitting defiantly, completely alone, in the middle of the road. The throng retreated out of the range of the water cannon.

Two smoking objects came over the roofs towards the barrier.

Billy shouted, 'There's bombs being thrown at the soldiers!'

Mike said, 'No, they're CS gas canisters.'

It took the troops by surprise and they rushed frantically to put their respirators on. The water cannon beat a hasty retreat; the driver wasn't wearing his respirator and the gas had affected him. The gas hung over the barrier enveloping soldiers and protesters alike. We could see people being sick on the ground. More gas could be seen rising to our left and Mike told us to put our respirators on. During riots on the Shankill, I was subjected to the horrors of breathing CS gas. It stripped your throat raw and made your lungs feel as if they had been rubbed with sandpaper. You then coughed your guts up and tears constantly streamed from your eyes.

As the gas cleared, a horde of youths charged down the street. It must have been the hard core, as there were nowhere near as many this time. Those who had got drenched or a whiff of the gas had decided enough was enough and called it a day. It was January and quite cold, so anyone who got soaked would have been freezing. Rubber-bullet guns were loaded. These bullets were meant to hit the ground first before striking the rioter. The soldiers that day fired straight at the mob. Each time one of them struck home we cheered. Mind you, they were hardy guys; once they recovered they came back for more. The sheer quantity of rubber bullets fired in such a short space of time was incredible. Volley after volley was fired and they kept coming back: advance, bullets, retreat. They were resilient, I'll give them that.

The water cannon was brought back a second time and this time it worked. Most of the crowd had moved away and were merely spectators. Or they'd gone up to Free Derry Corner to listen to the speeches.

We could hear over the radio someone from a helicopter saying, 'Your large water pistol seems to have moved all the people towards Aggro Corner.'

Rubber-bullet guns could still be heard firing. Mike pointed out CS gas rising by Aggro Corner. He informed us that the attackers seemed to have switched their attention to the barrier at Little James Street. Then, as the gas turned the air purple, he told us smoke grenades had been thrown.

There was a lot of chatter over the radio; I could hear another of Mike's men say they were under pressure at barrier 12 in Little James Street. A shot was heard over the noise of the fighting and the roar of the marchers. The soldier with the .303 rifle commented, 'That was a .303 just fired there.'

I hadn't a clue what had been fired, all I knew was that it was a gun. I assumed the man knew what he was talking about, given he was carrying one. A few minutes later came a distinct crack of a high-velocity round being discharged, followed by some more. I think it was three or four in quick succession.

Mike said, 'They were definitely from a SLR.'

Nothing came over the air about the shots. Mike took over the radio and kept us informed of what was going on. He was impatient and was walking up and down. There had been a blast over the radio about communications going wrong; more chatter in Army lingo.

Mike reported, 'The Paras' commander is asking for permission to go in for their arrest operation. Headquarters has answered but haven't given the go-ahead. What the fuck is holding them back?'

We could see the Paras moving into position near William Street.

Another burst from the radio and Mike said, 'Lieutenant Colonel Wilford is asking barrier 14 to verify there's still rioting taking place. It's just been confirmed.'

The youths were still throwing whatever they could find at the troops. Then, from round a corner, a group of them emerged with a piece of corrugated iron, a shield, and advanced slowly towards the barrier.

Mike said, 'They're notifying headquarters now about this shield and asking when the Paras are going in . . . Hopefully now . . . Fuck me, headquarters has said they'll let them know.'

We watched the action in William Street as rubber bullets were fired at the advancing shield. Mike walked a little further up the rampart and seemed to change the radio frequency. With his back to the rest of the squad, he started speaking to someone, but with the racket down below, I couldn't hear what he was saying.

Mike turned to us and said, 'They'll be going in now.'

We could see the paratroopers leap into their armoured cars, shouting and cheering as they moved. The roar of the engines was deafening as they raced up Strand Road. Mike told us they were going round the back, probably to barrier 12, to get between the rioters and the crowd at Free Derry Corner. A company of Paras ran up to the barrier in William Street, ready to go through on foot.

Mike announced, 'Operation Forecast has begun.'

The rioters scattered as the barrier was opened and the company of troopers filed through and gave chase. A lot of them ran up the first street, Chamberlain Street, which led up to Free Derry Corner. We saw many men running up Rossville Street, from the direction of Aggro Corner.

One of Mike's men shouted, 'Those bastards must have seen the pigs coming up Little James Street.'

We ran further up the rampart to get into a better position to watch the action at the Rossville Street barricade, where quite a few rioters had sought safety. It had been constructed with a lot of rubble that could be used to throw at the soldiers. Another MRF team was situated just beyond where we stopped and a sandbagged Observation Post was a short distance from where we were. We took off our respirators.

Mike handed me a pair of binoculars and told me to scour the flats and surrounding area for any activity, check for someone taking up a firing position. In front of the flats, across the waste ground, a young lad was running, pursued by soldiers. Two stopped and raised their rifles. I thought they were going to shoot him. One of the Paras kept chasing him and caught him round the head with his rifle butt. The boy was then arrested, lucky to have survived.

There seemed to be a slight delay of a minute or two from the paratroopers going in through the barrier at William Street and the men coming into Little James Street, in their Saracens (pigs). Paras from the William Street barrier were well into the area and had made arrests before the pigs had got through the Little James Street barrier. The armoured cars, when they managed to get all the way through, flew up Rossville Street, into the car park and the waste ground in front of the flats, swung round and stopped.

Billy yelled, 'Somebody's been knocked down!'

I could see a girl lying on the ground near the pig, and then starting to drag herself towards the flats. A middle-aged man seemed to be getting hit with a rifle and had blood pouring down his face. Troopers were jumping out of the pigs and taking up firing positions.

If this sounds confused, I confess that, after such a long time, I remember certain things more clearly than others. Due to the chaos and the constant noise, it was impossible to tell where the shootings were taking place. To make matters worse, the gunfire could be heard echoing from different positions around the blocks of flats. I could understand how soldiers on the ground might become completely disorientated, bewildered as to where the shots where actually coming from. Even in our position, we couldn't pinpoint from where exactly or by whom the shots were being fired from. The only exceptions were when we saw the Paras fire within sight of our vantage point and one IRA man with a pistol.

From this point onwards, I have tried to recreate events exactly as I remember them, however, they might not be in strict chronological order. My recollection of actions, although they might be slightly out of sequence, is accurate. Up to this point, I can confirm that everything I have written is a true account of events in the correct order. Because I was a non-participating observer until this point, events are very clear in my mind. After reading other accounts, I considered trying to correct any mistakes, but I felt by doing that it wouldn't be true to my memory of what happened that Sunday.

The paratroopers sped into the Bogside, going as fast as

possible to cut off the rioters' escape route, then ground to a halt in the car park in front of Rossville flats. At that moment there were two bursts of automatic fire, maybe six to ten rounds in each burst. The noise rang round the complex. One of Mike's men said it sounded like a Thompson. No matter who let loose with a machine-gun, soldiers or IRA men, they never seemed to hit anyone. Some pigs went towards the rubble barricade and stopped about 50 metres away.

Everybody was running like headless chickens, trying to get away. Some of the crowd were running over the waste ground towards a gap in the houses. Three soldiers were in hot pursuit. A number of shots were fired which sounded like high-velocity shots. I had no idea who fired them.

Pandemonium ruled. I could see soldiers and people running this way and that way. Looking through the binoculars, scanning the windows and balconies for any suspicious movement, I could see people watching the proceedings behind their windows. A few came out onto their balconies for a better view. Every couple of minutes I would make a sweep of the activities on the ground.

There were some Paras from the company that had come in by the William Street barrier already on the waste ground. Three of them knelt down and assumed firing positions, covering the second wave of paratroopers arriving in the Saracens. I think one of them fired at a group of people running through the car park. As I moved the binoculars, towards the direction from where the soldier fired, I saw a man lying flat out on his stomach, with what appeared to be blood slowly spreading out from under his head. I could observe some troopers jumping out of the armoured cars, also taking up firing positions. I saw a middle-aged man getting hit with a rifle a number of times and blood flowing down his face. Swinging round again, I focused on the car park and waste ground. Another soldier took aim and fired at a group at the top end of Chamberlain Street. The soldier looked as though he was going to fire again, but then suddenly ran off.

I refocused on the man lying in the car park; I could see he was a teenager, aged about 16 or 17. Some lads had turned him over onto his back. His face and shirt were covered in blood. The lads were agitated, seeming not to know what to do next. Women on the balconies were pointing and screaming. I couldn't hear what they were saying. Another burst of shots could be heard. I swung back towards the top of Chamberlain Street and could see a woman being carried into the first house.

It is impossible to confirm the sequence of events. I would be looking one way, then something would take place somewhere else, then I would turn towards it and refocus. Or a member of my group would shout and point in another direction and I would refocus the binoculars there. I remember feeling lightheaded, swinging from side to side and constantly refocusing the binoculars. I think most of the firing was done in about no more than 15 minutes, although it seemed an awful lot longer than that.

More Saracens arrived and I saw two lorries pulling up behind them with paratroopers piling out the back. Some Paras took up firing positions, covering others who were running for cover. The men just arriving would have heard shots being fired and wouldn't be aware of who was firing them. Meanwhile, rioters were still trying to throw stones from the rubble barricade. The retreating crowd had been alerted by the convoy, seen arriving at Little James Street barrier, because of the delay in letting it through. They had split three ways; some towards Rossville flats, others to the right into Glenfada Park North, while the third group headed towards the meeting at Free Derry Corner.

As the second batch of troops arrived at this juncture, I turned back to the car park; I spotted a man at the gable end of Chamberlain Street, slowly walking towards the corner of the car park. He was wearing a khaki-coloured parka with the hood up. I thought he looked suspicious. Suddenly, he pulled a pistol from his pocket and I heard three or four shots. I shouted at Mike, 'Gunman!' As he turned to where I was pointing, the guy disappeared into an alley.

Back in the car park, someone, who I took to be a priest, was leaning over the youth. He seemed to be waving others away. I scanned the windows of the flats again. Very few people were at them any more. I heard another couple of rounds fired by soldiers in front of the flats, but couldn't see whom they were shooting at. The youths beside the body were starting to lift him, when a guy took a run at the soldiers, waving and shouting at them.

I remember saying to Billy, 'What the fucking hell is that idiot doing?'

We couldn't hear what he was shouting. Some troops over on the other side of the car park turned to face him. One soldier was kneeling with his rifle raised in the direction of the man, who was still yelling and waving his arms. I was focused on the soldier as I thought he was going to shoot. A high-velocity round was discharged, but not from the man I was watching. Slowly panning back towards the arm waver, I spotted a paratrooper, kneeling behind a pig, who must have taken the shot. Then, back to the man who seemed to be wounded but continued his barrage of insults or whatever he was shouting. I thought, That's what I call a lucky man. Two men ran out, grabbed hold of him and dragged him round to the house in Chamberlain Street where I'd seen the woman carried into earlier.

Next, another man apparently overcome with the same madness, rushed out from the side of the flats, straight towards the soldiers, screaming at them. We watched as he stopped, and then we heard the crack of the SLR a split second later. He turned and staggered back round the flats and headed to a house opposite, in what I now know as Joseph Place. Was all this shooting driving people insane? Only people who were insane would be doing what these men were doing. We were mesmerised by their behaviour. Didn't they realise real bullets were being fired? To this day, I find it hard to comprehend what was going through those two guys' minds.

I switched my focus to some paratroopers at the house in Chamberlain Street, into which the wounded had been carried. It appeared as if they were arresting a lot of men who were all coming out of the house and being marched towards William Street.

While I was watching that, the troops from the lorries were making their way up Rossville Street. There was some firing, small bursts of three or four rounds. I switched my attention to the rubble barricade where some young lads were still trying to stone the soldiers. Shots were being directed at the barricade. One young lad fell backwards, possibly shot. It might have been at this point that the rioters became aware that real bullets were being fired. All hell broke loose, with most of the men behind the rubble trying to make a run for it. Guns seemed to be firing from all directions, including ones from another MRF team further along the walls. I kept the binoculars trained on the rubble barricade. I assumed some shots were from the troopers behind the Saracens parked about 50 metres down the street, from the barricade, some from the walls, but with the echoing I couldn't pinpoint the sources. It sounded like a major gun battle. There were different calibres of weapons being used; definitely not all SLR high-velocity rounds or rubber bullets.

There was a lull in the shooting before I heard three low-velocity rounds, quite distinctive from the high-velocity rounds. Some men dragged the young lad's body behind the rubble and ran for the safety of Glenfada Park. A priest leaned over the body, said something. After that, the body was carried off. While I'd been watching this incident, the shooting had intensified again. A very loud report reverberated in my left ear. I had been so engrossed in watching the activities at the corner of Glenfada Park, I had failed to notice one of the soldiers in our team, just beside me, taking aim and firing. I jumped so hard I suffered whiplash, which lasted for a week.

I hunkered down, shaking like a leaf. I could see Mike take aim and fire at someone or something on the ground. Billy thought this was funny and said, 'You're a fucking cracker, scared by your own side's bullets.'

I composed myself and stood up again. When I refocused on the barricade, I let out a gasp, 'Holy fuck, where did they come from?' There were more men lying behind it; five, possibly six. I could see some movement; maybe they were taking cover after the last fusillade. A soldier approached the barricade and spoke to an injured man, then walked back down the street. I presumed the injured man left the barricade, as when I turn back to it he was nowhere to be seen.

Paratroopers continued to fire from below the barricade, pinning down a group standing behind the corner of Glenfada Park. You could see the bullets pinging off the gable wall.

Billy nudged me and nodded at Mike. 'He's going to fire again.'

I looked back at the barricade. BANG. The noise was deafening, but knowing it was coming this time, I didn't jump.

Watching through the high-powered binoculars, I saw a young man's head explode and his body collapse in a heap.

'Fucking hell!' I could taste bile in my mouth, but I couldn't take my eyes off the scene. You never forget sights like that; they can never leave you.

Back at the barricade somebody was trying to crawl out. There were three bodies definitely not moving. It sounds stupid but it just hit me. Three bodies. Three shots fired from our position on the walls. After watching the accuracy of Mike's second shot, the three men had, I assumed, been hit by the two MRF men. Billy confirmed later I was right. Although gunfire was slowly becoming less frequent it was still audible. We were concentrating on the people in front of us when a burst of machine-gun fire came from the direction of Free Derry Corner. We ducked down as the bullets hit the wall not far from us. A SLR could be heard returning fire. Some firing could still be heard over towards Glenfada Park. We jumped up and fired a number of rounds in the general direction of Free Derry Corner before dropping back down to safety behind the wall. I wasn't aiming at anything in particular; actually firing the SLR was exciting enough.

The Paras had reached the corner of Glenfada Park and were arresting the group that had been taking cover there. They were giving them a very rough time. Then the troops herded them down Rossville Street, hitting them with batons and rifles, before loading them into the lorries.

Mike told us the Paras had been ordered to withdraw and we would now do the same. Checking my watch, I couldn't believe the time. From the time the first troops went in until now was only about half an hour. It had seemed like hours. How could so much happen in such a short space of time? We headed back to the Land-Rovers.

At that stage I wasn't elated or saddened; just numb, anaesthetised. I remember saying to Billy, 'There have to have been people killed. All those fucking bodies being carried like that. That guy whose fucking head exploded. Surely to fuck no one could survive a hit like that?'

We left Londonderry shortly after 6 p.m.; the sound of gunfire was still rattling round my brain. Billy and I must have smoked five cigarettes each, one after another; lighting the next one from the one we were finishing.

About half an hour down the road Mike, who still had the radio, said, 'They reckon at least 13 of the bastards are dead and a number wounded.'

I know I said, 'Jesus fucking Christ, only 13, with all that fucking shooting? I would have accepted 30 or fucking 40. How could so many rounds be fired into fucking crowds and only 13 killed? There must be 100 or more wounded, probably a lot critical and seriously fucking injured.'

I think shock had taken over at that stage.

I carried on. 'Well, General fucking Ford certainly got his suggestion put into place to-fuckingday. Ringleaders definitely got the fucking message, loud and clear. No fucking question about that ... Sorry, lads, it's one thing hearing it on the news, but to see it all in front of you is an entirely different fucking kettle of fish.'

Billy said, 'Amen to that.'

Mike reached under the seat and brought out a bottle of Scotch. He handed it to me. I wasn't slow in opening it and took a long swig from it before handing it round. I could feel the burning sensation the whole way down. A warm glow spreading outwards. By the time it came back to me a good hole had been made in it. My mind started to become calm. By the third drink, I had almost returned to normal. If I could

ever remember what normality felt like. I didn't know then
how much we would rely on alcohol to get us through what
lay ahead.

Arriving back at Palace Barracks, we were taken back to our
rooms to wash and put our own clothes back on. Mike left us,
saying he would be back shortly. By then, the purpose of our
being there was slowly returning to my thoughts.

Billy said, 'I suppose 13 dead taigs isn't a bad result for half
an hour of action. I'm sure the Provos will rethink their strategy and call off this insanity. Christ, surely to God, they will
wise up. Fifteen last month and another 13 today. They must
become conscious of the fact that Loyalists are prepared to
strike at Catholic targets and now the Army is going to do the
same. Will the Catholic population still support them? I don't
think so.'

I replied, 'Billy, we have to step back here and assess everything that's taken place since 1969 when it all started. A lot of
Catholics were burnt out of their homes, as well as Protestants.
Then the Provisionals were born out of the ashes. They started
their bombing campaign, shooting soldiers and policemen. The
Protestants are becoming more and more afraid that their way
of life, their country and freedom are being undermined. The
right to remain part of the United Kingdom is under threat.
Looking at it from our point of view, we're prepared to take
up the gun and defend what's rightly ours. Take our vengeance
and retaliation out on the Catholic community.

'We have to look at it from their point of view. First point,
they could look at it the way you just said and put pressure
on the Provos to end the bloodshed. Second point, they could
have been pushed too far and be exactly like us, wanting revenge. It'll be interesting to find out how many of the taigs
killed today were carrying weapons. To be perfectly truthful I

only saw one man with a pistol. He fired a few shots and disappeared. I know for certain the second guy that Mike killed had no weapon. Take it a stage further and, to be completely honest, I never saw any guns near the barricade where four or five of them were shot. What's more important, you know as well as I do that some of the Paras were given directives before leaving this camp on what the Government expected from them today and what General Ford had suggested a few weeks ago. We have to face the facts: that's why there's a MRF unit with unlimited powers to function as and when required.'

Just as I was finishing, the door opened.

Mike announced, 'It's been confirmed, 13 dead and 13 wounded.'

I was astounded. 'Come off it, Mike. Hundreds of rounds fired and only 26 people hit. I know you and the guy from your squad took three of them out. All that firing, it doesn't say a lot for the accuracy of the Paras' shooting. I don't believe it. They must have ferried bodies and wounded across the border to Letterkenny Hospital. Is there any figure yet for how many gunmen were hit or killed?'

'Not yet, they'll probably wait until the morning before debriefing the Paras. But unofficially I'd predict that all were aimed shots at gunmen, nail bombers and petrol bombers.'

Billy stared at him, 'For fuck's sake, how do you expect to get away with that? I never saw one petrol bomb thrown or heard a nail bomb blast. The place was coming down with the world's press!'

I added, 'I heard four or five different kinds of calibre of weapon fired so there must have been some IRA men shooting at someone. I never heard an explosion or saw a petrol bomb either.'

Mike looked at us. 'Look, lads, this is not a normal war

situation. We have to beat them militarily *and* in the propaganda war. What took place in Londonderry is no more than you're being asked to do. A bit more publicity highlighting the soldier's actions in front of the media, yes, but it's the same effect. There'll be an inquiry to appease the Catholics and the Republic of Ireland and the Americans, but it'll exonerate the soldiers' actions today. None of them will face prosecution for the killings. I can guarantee that.'

I said, 'I know you told us before about having a free hand and priority for anything required to be done to ensure victory, if you can tell us that an inquiry will be held and the conclusion's already decided, with no soldier being prosecuted, your powers must be even greater than I thought.'

His surprise looked genuine. 'You don't miss much, do you? You'd be considered as back-up or ancillary Army units. Only the very highest level of the British Government and Senior Officers know of MRF's existence. We're just instruments of those forces. In the end, we're no more than glorified pawns. Like they say, ours is not to reason why, ours is but to do or die. I think that sums it up rather nicely. Come on, lads, I'll get you a lift back to your car.'

He gave us another bottle of whiskey, which we gratefully accepted. There wasn't a drop left when I eventually headed for home from Billy's.

Having watched him speaking to Mike on the walls, General Ford knew his suggestion was going to be used that day. A lot of people, including some of the organisers, knew trouble was inevitable. John Hume expected violence and stayed away. Bernadette Devlin and Eamonn McCann were driving to Londonderry that morning. According to Pringle and Jacobson, Devlin and McCann had heard there was going to be a good turnout for the march. They were certain there would be violence, possibly some shooting. As they were approaching Londonderry they were even guessing how many people might be shot. This alleged conversation throws a completely new light on events. I wonder if they could name the soldiers or their officers who informed them there was going to be shooting. I think it would be easier for them to name the IRA men who told them there would be trouble and possibly some shooting later that Sunday. Two of the organisers had been prepared to let the march proceed, then joked about how many would be shot and killed. They must have known what the IRA was planning. Either that, or they are very sick people.

Who did Mike contact on the radio? Immediately after the radio conversation, he told us the Paras were going in straightaway. That person must have been important. Might a code have been used to supersede other orders and told to MacLellan? He may have contacted Lisburn headquarters, which in turn, may have ordered the deployment of one Para without delay. Suspiciously, the Brigadier was never asked that question at the Widgery inquiry.

There was a difference of opinion about what was said between Superintendent Lagan of the RUC and Brigadier MacLellan, overall commander of the military operation that day. MacLellan passed the remark to Lagan, saying, 'The Paras want to go in.' The policeman was concerned and asked him to hold back until the marchers were clear. MacLellan went back into the Ops room, returning shortly after and is alleged to have said, 'I'm sorry, the Paras have gone in.'

Lagan then commented, 'Well, I hope they're separated enough'; to which MacLellan replied, 'I'm assured that they are, but anyway it's too late to stop them now.' The controversial word is 'sorry'. Lagan is adamant MacLellan said it, whereas MacLellan denies saying it. The Brigadier had held back on ordering in the troops. Why? Even if he didn't use the word sorry, the statement still implies someone else had given the order. He then proceeded into his office without waiting for a reply from Lagan, which might indicate he was worried or preoccupied.

As I mentioned earlier, the truth, the whole truth and nothing but the truth will never be known. My eye-witness account is just another of many; the only difference being that I have no need to lie. I have nothing to gain by lying. My account fits events a lot more truthfully than any evidence given by either side. Although I was there as an observer with the MRF and subsequently when the dust settled, I was overjoyed at the result.

(Author's note. The description of events I witnessed have been detailed above. Below I address information in the book, *Those Are Real Bullets, Aren't They?* There are, in my view, some discrepancies in eyewitness accounts).

When the lead pigs roared onto the waste ground, confusion reigned. The echoing sound of a Thompson machine-gun was heard, not only by soldiers but also by civilian witnesses. Father Daly stated that he saw some youths acting suspiciously at the back of the high-rise flats. He did not explain in detail why they looked suspicious or where they went. Were they getting ready to use guns against the soldiers and Daly couldn't stop them? When the Paras rushed in, why did a priest think he was in danger if he thought it was the usual snatch squads coming in? If he was wearing his dog collar, why run? Or, maybe, after seeing the suspicious youths preparing to shoot, he recognised the danger he was going to be in, stuck in the middle, once the guns were fired.

Daly described how he sprinted past Jackie Duddy, heard the shot and saw the young lad fall. Why did he not stop and try to help the lad, even if he thought he'd only been hit by a rubber bullet? He must have realised the guy would have injured his face badly, falling on it while running at full speed. Another two young lads stopped to help.

There is another discrepancy in people's statements. Father Daly said he had just passed Jackie when he was shot. People said they saw a soldier lean across the bonnet of his pig and open fire. Daly states he was hiding behind a wall when the lead pigs arrived in the car park, stopping 30 feet from were he was. Here is the question; if the young lad was hit while running with the priest and the pigs didn't arrive until after he was behind cover, how could people see a soldier stand upright, rest his arms on the bonnet of the pig, while it was still moving, and fire at Jackie Duddy? I think my account is a bit more realistic, observing a soldier from C Company fire the shot.

Sometimes one is given the impression of every member of the Parachute Regiment in Londonderry that day just waiting for the nod to go on a killing spree. This is not accurate. There were well over 100 soldiers involved in the arrest operation and, if they had all been so hyped up, I would have expected many more people killed or wounded than the final total of 26. The Army states that soldiers fired only 108 rounds that day. I heard a lot more than that. Obviously, I wasn't counting, but the number appeared to be at least twice or three times that figure. Of course, the rounds the Provos fired must be counted too, even if they deny it. What they want people to believe is their weapons were in cars driving round the Creggan, in case they were needed.

The shooting went on for approximately 30 minutes, with a concentrated period in the middle of ten to 15 minutes. Are we to believe it took them half an hour to get from the Creggan to the Bogside to protect their people? Another detail, which I didn't discover until much later and by accident, was that extra rounds were given to certain troopers involved by the MRF, so when they were asked how many rounds had been fired they could declare only a small amount, even if they had used a lot more, or claim they hadn't fired any and hand back their 50 rounds. The whole operation was handled perfectly, when you know the full facts.

Their plan for an arrest offensive, to teach the Derry Young Hooligans a lesson, was sound and badly needed from a Unionist perspective. The dirty tricks war had started.

In the aftermath of Bloody Sunday, the shock waves reverberated worldwide. Photographs and television footage showing a body being carried out by a priest and some men, bodies lying with coats thrown over them, blood seeping from underneath, sickened people everywhere although there were those, including myself, revelling in the result. After the initial revulsion of seeing someone's head explode, I settled down and looked at what many Loyalists then saw as the positive side of the operation. I hoped that someone would pull it all back from the brink, see the number of Catholics being sacrificed for a cause that was doomed before it got started. But I didn't realise how naïve I was. The Catholics were being put into the same position as we had been – under threat.

Now, young men from both communities were being sucked into a spiral of violence. Revenge was on all our minds. Downward, downward, civilisation spiralled and all we Irish seemed capable of doing was quarrel and fight over who was to blame. It was madness.

After the Widgery inquiry, I'm sure no one expected a future prime minister to order a second inquiry. But, it happened and it was another farce. No soldiers were prosecuted.

Bloody Sunday helped win the propaganda war for

Republicans. It wasn't long before reports came through on how their ranks had swelled with new volunteers. You should never underestimate the ability of the higher echelons of an organisation, whoever they may be, to write off the lives of those much lower down the tree, if they think it will help advance their cause one step closer to success. The dead on that day were victims of hidden agendas.

Monday 31 January was just a normal Monday, back to work as usual. Everyone was talking about the previous day's events. It was very hard to concentrate on doing any work. Every time it was mentioned, my mind automatically returned to the bullet shattering the guy's head. I think of it still.

Reginald Maudling, the British Home Secretary, made a statement to the House of Commons: 'The Army returned the fire directed at them with aimed shots and inflicted a number of casualties on those who were attacking them with firearms and bombs.' He also announced that an inquiry would be held to look at the circumstances of the march. Looking back, I feel the same as I did then. It's perfectly simple; when the Government didn't denounce the killings, were prepared to state the case for the soldiers in Parliament that the killings were justified, they must have known beforehand they were going to take place.

The very next day, Edward Heath announced that the Lord Chief Justice Lord Widgery had agreed to head the inquiry into the 13 deaths on Sunday, 30 January 1972.

During an Opposition debate, the Minister of State for Defence gave an official account of events and went on to comment, 'We must also recognise that the IRA is waging a war, not only of bullets and bombs, but of words. If the IRA is allowed to win this war, I shudder to think what will be the future of the people living in Northern Ireland.'

The British Army's account states: '. . . throughout the fighting that ensued, the Army fired only at identified targets, attacking bombers and gunmen. At all times the soldiers obeyed their standing instructions to fire only in self defence or in defence of others threatened.'

When they were prepared to issue these sorts of statements and not pursue murder inquiries into the deaths it only strengthens the evidence in favour of complicity in the sanctioning of the actions taken that day. The new propaganda unit was working hard to combat Republican accounts of events. It worked on the Protestant community because that was the way things were. Loyalist opinions always tended to favour the Security Forces' explanations.

If there was an award for the most ridiculous, unbelievable statement to come from any politician's mouth, I think Harold Wilson must rate as the all-time number one contender. On Tuesday, 1 February 1972, while Leader of the Opposition, he put his foot firmly back in his mouth and inflamed the situation in the Province yet again. He said, 'The only solution to the dilemma is an United Ireland.'

It made everyone nervous. We could all see a situation similar to that of 1912 arising – when the people were prepared to fight to remain British – if Labour regained control of the Government. Wilson wasn't the only politician who came up with an absurd answer to the quandary. William Craig, the Northern Ireland Minister of Home Affairs, suggested the West Bank area of Londonderry should be ceded to the Republic of Ireland. All these statements did, however, was to strengthen our resolve to defeat anyone who stood against us, including the British Government.

On Wednesday 2 February, 11 funerals of the 13 people who were killed took place, with thousands attending from all over

Ireland. Throughout Ireland prayer services were held at the same time as the funerals. Practically everyone in Dublin, over 90 per cent of workers stopped working to pay respect. A huge crowd marched to the British Embassy carrying 13 coffins and black flags. They attacked the building with stones and bottles, later switching to petrol bombs and eventually burning the Embassy to the ground while Irish police watched and did nothing.

I remember watching the pictures on television and they frightened me. I personally thought the fight was to defeat a small number of men involved in the civil disobedience and insurrection within our homeland. This show of solidarity by thousands and thousands of people taking to the streets, in support of the men who were killed, sent shivers up and down my spine.

At that point I knew the writing was on the wall; civil war was now looming on the horizon. There would be no turning back; too much was happening, too many people were dying, and too many people wanted revenge. We were anticipating an invasion by the Republic's Army, as was threatened in 1969. Backs were up, moderation had been kicked into touch, and people's views were hardening, with extremist positions resurfacing. All that was needed was somebody to give the nod and hostilities would begin in earnest.

About a year later, Billy, Mike and myself were having a drink in Billy's house. We were talking about Sinn Féin, and the topic of the slaughter of innocent Catholics by the Army came up. Billy and I were haranguing Mike about the soldiers not being able to shoot any of the IRA men attacking them; that they could only hit poor people out for a bottle of milk at four in the morning or just walking down the road. And how they had a different excuse for every time it happened.

Mike stared at us intently before speaking. 'Wait a fucking minute, you wankers. The pair of you have got the whole thing wrong, as per fucking usual. Can you not work it out for yourselves? This is another strand of our overall strategy to combat the Provos. There are literally thousands of troops stationed in Northern Ireland . About 90 per cent of them have never had a bullet fired at them. They've never even had to use their own weapons. So, we issue a directive to all soldiers in the most dangerous areas, where they're more than likely to come under fire. Most of the attacks on them are generally from single snipers firing a few rounds then disappearing.

'Once the first shot's been fired, if they have an inkling where it came from, then they're entitled to return fire. If someone happens to be in the same area, it could be construed they were caught in the crossfire. The more bodies caused by IRA attacks, the more pressure on the Catholic community to make them stop. Now do you get it?'

I remember studying his face, trying to work out if he was having us on. He was deadly serious.

Billy asked, 'So, what you're telling us is that on many occasions these witnesses could be telling the truth, that some of the people being shot really were just in the wrong place at the wrong time?'

Mike confirmed it. 'It's so simple, isn't it? Don't get me wrong, every effort will be made to engage the gunman, but if anyone happens to be in the surrounding area it would be possible for them to get hit by a stray bullet. Only sometimes it may not be a stray. The locals in staunchly Republican districts generally get word that an attack's imminent and know to keep their children and themselves inside. They'll know the IRA will have attacked the Army and the soldiers will have fired back. No matter what lies they tell to the media, in their hearts and minds they'll know the Provos provoked the return fire. We've got weapons the IRA use, from IRA arms dumps that have been uncovered in searches and kept in certain barracks that come under continuous sniper fire. So, when the opportunity arises they can be used and the postmortem results confirm the type of bullet used is from a gun known to be used by the Provos.'

It was ingenious, in MRF terms at least. Their techniques were designed to end the conflict quickly: the recruitment of informers; Loyalists trained to kill anybody remotely Catholic; soldiers with the power to shoot anyone convenient to an attack; a propaganda department trying to outdo and contradict the Republicans' version of events; new interrogation methods; and, finally, the IRA's own weaponry being used against them. The only problem with the plan was that it didn't allow for the determination and resolve of the PIRA.

It seemed that the PIRA didn't care how many innocent Catholics were murdered, until the early 1990s when Loyalists intensified their retaliation and outdid them in body count. The whole concept of the war had changed. C Company of the UFF went from retaliation to all-out assault against Catholics. That is, when, according to Loyalist analysis, Adams and company decided to call a halt to the campaign of violence.

1972 TRAINING

O N 2 FEBRUARY 1972, a Catholic man was killed when a bomb exploded without warning outside the Catholic-owned Imperial Bar in the staunchly Republican town of Stewartstown, County Tyrone. As the funerals of the victims of Bloody Sunday were taking place, all businesses had closed in Republican areas as a mark of respect. Louis O'Neill died instantly and five others were seriously injured as the bar collapsed around them while they enjoyed a quiet drink. Because the owner had defied the order to close the bombing was intended to give the impression that the Provos had carried out the attack. It worked. Newspaper reports suggested that the Provos had indeed planted the device. Some people suspected the Loyalists and, in fact, it had been organised through a MRF contact with an Out of Bounds order.

Saturday saw us back at Palace Barracks. There was an air of expectation amongst us as we waited for the usual pep talk before training took place. The Captain entered the room and gathered his thoughts for a moment before speaking.

'I hope you all enjoyed your little venture last Sunday. I'm afraid it didn't go exactly as planned. Some of the troopers went a little bit over the top – even those not issued with specific instructions or extra rounds seemed to go berserk. One of them fired 22 rounds and can't remember what he fired at. [I think at the Widgery inquiry one soldier said he fired 19 rounds through someone's bathroom window, but there had been no report of any window with any bullet holes in it anywhere.]

'Unfortunately, because of these over-zealous actions taken by rogue troopers and the political backlash it's caused, two negative results have occurred. First, the opposite effect of what was intended has happened. Instead of driving men away from the IRA, quite the reverse has been taking place. Reports from well placed sources indicate hundreds of men of all ages have been queuing up to enlist in the PIRA all over the country. Last Sunday's events have inflamed the whole situation and, instead of helping to bring a swift end to the conflict, it appears to have escalated the campaign.

'Secondly, I'm sorry to say our operation has been put on hold for a while, until the bigger picture can be examined and the powers to be give us the OK to restart our operation. We'll sanction some missions to break you into the mould slowly and gently, but the main operation is on the back burner until further notice. Today, your contacts will brief you on what to prepare for in the coming months.'

This was disheartening news, as we had all been expecting the green light to begin hostilities in the near future. Mike took us aside after the Captain's talk. He seemed just as annoyed as we were. He had expected the order to be given for operations to commence soon.

He said something then that still baffles me. 'We knew Martin wouldn't let us down. He was vital to the commencement of hostilities and sure enough he did it. The whole operation depended on him firing the vital first shot. Without that, Operation Forecast would never have got off the ground. With hindsight it would perhaps have been better if he hadn't.'

This statement wasn't elaborated on, and we assumed Martin was the name of a paratrooper (like Charlie, who had been significant on Bloody Sunday). Until now. When doing research for this book, I discovered what Charlie and company meant. During the Saville inquiry an informer from 1972 said under oath that Martin McGuinness had fired the first shot. It was then I recalled Mike's statement from all those years ago.

We had thought it could only mean one thing; that between Sunday and Saturday the MRF informer had confirmed their suspicions that Martin McGuinness would be uncontrollable and would attack the Paras once they entered the Bogside. The second scenario was dismissed out of hand as being beyond the bounds of reason. Now, after discovering who Charlie was, there must have been more to it. If Martin McGuinness was so important to the whole operation, then it stands to reason the MRF knew he was going to fire at soldiers on their orders, therefore, he had to be working for them. That is the missing link. He was the ace up the sleeve and the key to whether the operation achieved its intended goal. The MRF could not leave such an extremely important event to chance. They had to be certain he was going to fire at soldiers.

Mike continued: 'We're going to do dry runs in and out of Republican districts. We'll be armed and OOBs put in place so that all concerned will get used to how it's expected to work, including Security Forces personnel. It will be practised almost every night and some days in all areas. Then we'll progress to taking a few shots at nothing in particular, just for you to get the feel of your weapons; the way they fire from a car, with a window down. The noise, as you know, can be quite loud on the firing range, but when you fire in a confined space, multiply that by three. You'll soon understand why earplugs are worn on the firing range. It's the same if you fire a Sterling submachine-gun – thunderous from inside a car, and the shell cases are flying around bouncing off the windscreen. Remember, they will be *very* hot. If you can lean out of the window, it cuts down the noise and the likelihood of getting hit with empty cases.

'Tomorrow you'll be shown how to steal vehicles and hot-wire them. If there's a special job to be carried out, that we need a team to do, we'll supply the car. Clean weapons, never used before, will also be left in the car. You'll be told where to pick up the motor and where to leave it, and the weapons, when you've completed the mission. We'll take care of the rest.

'Hopefully, we'll be operational within the next two months. In the meantime we'll be stepping up your training. I'll be trying to sharpen your reflexes, to make sure you're ready for something untoward. You'll be given a short course in unarmed combat, on how to defend yourselves if the need ever arises. I'll always be there in the background if ever you need me and I promise to keep you up to date on as much as I can. When operations are going down I'll come across and let you know, and we can listen on my radio and hear if it was successful or not. If we're close enough, we can take a drive past and see what damage has been inflicted on the bastards.

'You'll be given a couple of lectures on surveillance techniques, both in the art of carrying out surveillance and how to watch your back, in case you're the subject of someone else's interest. It's difficult for either side to carry out surveillance in each other's areas because any strange faces are soon noticed and challenged. So, a lot of your information on targets will be done through the military and passed on to the different units that are ideally placed to carry out the assassination of targets. We don't expect every time an ASU goes out, that they'll kill somebody. The fact that an attempt has been made and shots fired, even if they wound or miss altogether, is part of the terror tactics you're involved with and hopefully it will scare the shit out of them.

'Killing in the heat of battle isn't difficult. It's easy because the body's defence mechanism takes over and you kill without thinking. It's kill or be killed. It's easy to stab a man if he's coming at you with a knife in his hand. Snipers are a breed apart; it's like no other kind of warfare. A sniper with a telescopic sight on his rifle kills from a distance. He's usually in no danger himself yet he gets to see his victim close up. He looks through his scope and sees the eyes of his victim. You have to be a special sort of man to kill like that and stay sane.

'After interrogating someone – Catholic or Republican – you'll need a lot of inner strength to then put a bullet in his head. Even though you'll probably hate them, when you question somebody, it becomes personal. You'll have spoken to him, maybe discovered some intimate details about him: his name, where he lives, whether he has a family. He'll be crying, sobbing his heart out, begging you to be merciful and spare his life. That's when you have to get mean, be hard, know why this individual has to be executed, because it's necessary to show the IRA bastards that you're serious. For every attack they carry out, retaliation and retribution will follow closely on its heels. They must be pressurised into thinking that whenever they kill, they're condemning their own people to an agonising death. We'll start a process that will help you to handle the execution of these men.

'If a team picks up a Catholic and takes him for interrogation, you'll be taught techniques on how to extract information from them. You'll be given expert guidance on how to understand people's body language; how to detect if they're lying or telling the truth. What you must understand is the need to put the fear of God into the Catholic community – to make them understand that ruthless men are out there who are prepared to exact a terrible retribution on them. The more injuries or mutilation done to a body, the more scared out of their wits they're going to be. The best place to shoot someone, to make sure of a kill, is a shot to the base of the skull, angled upwards. It kills instantly.

'Fear is the key. Terror, anxiety, apprehension and foreboding about what the future has in store for them. Exactly the same as you were feeling about the Provos' campaign. Nothing is going to be left to chance. Maybe this slight delay is to our advantage and will give us the time to make sure you're all ready for when the action really starts. Believe me, I'd say it's an odds-on favourite it's going to be given the green light.'

When Mike laid everything out in front of us like that, it put the fear of God in me. Although I felt disappointed that the action was delayed for a while, a tiny part of me felt relieved. The reluctance was still buried in my sub-conscious, niggling away at my resolve. I still hoped that somehow peace would break out and we would be sent home, to live the rest of our lives as normal human beings.

At that time I still did believe in a merciful God, and I was able to pray and pray hard to him, asking him to spare the taking of any more innocent people's lives. Did he listen? No, he didn't. He didn't listen. I remembered a quotation from Acts 10, verse 34, 'God is no respecter of persons.' I think that just about sums it all up.

The next day and during the weeks to come our training was stepped up dramatically. Everything they had described to us happened: we were taught how to steal and hot-wire cars, surveillance techniques, interrogation methods, unarmed combat and training to increase your reflexes. More assault-course work left me as breathless as ever; I remember thinking I must give up smoking, but it was a long time before I did.

On Tuesday 8 February, Mike called to see Billy (I was in

Glengormly with some of our mates at the time). He told Billy a team was going to do a job as another test of the OOB system. It was to take place in the Ardoyne district off the Crumlin Road. Billy told me the next day that they'd sat in Mike's car and listened to the radio. They'd heard the instruction for an OOB being transmitted. Approximately half an hour later reports started to come over the air that a shooting had occurred on the Crumlin Road. About 15 minutes after that, it was confirmed that there had been one fatality.

A Catholic man was shot dead by Loyalists near Ardoyne, on the Crumlin Road, in North Belfast, close to where he lived. He was walking past the Ardoyne fire station when a car came down the Crumlin Road, slowed down and a single shot was fired, which hit him in the head. I remember thinking it must have been an exceptionally accurate shot from a well trained man.

It horrifies me now to recall that I felt disappointed I hadn't been there with them, listening to what was taking place.

The following day William Craig, the former Northern Ireland Minister of Home Affairs, announced he was forming the Ulster Vanguard Party. It was to be an umbrella movement for the right wing of Unionism and over the next few months held a number of demonstrations and rallies throughout the six counties. That same day, a controversial report detailing the interrogation techniques used by the Security Forces during internment was published. These included: in-depth interrogation; food deprivation; hoods; use of white noise to cause disorientation; sleep deprivation; and being forced to stand for long periods leaning against the wall with their fingertips. Two members of that committee said the methods used were justifiable; the third disagreed.

Three times that week we carried out sorties in and out

of the Republican New Lodge Road area, the first two in a car supplied by Mike. Billy drove the car the first time and I drove the second time. We were all armed and I wasn't a bit nervous. We drove up and down the streets with no problems. Very few people, if any, paid much attention to us. At that time, the Loyalists had not commenced their murder campaign and drive-by shootings had not begun. I dare say if we had parked, we might have become a bit more conspicuous and we would have been noticed. Perhaps they thought we were an IRA unit patrolling the area. For the third sortie we stole a car to use for our tour of the district. It was then concealed in a garage for future use. At no time did we encounter any Security Forces patrols. After each foray, the feeling was good.

On each trip we could have opened fire on a number of occasions at groups of young men standing about street corners, and then made it back safely – a quick dash in, open fire and beat a hasty retreat. You were only talking about five to ten minutes max. We grew to appreciate these exercises; they were settling our nerves. You became aware of your capabilities, the immense power that was in the car beside you. Two Sterling submachine-guns, a 9mm Browning semiautomatic pistol and a .22 Star semi-automatic pistol posed a considerable firepower. While driving, I was conscious of the weight of the gun beneath my arm, that sense of power.

Tuesday 22 February, and the Official IRA (OIRA) carried out their retaliatory action against the Parachute Regiment for Bloody Sunday. A bomb exploded outside the regiment's headquarters in Aldershot military barracks. Another total fuck up: seven people – five women and two men, including a Catholic padre – died when the device detonated without warning. It seemed as if they were killing more of their own religion than ours.

During the week we stole another car, did a couple of laps round the New Lodge and ventured onto the Antrim Road and into the Newington and Little America districts. Mike always followed close behind in another vehicle, but we never encountered any patrols or VCPs. If you can imagine the picture: we were four men in a car, all armed, coming down a street, spotting people either in groups or on their own, pretending to stick a gun out of the window and saying, 'Bang, bang, you're fucking dead, you bastards.' It sounds ghoulish but I was gaining in confidence. The craic was good and later, over a few drinks, it improved.

On Saturday 4 March we were at Palace Barracks as usual when news started to filter through about another significant incident that had a traumatic impact on the population of Northern Ireland. A bomb had gone off in a crowded restaurant in the centre of Belfast. The Abercorn Restaurant was wrecked when the device detonated without warning. Two young Catholic girls, Janet Bereen and Anne Owens, were killed and over 130 men, women and children were injured, some very seriously, with loss of limbs and multiple injuries. Two Catholic sisters lost their legs that day and rumours were flying that they had planted the device, which had gone off prematurely.

While our training continued, we set up contacts throughout Belfast with different groups. Although we had been armed by MRF, we still pursued our own quest for more weapons. Guns were being procured in Scotland and smuggled into the country. Bass drums were used, but another ingenious method was also very effective. A member of a team knew these two wonderful old ladies who loved to travel to Scotland. Once a month he would tell them a charitable organisation wanted to pay for a trip across to Scotland, their being pensioners. They loved the idea and soon they told this man they really looked forward to their weekend breaks away from all the trouble. Little did they know the purpose for their outings.

Their breaks took place from Fridays to Sundays. During the Saturday night their car was taken away and the spare tyre filled with handguns and ammunition. It was then returned to where they had left it for the night. Another car with two men was always sent to shadow them, with an extra spare wheel, just in case they got a puncture. We thought it would have been hilarious if they had had one and some kind soul had stopped to help them. With the weight of the wheel they couldn't have lifted it out of the boot of the car. Hence the back-up, just in case. On Sunday night the car was taken away again and the stuff removed. They were never stopped and searched. It was a brilliant scheme.

On 13 March Harold Wilson met leaders of the IRA in Dublin to have talks. In a press conference he said, 'Internment should be ended and security should be transferred to London. IRA terms should be put on the agenda for talks.' If there was one person that drove the Protestant people ever closer to the brink, it was Harold Wilson.

That same day, Loyalists carried out a shooting. A 19-year-old Catholic lad was shot and killed as he went to answer a knock on the front door of his house at Ravenhill Avenue, in Loyalist East Belfast. It would appear this young man had been attacked and beaten on a number of occasions by some of the Tartan gangs that roamed different Protestant districts of Belfast. During the last beating he received, he was told they would get him. Each gang wore denim and tartan in different colours to denote which area and group they came from. They were controlled by the notorious Loyalist paramilitary and paedophile John McKeague.

They caused a lot of trouble in Loyalist neighbourhoods and

eventually most of them were taken under the UDA's wing. The police implied this young man could have been shot by either one of the two IRA groups for refusing to pass information to them regarding Loyalist paramilitaries' activities in his district. His murder appeared to have been sanctioned because the rumours were that he was doing exactly that. I always had my doubts, but an OOB was in force for that area at the time of his murder. His girlfriend identified two of his attackers but nothing was done about it, as it couldn't be substantiated that they had taken part in his murder. MRF had, I surmised, interfered with police investigations.

During the course of 1971, recruitment for 'young lads' into the ranks of these Tartan gangs was going on. The leader of these gangs was a wiry, sly, sadistic man. John McKeague had been around for a number of years and was known to have connections with Gusty Spence, a senior figure in the UVF who had been jailed in 1966 for murder.

McKeague used gelignite from Spence's team to set off a number of explosions, subsequently blamed on the IRA (see first chapter, 1968–70 The Early Years). When the Troubles started in 1969, McKeague was one of the main instigators of an assault on Catholic homes, which resulted in hundreds of houses being burned to the ground. He and four others were arrested and charged with causing the explosions, but on 21 February 1970 they were all acquitted. During their trial two small bombs exploded near the courthouse – in an attempt to influence the outcome of the trial.

Billy and I met the man once and took an immediate dislike to him. His sunken eyes were of an intensity that bordered on fanaticism; and there was something casual but alarming about him, as if he would be just as happy strangling a dog as he would be cooking spaghetti Bolognese. He was the perfect instrument of pain and a cruel death. When we were introduced to him, we didn't know much about him, except that he was thought to be a bit of a nutcase.

It was later in 1972 when his name cropped up in a conversation with Mike. He told us that Special Branch had recruited McKeague as an informer. His illegal sexual behaviour made it easy to blackmail him into working for them. A blatant and shameless homosexual, he was given over to the MRF, who used him in his role as leader of the Tartan gangs. Special Branch was also still using him for information on other Loyalists. I conclude that Special Branch knew what the MRF was engaged in and felt he could be of use to both them and the MRF.

There had been another horrific murder in the early 1970s that revolted the entire population of the Province. Both sides of the community were appalled when the dismembered and charred body of ten-year-old Protestant Brian McDermott was discovered on the banks of the River Lagan. Initially, we laid the blame squarely on the shoulders of Republicans. There were reports of black magic circles and the boy having been killed in a gruesome ritual. Some time after this murder Mike told us that he had seen a file which stated that evidence pointed either to McKeague or another leader of a group calling themselves Tara, William McGrath, being responsible for his murder. (McKeague and McGrath knew each other and they may have been involved together – both were well known as sadistic homosexuals.)

Back in those days, homosexuality was taboo, something that was never discussed publicly. Today it's accepted as the norm; they're even paid money to appear on television and have their own shows. They can have parades in different cities throughout the world. But in the 1970s they were for the most of the time kept firmly in the closet. When Mike told us about these two gays, we were astounded. He revealed that McGrath was in charge of a boys' home, Kincora, and there were some very important people from Northern Ireland and across the water aware of a paedophile ring connected to the home. It was a top-secret operation involving politicians and royalty. He told us McGrath was an agent run by MI5 and that all top men in the police, Special Branch and Military Intelligence were aware of the abuse at the boys' home. No one wanted the boat rocked so the main participants were granted immunity from prosecution. The very thought of what was going on disgusted Mike, but it was all part of the overall strategy of the dirty war.

In 1980, thanks to a tip-off from a leading Catholic politician to a reporter from the *Irish Independent*, the Kincora Scandal, as it became known, was finally made public. McGrath and two others were charged with offences and given jail terms, McGrath only receiving a sentence of four years. He took his secrets with him to the grave, never once giving any names of those involved.

The man who Special Branch and Military Intelligence most worried about though was McKeague. He swore he wouldn't suffer the same fate as McGrath and told them he would name the people involved unless he was immune from prosecution. That's where he made his big mistake, especially since he knew how the game was played. If a problem arises, kill him or her; problem over. (In January 1982 two members of the INLA walked into his shop in East Belfast and shot him dead.)

On 16 March 1972, a 20-year-old Catholic girl was killed by a bomb left in a ladies' toilet in the centre of Lurgan, in a Catholic part of the town. Groups of young Catholics used the toilets as a meeting place and they were the intended targets. The outcome was the same; as long as it was a Catholic killed, fear would be creeping into Catholic minds. Who would be next?

On 18 March, we had arranged to skip the usual training to attend a massive rally in Ormeau Park, organised by William Craig's Vanguard Movement. It was estimated that in excess of 60,000 people turned out for the rally, and it was at this venue that Craig made his controversial statement, 'If and when the politicians fail us, it may be our job to liquidate the enemy.'

The crowd erupted with approval at those words. Had we found the new Lord Carson?

I had often wondered how masses of people followed and obeyed men like Hitler and other dictators; how so many people could be taken in and become fanatics to the point that they would carry out atrocities on behalf of these men. I watched TV programmes on the anniversary of the liberation of the extermination camp Auschwitz and recall a German soldier, who was a guard at the camp, being interviewed. He was asked if he felt any remorse about what went on in the camp. I was stunned by his answer: 'No, we were told what was taking place was right and necessary for the greater good of Germany, and that's what we believed, so we didn't see anything wrong in what was taking place.'

Looking back, we were exactly the same; we were listening to words of war and hatred directed at not only IRA men or supporters but all the Catholic community. Words we wanted to hear. If William Craig had told us there and then to go and attack Republican areas, kill and destroy Catholics, the crowd would have done precisely that. Ultimately he hadn't the courage or conviction to follow through with his prognosis for the future of Northern Ireland.

On 20 March there was another day of carnage, in Donegal Street; another Belfast street ran with the blood of ordinary innocent folk going about their normal day's work or doing a wee bit of shopping. A mate and I had just turned a corner and we could see people running here, there and everywhere. We knew a bomb warning must be in place as the people were being directed away from a side street. Just a couple of minutes before noon a 200-pound bomb exploded in a Cortina car parked in the street, devastating everything and anyone in its vicinity. We were knocked backwards, head over heels, onto the ground by the force of the blast. As we lay there trying to make ourselves as small as possible, debris, fragments of the car and shards of glass fell around us.

After a few moments, still reeling with shock, we started to move towards the scene of the blast. As the dust and smoke started to clear, our shock turned to horror as we approached what looked like something from a war movie. People were lying everywhere, blood was everywhere, devastation was everywhere, bits of bodies were everywhere. Screams and awful crying and wailing filled our ears. A couple of policemen appeared to be dead.

I had done a First Aid course and carried a card stating I was qualified to treat injured people. As I surveyed the carnage in front of me, I felt as useful as a snowball in hell. Eventually, instinct took over and I moved to comfort the casualties and try to help as best as I could. An old man lay on the footpath, outside what I think had been a shop minutes ago; a number of us tried to console him as he lay semi-conscious, oblivious to the fact that he'd lost half his leg.

I find it impossible to describe what it was like to be caught up in this situation. Words cannot describe the slaughter, the blood, or my emotions, my anguish. The soul-destroying screams and the heartbreaking crying of children are all permanently embedded in my memory. Every ambulanceman, policeman, soldier, doctor, nurse, fireman and paramedic that had to cope with seeing those sorts of casualties deserves a reward for their endurance and bravery throughout the Troubles.

Apparently the PIRA had left inadequate and misleading warnings. Whether this was done deliberately or not is open to conjecture. The first warning at 11.45 a.m. was made to an agency in Church Street, saying that a bomb had been placed in their premises. The second warning came at

11.52 a.m. to the *Irish News* (a mainly Catholic newspaper), stating that a big bomb had been left in Church Street. The police started to clear Church Street and direct people towards Donegal Street. The third and final warning was given to *The Belfast Telegraph*, stating that the bomb was actually in Donegal Street. The newspaper passed the information to the police at 11.55 a.m. The car exploded at 11.58 a.m. The evidence speaks for itself; they intentionally gave the wrong location, knowing they were directing innocent folk to their deaths.

Shortly after this atrocity, Prime Minister Edward Heath told the Northern Ireland Prime Minister Brian Faulkner he was going to implement one of Harold Wilson's suggestions. He was going to remove security powers from Stormont. Faulkner and the Unionist Government refused to hand over security powers. Heath told him he would abolish Stormont and introduce Direct Rule.

On Friday 24 March, Edward Heath announced that the Stormont Parliament was to be disbanded and Direct Rule from Westminster would be introduced, with effect from 30 March 1972. He cited the main reason as the refusal of the Unionist government to accept the loss of law and order powers to Westminster. On Sunday 26 March, William Whitelaw was appointed the first Secretary of State for Northern Ireland.

During our training that weekend we had been told, because

of all the events in the political arena, that once again our operation had been put on the back burner. Apparently, the Prime Minister wanted to see if Direct Rule would persuade the IRA to at least call a ceasefire or persuade them to halt their campaign of violence all together. You could sense the feeling of apprehension in the room. Everybody had a dark cloud of doom hanging over them. Were deals being done behind our backs? Had Wilson persuaded Ted Heath he could get the IRA to stop if a lot of concessions were made to them? It sounded ominous. A lot of questions were asked, but the answers were circumspect and cautious. We left Palace Barracks that Sunday with heavy hearts. What the fuck was going on?

It was announced that the Ulster Vanguard Movement was calling a two-day strike, starting on Monday 27 March, against the abolition of our parliament and the imposition of Direct Rule. The strike caused public transport to be halted and cuts in power supplies. Many firms closed. On the second day a huge rally was organised to finish at Stormont. Over 100,000 people participated. The final sitting of the Northern Ireland Parliament at Stormont finished that day. On Thursday 30 March, the legislation introducing Direct Rule was passed at the House of Commons.

As the UDA turned more military-minded anybody speaking out against it met with speedy punishment. During March 1972, Ingram 'Jock' Beckitt from the Shankill area said what he felt about the criminal elements within the UDA. He was the sort of man who didn't mince his words – one of Belfast's hard men. (It was rumoured that he'd once fought six policemen to a standstill in a bar brawl.) He and his brother 'Pinky', whom I met later in the year, were well known to locals and had a good reputation as being honest men who were opposed to criminal activity. 'Jock' was one of the founder members of the

UDA. He was not afraid of voicing his opinion and would talk in the bars and clubs about men using the UDA as an excuse to pursue criminal activities. At one meeting he had pointed at a group of men and described them as a bunch of thugs.

Speaking in a club later, 'Pinky' declared his support for his brother's stance. He was promptly attacked and badly beaten by a group of men. When 'Jock' heard about the assault he headed straight for the club. Two armed men were waiting for him and shot him as soon as he went inside. They loaded his body into a car and set off to dump it. When the car stopped, as his attackers tried to lift him out, he regained consciousness and tried to fight off the men. One of them shot him in the head.

The people of the Shankill were in a state of shock at the murder of the big 'Honest Prod', as he was affectionately known. Harding Smith, another founder of the UDA and a good friend of 'Jock', realised that something would have to be done to get rid of the criminals within their ranks. Thomas Boyd and William Spence, the two gunmen and known criminals, were both murdered later in their homes. Throughout the Troubles many men were killed for similar offences.

During the first week in April, we had started to believe tentatively that maybe Direct Rule was going to be enough to end the killing at least. Of course, it also strengthened our feeling that a deal had been agreed behind Protestants' backs and the sell-out had begun. We were wrong.

At training that weekend, we were told to start preparing ourselves for action. The room filled with tense conversation as they broke the news. The Captain said that all other avenues had been exhausted and the time was coming to launch our offensive. Informers were in place, one or two in fairly high places within the ranks of the Provos.

We were regarded as ready to carry out our objectives and all that remained for him to say was, 'I wish you all the best. Your contacts will speak to you and help in whatever you need.'

Butterflies flew around my stomach as we left that Sunday.

The tenth of April was the day Lord Widgery released his report on Bloody Sunday, which largely exonerated the Army. It was exactly the result that Mike told us would occur. The cover-up was complete. Republicans referred to it as the 'Widgery Whitewash'. I'm sure even he didn't expect a second tribunal over 26 years later. As I mentioned, the outcome can only establish who were the better liars and no clear picture will ever emerge of who did this or who did that. Maybe when people read what I have to say, it will help to achieve a more honest conclusion.

On Monday night, Mike was over, in the background, following and observing. A dozen of the team had gathered at Billy's house. I often wondered what his parents though he was doing, with so many friends who came and went from their parlour. They never did ask. When it was dark two men were sent out to steal a car. Half an hour later they returned with a Cortina and parked it round the corner. Four more men were selected and they drove off towards the New Lodge Road. The purpose of the exercise was to pass a gable wall, pick out a spot on the wall, and drive off. Then they were to return a minute or two later, fire two or three shots at the spot, see how accurate they were, and return to base.

The second group was sent to the Newington area, off the Limestone Road, and the same action was to be followed. The third team did the same in the Little America area, between the Antrim Road and the Cavehill Road. Mike followed each time and, when we had finished, he gave us an indication of how accurate each unit had been. The car was then taken by some of the Glengormly men back there with them, to a place we had found behind some garages. That was the third car stashed, essential for operations.

If a car had to be brought from its hiding place and happened to pass a patrol on the way, that patrol would be on the look-out for stolen cars taken that day. The longer a car remained hidden away, the further down the list it went of each patrol. For a really important operation a new set of number plates matching a car of the same make and colour would be fitted. We did the same action three more times that week. At no time did we encounter any Security Forces patrols. Mike was upbeat; the accuracy wasn't bad at all.

On Wednesday 19 April, Edward Heath confirmed that the plan to conduct an arrest operation, if a riot developed on the protest march on Sunday 30 January, was known in advance by ministers. I found this admission startling. It also confirmed Mike's information that the orders had come from the top and been sanctioned at Cabinet level.

On 20 April, two men got into a taxi at the Catholic depot in Clifton Street, North Belfast. The driver drove his killers up the Crumlin Road and was told to stop about half a mile up the road, beside streets leading into the staunchly Loyalist Shankill district. There, he was shot five times. The killers were observed running down one of these streets as they made their escape. The man staggered towards a house where he collapsed. He died in an ambulance on the way to hospital. It was the first time I was in the car with Mike as we listened to the reports of the attack. Another OOB was in place at the time.

On 22 April, Francis Rowntree, an 11-year-old boy, died after his skull was fractured after being hit on the head by a rubber bullet. The bullet had been fired by soldiers during riots in the Divis Street area two days earlier. This was the first of three deaths caused by rubber bullets. Republicans claimed that the rubber bullet had been tampered with and, instead of being hit with the bullet, it was an Ever-Ready battery which had hit the child. An Army spokesman claimed it was impossible for the bullets to have been doctored, adding that 'they were designed to be effective without causing injury'. The guy must have come from Cloud Cuckoo Land, as it was very easy to improvise these weapons.

An ex-military policeman (Red Cap) confirmed to me about five years ago what Mike had told us about these bullets, that the practice was widespread throughout all battalions in the Province. Soldiers would doctor rubber bullets by chopping off a couple of inches to enable two or three charges to be inserted, along with batteries, coins, or nuts and bolts, to make them more effective and deadly when fired. I witnessed it being done in Palace Barracks.

We had spent the whole month doing dummy runs, in and out of the target areas, familiarising ourselves with dead ends and cul-de-sacs; the last thing you would want to do would be to drive into a blind alley if something went wrong. Sometimes Mike would have gone in beforehand and placed a piece of wood against a wall. He would then tell us to inform whichever team was going out that a target was standing at such and such a place. The unit would be despatched and the driver would know exactly the spot he was taking them to and his escape route.

Mike would later retrieve the piece of wood to see how accurate the units were. One night he returned and said to Billy, 'Who's the cunny funt?' Someone had drawn a wee smiling head and a heart on the wood, then fired two rounds into them. I'm sure people would have heard our laughter a mile away.

On 4 May, a Catholic man was a victim of a ferocious attack

187

just off the Antrim Road. This murder took place a long time before the Shankill Butchers were around. The young man was found with multiple stab wounds in an entry between Baltic Avenue and Atlantic Avenue, a small Catholic enclave between the Limestone Road and the Duncairn Gardens, in North Belfast. He was waylaid, taken to a house in Tiger's Bay 200 yards away, where he was badly beaten, tortured and stabbed 18 times. When they had finished he was dumped up an entry. The whole of Belfast was made up of narrow streets with small houses, each with a back yard and a door leading out to an entry for putting your bins out and so on – ideal places to dump bodies. This was another killing intended to put the fear of God into the Catholic communities. It's brutal to kill anyone in any fashion, but to stick a knife into them 18 times frightened me. An OOB had been in place. Mike told us later he thought a tartan gang had been responsible.

During the next week no one was murdered. There were a number of attempted murders and drive-by shootings, riots, petrol bombings; days wouldn't have been the same if absolutely nothing took place. Journalists would be getting the sack if all the nasty stuff stopped. Eventually it did come down to that; I heard that foreign reporters and news teams actually went and paid the young lads to start riots with the Security Forces, in order for them to catch it all on camera.

That brief lull was the calm before the storm. Thirty-seven more people were to die between 11 and 31 May. This was a milestone, when the blood lust started to take control of all our minds, across the divide. Revenge for revenge's sake, reasoning out the window. It was going to be a battle to the death.

The only question was: who could kill most and to what depravity and debauchery would each side stoop, to outdo the other?

A lot of the information passed to Loyalists came from undercover soldiers scouting around Republican districts. It's the only way to explain how they ended up in compromising situations. Now and again they would spot someone who was on their wanted list and decide to apprehend the men themselves, or try to kill them and blame it on Loyalists. They had been caught out on a number of occasions, when witnesses had observed their actions. Then the Army's new propaganda machine kicked in and came up with strange justifications as to why these incidences had happened. Their misinformation would never better the Republicans' propaganda machine though; they didn't even come a close second.

On 13 May, a Loyalist car bomb exploded without warning outside Kelly's Bar at the top of the Whiterock Road. The bar was packed and 63 people were injured. Once again, the question arose: whose bomb was it? William Whitelaw, the Northern Ireland Secretary, announced in the House of Commons that it appeared to have been an IRA bomb that had detonated prematurely. Accusing the Provos of trying to provoke a Protestant backlash he said, 'Facts did not support the theory that it was Loyalist extremists who had planted the bomb.' In fact, it was a Loyalist device. We were sitting in Mike's car waiting for news of the operation taking place. A barman injured in the bomb attack died from his injuries on 23 May. An OOB had been in place. You can see how it was working. Even the Secretary of State didn't know what the MRF was authorising.

A Catholic man had been spotted leaving Unity Flats and walking up towards the Shankill. He had drawn attention to himself by doing that, putting himself in danger. No Protestant would have passed from Unity Flats into the staunchly Loyalist district. He was stopped, and asked who he was and where he came from. Unable to provide verifiable answers, he was taken for interrogation. After being badly beaten he was taken to Hopeton Street and shot once in the head. A number of personal items were taken from him before he was killed. It's possible that during his beating and torture, he did eventually break and give his proper name. He had been interrogated at Palace Barracks on one occasion previously and the MRF would have put his name on the lists passed onto their contacts. Once his name was discovered on their list, his fate would have been sealed.

The IRA mounted a gun attack; this time on Protestant workmen leaving Mackie's engineering works just off the Springfield Road. Although the company was based in a Catholic area, its workforce was almost 100 per cent Protestant. My mate Billy worked there and had to make a dive for safety as the gunmen opened fire. Fortunately, no one was killed.

On 27 May, a Catholic man was shot dead while walking along Finaghy Road North towards his home in Andersonstown. He had just left his girlfriend's home when a hit team out looking for some vigilantes noticed him and opened fire. An OOB had been in place at the time of the shooting. Once again, we were sitting in Mike's car as reports came in when the operation took place.

The same day, another young Catholic man was shot outside a training factory belonging to Mackie's. He was found lying in a pool of blood some time later. The gunman had walked up to him and fired two bullets into his head, before driving off along the West Circular Road towards Ballygomartin. An OOB had been in place at the time.

On 28 May, in the early morning, the Provos were transporting a bomb either to or from Anderson Street in the Short Strand district of East Belfast. The bomb exploded prematurely outside a car, probably as it was being carried, killing four active service members of the PIRA. It also killed four civilians, two men and two women; one of the women was a mother of three children. Everyone that died sustained massive injuries; one body was blown 100 metres into the air. It appeared they had all been close to the bomb when it detonated. Did we celebrate that day? You better believe it. I'm ashamed to say it was like a party atmosphere.

On 29 May, once again during an OOB, a Catholic man was shot twice in the stomach as he made his way from Durham Street to Unity Flats. He would have had to walk across Millfield, which runs from the Shankill to the Falls. It became a notorious murder spot; Catholics seemed to be oblivious to the danger they faced while using it as a short cut from one Catholic area to another. The Loyalist district of Brown Square was directly off Millfield. If I had a fiver for every OOB put on Millfield, I would be a very wealthy man. A soldier on duty at Unity Flats heard the shots and saw the man stagger and fall. The gunman was still able to make a quick getaway.

We were ending May on a high; eight of them killed by one of their own bombs and the officials pulling the plug on their military campaign. Plus, Loyalists were now striking back. Surely they must decide their war was fruitless.

The following day, a 12-year-old Protestant girl, Joan Scott, died. She had been hit during a sniper attack on a RUC patrol on the Oldpark Road three days earlier. The killing of any child always weighed heavily on my mind. I knew our aim was to inflict as many casualties as possible, including men, women and children, but the thought of taking a child's life was repellent. I don't think I could have lived with myself.

The month of May finished with 39 people dead and many more injured. Rioting was commonplace. People were being driven from areas in which they had lived peacefully all their lives.

Gun battles were a regular feature in our nightly vigilante duties as soldiers took on IRA snipers. Explosions erupted all over the place. On many nights, Loyalists went across to the streets close to the Duncairn Gardens and fired a few rounds up and down the street, or shot into someone's window or planted a small pipe bomb – anything to cause fear within the Catholic community.

On 4 June, a Catholic shop owner was shot dead on the Antrim Road in North Belfast. He had been out for a few drinks with his wife and brother. It was after midnight when they pulled up outside his music shop to check his answering machine. The gunmen were waiting for him. As he came back out of the shop, six shots were fired. He was hit in the chest, and a number of bullets hit the van where his wife and brother were waiting. Someone had called him during the day to arrange a very lucrative business deal, saying he would leave a message at the shop and to contact him straight away, no matter what the time. An OOB had been in place at the time.

On 11 June, a Catholic greengrocer was gunned down by a Loyalist hit team while sweeping the street outside his shop on the Catholic part of the Oldpark Road. Tensions were running high in Catholic areas as earlier that day police and soldiers had blocked a Republican rally in support of prisoners who were on hunger strike.

The rally was to have come from Divis Street across Millfield, past the lower Shankill to the Crumlin Road Prison. The police and soldiers stopped the march at Divis Street. Violence flared as the marchers were prevented from going any further. Loyalists had gathered at a number of flash points along the route. A lot of blood would have been spilled if the demonstration had been allowed through. Heavily armed men were waiting and would have opened fire at a number of places. In the end the parade was stopped.

The IRA had already had a few cracks at the Army in the area, and the MRF decided to provoke them even further, by sending in a hit team to shoot someone. It worked, as the IRA confronted the Army and Loyalists all over the district. Heavy gun battles raged in Ardoyne, the Bone, Crumlin Road, Manor Street and New Lodge, as well as many other places throughout Belfast and Northern Ireland. The gunfire was so sustained an ambulance couldn't get into the area to retrieve the body of the dead man.

This was the first gun battle in which we had been involved. Talk about the ultimate adrenaline rush – it was as if someone had fired a syringeful straight into your blood stream. My senses were so heightened I could hear them humming. There was no time to think about being nervous: it was kill or be killed. We were taking the IRA on and giving them a taste of their own medicine, showing them we were better armed than before and prepared to fight back.

During the next few days there was a flurry of political manoeuvring to get talks started between the British Government and the IRA. On 13 June, the IRA invited William Whitelaw to meet them in Free Derry. Whitelaw turned the offer down and confirmed that British Government policy was not to 'let part of the United Kingdom default from the rule of law'. The Catholic Social Democratic and Labour Party stepped in and seized the opportunity to push for talks.

On 14 June, John Hume and Paddy Devlin met members of the IRA in Londonderry. At the meeting, conditions were expressed by the IRA representatives: 1) there should be no restriction on who represented the IRA; 2) there should be an independent witness at the meeting; 3) the meeting would not be held at Stormont; 4) political status should be granted to Republican prisoners.

SDLP representatives met William Whitelaw in London the following day and set out the IRA's terms. Whitelaw agreed to the proposals.

A man who had been shot twice on Bloody Sunday, John Johnston, died on 15 June – the 14th person to die as a result of injuries sustained during the violence that day.

We had been following the reports of the proposed meeting between the Government and the Provos with great interest. Considering the IRA had made the first move we had begun to believe the message was beginning to get through to their leadership; that the cry throughout the centuries of 'No surrender!' from the Loyalist people was as much alive as when our forefathers shouted it. Our reasoning was, they must be under pressure to make such an offer.

On Monday 19 June, an interesting development took place. Catholic Desmond Mackin was shot dead by the Provos in the Cracked Cup Social Club, on Leeson Street, Lower Falls. This street was known as the Republicans' heartland, similar to the Shankill for Loyalists. Mackin was involved in a difference of opinion with PIRA members, which stemmed from a feud between the Officials and the Provisionals.

It was around this time we had our first successful operation. We drove past a number of youths then slowed right down to allow our gunmen time to aim and fire. Two of the youths were hit and wounded. We felt good; at least it was a start.

1972 OFFENSIVE

'Cry havoc and let loose the dogs of war!'
William Shakespeare

ANOTHER MEETING TOOK place between the SDLP and
William Whitelaw. Meanwhile a well known Republican,
Billy McKee, was on hunger strike, in an attempt to persuade
the powers-that-be to grant 'Special Category' status to paramilitary prisoners incarcerated for political offences. Whitelaw
granted this request, however, the authorities still snubbed Billy
McKee and informed the UVF leader, Gusty Spence, of the
'Special Category' decision. Spence then relayed the news to
the IRA. In effect, control of the prison was handed over to
the paramilitaries, who took charge of their wings: 'A' wing
was Republican and 'C' wing was Loyalist. Eventually, Crumlin
Road Prison would be used for remand prisoners who, once
they were convicted, would be moved to Long Kesh where
each group had separate compounds.

On Thursday 22 June, the IRA announced that a ceasefire
would come into force from Monday 26 June, provided that
a mutual response came from the Security Forces. We were
jubilant on hearing this news. Had they had enough? It certainly seemed that way. Then the doubt started to creep in.
Why has this happened? Heath had said he wouldn't negotiate
with the men of violence. Had there been some sort of deal

done behind our backs? Fear and suspicion was growing again, and we watched events very closely over the coming days.

On 23 June, a 17-year-old Catholic lad and his girlfriend were standing at the Northern Bank at the junction of Antrim Road and Atlantic Avenue with a group of friends (a favourite place for young Catholics to hang about at the time). A Loyalist hit team slowed down as they approached the corner, before opening fire on the young people. The lad was hit and died, while a young girl was wounded in the neck.

At midnight on 26 June, the Provisional IRA put into place a bi-lateral truce. We did not know then that Whitelaw had agreed to hold secret talks with the Provos, on behalf of the British Government. The truce at that time sparked off fear amongst Loyalist groups. We were in no doubt that some kind of political power-sharing deal was being instigated, which would lead to a British withdrawal and leave us out in the cold.

On 27 June, William Galloway, who lived in the next street to me and was a very close friend, was murdered during a riot at Edlingham Street and Duncairn Gardens. This street ran from the Republican New Lodge Road to the Loyalist Mervue Street, on the edge of Tiger's Bay. Duncairn Gardens marked the dividing line between one side and the other. A crowd of young lads had gathered on the Republican side of Edlingham Street, hurling abuse and a few stones. There was nothing strange about that, just another daily skirmish; before long, more of us arrived and joined in the fray.

All of a sudden, a whistle sounded and the Catholic crowd parted. A hooded man with a Thompson submachine-gun was revealed. He fired a burst at us. I dived for cover and tried to make myself as small as possible. The gunman disappeared. A huge cheer went up from the Catholic crowd and they all dispersed up entries and down nearby streets.

Raising my head slowly, I could hear screaming and saw someone lying on the ground about ten feet away. A woman was shrieking about 30 feet behind me to the right. Looking across at the Republican side, it was empty. Not a sign of anyone; not one person even watching the scene of turmoil. This was unusual, as shootings or bombings always attracted morbid onlookers who wanted to see the gruesome scene, so I reckoned they must have been told to stay off the streets. I went over to see the body, and I realised it was Billy Galloway. He wasn't moving. His head was in a pool of blood and as we felt for a pulse we could see that part of the back of his head seemed to be missing. The woman behind me had been hit in the leg. I recognised her as a mate's mother.

Later, as darkness began to settle over the area, it was our turn to bring the weapons out. People opened their doors – front, back and yard – to enable men to run through the houses from the front to the back entries and through another entry door into another house and the adjoining street. It meant you didn't have to go across the top of any street where the gun battle was raging. The Welsh Guards were deployed on the Duncairn Gardens to act as a buffer zone between both sides. They shot and wounded the father of one of my mates as he tried to go across the top of the streets, instead of through the houses.

People egged you on as you flew from one house to the other. 'Go get the murdering bastards.' 'Go on, son, get a fucking taig for me.' 'Good on you, lads.' I honestly believe ordinary folks didn't think that Loyalist organisations had the capability to strike back and engage the IRA head-on. After the troops intervened, we slipped away. Our fight wasn't with the British Army. Although there had been gun battles a few weeks before, this was different. A young lad known to a lot of people had died on the streets where we had played as youngsters. It felt good passing through houses with people praising you as you went.

I could feel hatred taking over my mind and my body, consuming me uncontrollably. Once it was there, once it was in you, nothing you could do would ever exorcise it.

That same day a Catholic man, Bernard Norney, was shot and killed while attempting to drive through an IRA roadblock on the Whiterock Road, in West Belfast. It felt good they were killing their own again.

But we were cracking up. Now there was a ceasefire they were going to be allowed to set up roadblocks in Republican areas. There were still no-go areas in place. Tempers were smouldering. The UDA began to organise no-go areas in their own districts. This was mainly due to rumours spreading that concessions were going to be made to the IRA. Men armed with whatever they could find manned the roadblocks, checking everyone going in and out.

On 1 July, a Catholic man was abducted as barricades were erected all over Belfast in Loyalist areas. Everyone was stopped and questioned, asked for identification to prove who they were. If they were found to be Catholic, they would be taken to a romper room, subjected to beatings and torture, and then shot there or taken to sites where they were unlikely to be seen and killed there. This man was one of those victims. He was taken to a playground off the Shankill Road and shot five times in the head and chest.

Some Protestants were also given a beating if they were hostile or didn't want to produce their driving licence.

Most of these types of killings would occur within areas behind barricades so there would be no need for an OOB. Units that had MRF contacts carried many of them out; we were given a no-holds-barred directive. In other words, we were encouraged to murder in any way we wanted, the more gruesome the better, to create an impact. Consequently, this attracted men who had serious sadistic tendencies.

Also on 1 July, an Englishman who had just returned from a job interview in London took a lift from a man for part of the way back into Belfast from Aldergrove Airport. He was stopped at one of these roadblocks and asked for identification and his destination. Not realising what was going on, in all innocence he said he was going to Unity Flats. That reply was enough for him to be taken for questioning. His hooded body was found off the Ballygomartin Road, shot a number of times.

The following day saw two Catholic men abducted at a roadblock and later killed. Although they were together when their car was stopped by a Loyalist squad, they were split up and taken to separate locations for interrogation, somewhere in the Shankill district. One of the men was found in Forthriver estate hooded and shot; the second man was found the next day in the back of the other man's Mercedes, in the lower Shankill, also hooded and shot. While this was not a planned abduction, one of those wrong place/wrong time killings which occurred on numerous occasions in the future, a MRF contact notified when the bodies were going to be dumped and OOBs were ordered.

Republicans hit back swiftly. Two Protestant men were picked up in the Oldpark and Cliftonville Road district as they walked home after spending the night drinking in an illegal drinking club, the Jolly Rodger on Alliance Avenue. At some stage of their journey home, probably near the Catholic Bone district, they were spotted by a group of vigilantes with armed back-up. They were taken to a nearby house, beaten and tortured. After undergoing many hours of brutality and cruelty they were taken to a piece of ground near Cliftonville Cricket Club, where both men were shot.

Unknown to everybody a secret meeting between the Provisionals, William Whitelaw and Northern Ireland Office ministers in the Chelsea home of Paul Channon, Minister of State for the North, took place on Friday 7 July. The IRA delegation included Gerry Adams, Seamus Twomey, Sean MacStiofain, Daithi O'Connaill, Ivor Bell and Martin McGuinness. Adams had been released from detention especially to enable him to take part in the talks.

The whole Protestant population knew nothing about these talks until Monday 10 July, when Whitelaw admitted the secret talks had in fact taken place. Everyone was in a state of shock and bewilderment as to why the Government would stoop so low to even contemplate talking to gunmen and bombers, never mind releasing a detainee from prison to attend. Was the writing on the wall for the state of Northern Ireland?

On Sunday 9 July the IRA had been on ceasefire for about two weeks. There was a dispute over housing in the Suffolk and Lenadoon area, on the border of South and West Belfast. Shots were fired in Horn Drive at soldiers. A gun battle ensued and quickly spread throughout West Belfast.

We had been at Palace Barracks that day for our report on what had transpired in the previous month and to discuss any new ideas for the next month. News reached us that the ceasefire had broken down and gun battles were starting in West Belfast.

Mike approached Billy and me, and asked us to wait in a room for a few minutes. He returned carrying combat clothing and instructed us to put it on, adding that he would explain our mission later. Butterflies roused in my stomach. We had just finished dressing when Mike came in, kitted out and carrying three SLR rifles.

He explained. 'We're going to give the Army a bit of a hand in West Belfast. We'll be positioned in Corry's timber yard on the Springfield Road, to cover Ballymurphy and make sure there are a few civilian casualties. They can be claimed to have been hit because of IRA activities. The Army can, in all honesty, say they weren't to blame for anybody who wasn't a gunman being shot.'

We looked at him disbelievingly, but, when he said, 'Right, let's move,' we realised it was genuine.

Three Land-Rovers were waiting and we set off up the Sydenham bypass. Arriving at the timber yard we leapt from the vehicles and automatically ducked at the sound of gunfire. It was so intense we thought it was very close. Sandbags had been put in place and we took up position, nervously looking over the tops. We had a good view of Ballymurphy and Springhill estates.

In the book *Ballymurphy and the Irish War* author said it was unlikely that Loyalist gunmen could have gained access to the timber yard. He was wrong. True to form, in the book *Lost Lives* by David McKittrick, Seamus Kelters, Brian Feeney and Chris Thornton, the Army denied any involvement in the Springhill killings. I believe they finally admitted there were Army personnel present but omitted any specific details.

The first person that died was a member of Fianna, the junior wing of the IRA. John Dougal was shot by someone in the timber yard. I heard the shot and I saw a man fall. The gunfire intensified at that point and no one was venturing outside. I could hear the bullets ricocheting off metal now and again, and the dull thump as bullets hit the wooden fence or the sandbags.

There was firing from all along the perimeter fence. The intention was to create such an intense noise that the only people who would be moving about would be the IRA men engaged in the shoot-out. A second person was hit and was lying on the ground. I didn't see it happen but Mike pointed the body out to us. I remember him saying, 'Wait a minute or two, somebody will try and help her.' I wondered how he knew it was a woman, as I couldn't tell from where I was standing. All of a sudden two men and then a third ran out to help the person on the ground. Mike fired a round and I saw two men fall to the ground. I heard Mike laugh, 'Not fucking bad, two for one.' Just then more shots were fired and the third person collapsed.

It was Mike's shot that hit the priest and the second man. The last to die was a 14-year-old schoolboy who turned out to be a member of Fianna. Five people were known to be dead and quite a few were wounded. There have always been rumours that the IRA would smuggle bodies and the wounded across the border in order to minimise publicity about their losses. I can't confirm if it was fact or fiction.

Once the firing eased off, we packed up and returned to Palace Barracks. Everyone was in good spirits. Before leaving, Mike told us that all teams were being told to halt operations for a short period, in order to allow time to see what would develop now that the ceasefire had broken down.

As we were driving home, I remember discussing with Billy that Mike appeared to be of a much higher rank within the MRF than he admitted and that he was a superb marksman. We went to Billy's house, where we opened and finished a bottle of Scotch.

That incident gave me an understanding of Mike's reasoning. For a man with the intelligence and resolve to rise above the tangle of right or wrong, there was no problem that couldn't be solved simply, quickly and permanently by a gunshot. I would speculate that Mike had never met anyone else who had the inner strength to live by this philosophy. But you can become addicted to killing and become dependent on the brief sensation of ultimate domination to mask your feelings of guilt and horror. Mike saw killing as nothing more or less than an effective tool, and he used it with the intuitive precision of a master craftsman.

On 11 July there was widespread rioting, burnings and shootings across the whole of Northern Ireland. Some of the major gun battles took place around Andersonstown and Ballymurphy. A team of Loyalists was sent in to stir things up a bit; their target was a member of the OIRA's Fianna youth wing. An OOB was in force for the Suffolk area when a single shot rang out, hitting their target, and killing him. Troops were close to the area and heard the shot, but the men made their escape easily. A call was made to the Samaritans claiming the UVF carried it out, but it was never made public.

A Catholic youth was abducted shortly after leaving the Imperial Hotel on the Cliftonville Road. He was taken to a romper room but passed out during interrogation. He was then hooded and taken to Adela Street, near Carlisle Square, where he was shot four times in the head and chest. An OOB was in place at the time.

The twelfth of July is, of course, a significant date on the Protestant calendar. During this day thousands of Orangemen walk in a number of towns across the country, with the main parade taking place in Belfast. The killing still went on. During a gun attack on McCabe's Bar, Loyalists killed a Protestant man and a Catholic man. An OOB was in place at the time.

Over the next week or so, the IRA intensified their attack

on the Security Forces, with the Army taking the brunt. On 13 July, three soldiers, Martin Rooney, Kenneth Mogg and David Meeke, were shot by snipers in Belfast. James Reid, an IRA man, was shot dead by soldiers in a gun battle in Ardoyne. Thomas Burns and Terence Toolan, both Catholic civilians, were shot dead by soldiers.

British soldier James Jones became the 100th person to be killed in the Troubles, shot by a sniper while inside Vere Foster School British Army base in Ballymurphy.

On 19 and 20 July two Protestant 'have-a-go heroes' were shot and killed, and a Protestant baby boy died in a bomb explosion. Henry Gray, a 71-year-old pensioner, died while trying to stop men planting a bomb in the Whitehorse Inn, Springfield Road, Belfast. On the same day, a baby, Alan Jack, who hadn't reached his first birthday, died when a bomb exploded in Strabane, County Tyrone. There was an inadequate warning given. The next day Robert Leggett died while attempting to stop a bomb attack on his shop, also on the Springfield Road. By this time, we were traumatised by the ferocity and intensity of their ability to strike whenever and wherever they chose. It seemed the armaments received from Gaddafi had boosted their confidence and capability. It instilled fear and apprehension in us. What we didn't know was that worse was to come.

Another milestone in the Troubles: 21 July. It became known as Bloody Friday. A total of 22 bombs exploded in and around Belfast within a space of 75 minutes. People were panic-stricken; no one knew which way to go. Not only were there actual devices planted, there had been a large number of hoax alerts which overwhelmed the Security Forces. Total bedlam ensued as one by one the bombs started to explode. Men, women and children were frantically trying to find somewhere safe. Where could you go? As you went one way, you found the police trying to clear people away from that area. When you turned in another direction, the same thing happened again.

I had been shopping in town when a huge bomb went off in Oxford Street Bus Station. Once again I was extremely fortunate. I had just turned a corner and was shielded from the blast. For those who have never had the misfortune of being close to an exploding bomb, when the device explodes, any windows close to the detonation are blown inwards, showering anyone inside with razor-sharp shards of glass which can rip you to pieces or even kill you if they pass through a vital organ. Then, as all the air is pushed out with the explosion and leaves a vacuum, it comes rushing back and any glass panes remaining in the frames are sucked outwards. People standing nearby are then showered with shards of broken glass.

This all happens in a split second. I was lucky I wasn't under a window, but I could hear glass smashing all around me. I stood frozen to the spot for ten to 15 seconds before moving. When I turned the corner, the scene was horrific; similar to the bomb earlier in the year, only this time the dead were unrecognisable. In the end, the emergency services were literally shovelling bodies into black bags. Six of the nine killed were at the bus station, including two young soldiers trying to clear people away from the area.

Moments later, I became aware of the screaming – screaming that would never stop for those witnesses who survived, so long as they lived. It was sickening to watch it on television, but to witness it close up was indescribable.

This bombing was a defining moment in the Protestant community. You could feel the resentment growing like a cancer, in even the most liberal men. I had been in town and seen the terror etched on people's faces, probably on my own as well.

Protestants and Catholics became even more alienated and po-larised. Support for the up-and-coming Loyalist Paramilitaries was growing, and membership was increasing daily. Bloody Friday was our Bloody Sunday. It drove young men right into the Loyalist groups' arms by the hour. Over the days following the attacks, I could sense the whole conflict slipping and sliding into the abyss.

Payback time was about to start. A Catholic man was shot when he answered the door of his house in Clovelly Street, off the Springfield Road, after midnight. He only opened the door when one of the gunmen mentioned the name of a friend. He was hit twice in the chest and died later in hospital. An OOB was in place at the time. Soon afterwards, several Catholic fami-lies moved out of the street; some to stay with relatives, others into St Paul's Primary School, in the Beechmount district, of the Falls Road. The tactics seemed to be working, and fear reigned in the Catholic community.

That same night, a Catholic man was killed as part of a plan to have the IRA blamed for the murder. Information had been passed to the MRF that one of the man's sons had fallen foul of the Provos and some sort of action was going to be taken against him. So they arranged for a team to get there first. When the men arrived at the door and asked for the son, the father who had answered the knock slammed the door in their faces. Two shots were fired through the door hitting him in the thigh. He bled to death a short time later. The men fired further shots as they left the scene. The family blamed the IRA. However, if it had been them, they wouldn't have shot through the door, as it wasn't the father they were looking for. The house had been watched on a number of occasions in the past. An OOB was in place at the time.

On 22 July, a Catholic man and woman were abducted and

taken for questioning. The man was subsequently beaten for information; the woman wasn't touched. A witness described how he had heard six shots in Forthriver Road and observed two cars proceed down the road. Both cars pulled into the kerb, then the occupants got out of the cars and started talking. They did not seem to be in a hurry. After a few minutes one of the men walked over to one of the cars and fired another six rounds into the vehicle. The man and the woman had both been hit six times. An OOB was in place at the time.

The same night: a Catholic man who came from Fallswater Street in the Falls Road was escorting his girlfriend home to Ardoyne. What follows is an excellent example of an OOB in force. About a dozen men in combat jackets stopped a taxi at an illegal roadblock on the Crumlin Road. The men asked everyone in the taxi their name and where they where going. They flung the man out of the car and let the taxi carry on with the rest of its passengers. His girlfriend and the taxi-driver reported the kidnapping to two police stations, but the officers seemed to take no action.

The man who had been removed from the taxi was taken to the Lawnbrook Social Club, off the Shankill Road. There he was to meet one of the most psychopathic killers the Troubles ever produced – Lenny Murphy. Murphy was putting together a team of his own at the time and was drinking with some of his mates. There was quite a crowd in the club. The man was held in the back of the club until all non-paramilitary people had left. I was in the club with Billy and some of our team. One of Billy's mates had whispered to him and his party to stay behind as there was going to be some more entertainment. Not knowing what he meant, another round of drinks was ordered.

When there were only Loyalist group members left, the man

was brought into the room. He was obviously drunk, and had blood oozing from a wound on his head and a few cuts on his face. He was placed in the middle of a circle of men, and Lenny walked round the circle, staring at each man present, as if he was assessing each man in turn. He then went over to the man, hitting him as hard as he could, and the rest of the men began to punch or kick him too. Each time he fell to the ground, some water was thrown over him and he was hauled to his feet again, to be hit some more.

As he lay on the floor, barely conscious and unrecognisable, Lenny pulled out a knife and stabbed him repeatedly, constantly yelling questions about IRA men in his district. The man drifted in and out of consciousness, until, after what must have been hours, he was killed.

His body was later found in a stolen car in Liffey Street. He had been shot seven times. At his inquest a detective stated: 'There had been five murders within Tennent Street's sub-stations area and the police were under pressure that night.' The coroner summed it up perfectly: 'Tensions had been high after the previous day's Bloody Friday bombings.'

I will never forget Lenny Murphy's eyes. Although the irises were the colour of blue ice, the pupils were like black coals, burning with a dark madness. When I first encountered him, those eyes bore into mine, making me feel light-headed. It was as if his insanity was crossing the two feet between us, firing along my optic nerve into my brain. I think that was how he judged people, their reaction to his stare. I realised I must at all costs keep my eyes open and stare back unflinchingly; one moment of weakness and he would have owned you.

I didn't know what a demon was until then. He was a man who had no perceivable conscience or sense of remorse. He had an incredibly short fuse and a bent towards cruelty and brutality. He could murder with a butcher's knife and, hell, he'd probably laugh while doing so.

On 26 July, two Catholic men were discovered in the boot of a car. One of the men was badly beaten and had been shot six times. The other was bound at the hands and feet, beaten and shot three times in the head. The two men didn't know each other, but they had been abducted by the same team. One was a businessman from Muckamore, near Antrim, and had left there to visit various wholesalers in Belfast, trying to get his business off the ground. The car had been taken to the lower Oldpark, dumped and set alight. An OOB was in place at the time.

On 28 July, a Catholic man from Andersonstown was taken to Dundonald, on the outskirts of Belfast, where he was shot in the head. He drove a mini-van for the Hastings hotel chain and was last seen leaving the Midland Hotel in the early morning, carrying a payroll of £1,000. Information had been passed to a Loyalist group regarding the man's movements. He had been stopped and his driver's licence confirmed that he was a Catholic. When his body was finally discovered, the payroll was missing. An OOB was put into place when he was picked up.

On 29 July, a Catholic man was shot dead outside his home in Blackwood Street of the Ormeau Road. The victim had been followed home the previous night and was supposed to be kidnapped. As the men lying in wait approached him, he recognised one of them. Panic broke out and he was shot where he stood at his front door. An OOB was put in place, enabling the assailants to escape. Ten years later, four men were jailed for his murder.

Ten days after the Bloody Friday atrocity, the Provisionals made another blunder. The date of 31 July 1972 will burn in my brain forever. If you ask the question why Loyalists chose to carry the fight to Republicans and their supporters, I can cite the cold-blooded atrocity which took place in the small, peaceful rural community of Claudy, in County Londonderry, that day as a reason. Claudy was a picturesque village where everyone knew each other and, more importantly, Protestants and Catholics lived side by side in friendship and harmony. The Troubles were a million miles away from this tranquil neighbourhood . . .

. . . until the Provisional IRA decided to retaliate against Operation Motorman (the ending of no-go areas by the removal of barricades in the Bogside and Creggan districts of Londonderry) and restore law and order to this part of Ulster. It had been the biggest British military operation since the Suez Canal crisis in the 1950s. In all, 12,000 British soldiers were involved, backed up by tanks, and bulldozers smashed their way through the barricades. The aim was to put an end to no-go areas and restore law and order to all districts in the Province. During the process, soldiers shot and killed two young lads during the operation in Londonderry; one was a civilian, Daniel Hegarty, the other was Seamus Bradley, an IRA man.

Three car bombs had been placed on the Main Street of Claudy. No warnings were given in time. The bombers drove to Dungiven to find a telephone but the callbox there wasn't working, because of an earlier bomb attack on the Claudy and Dungiven telephone exchanges. The bombers then went to a shop and told assistants there to warn police about the devices parked in Claudy. As their phones were also out of order, one of them had to run to Dungiven RUC Barracks to relay the message.

By this time the first bomb had exploded – at 10.20 a.m. outside McElhinney's public house on the Main Street, killing and injuring a number of people. The police had discovered the second bomb in a mini-van outside the post office and had started to clear people away from the area. Unknown to them they were sending people towards the third device, in another mini-van parked in front of the Beaufort Hotel. As the warning was being given to police at the scene, regarding three explosive devices, it was too late. The second and third devices detonated, killing and injuring more local people. A total of six people were killed outright, three more died as a result of their injuries, and over 30 were injured.

The poet James Simmons composed a heartbreaking poem after the events in Claudy village, which summed up the intense emotions we all felt when the news of the tragedy hit the headlines around the country and abroad.

The start of August was the same as the end of July, with the IRA keeping up the offensive on the Security Forces and their bombing campaign on business premises. The attacks on Protestants also continued. We seemed to be unable to mount a sustained onslaught on the enemy. Fear and doubt had taken over. We discussed the situation for hours, and our consensus was that we were being overwhelmed by the Provos' responses to our attacks. They were being met with swift retaliation, even though they were fighting the war on two fronts. I was aware that each time we killed a Catholic, we were condemning some Protestants to death. The Provos had the bit between their teeth and we were in danger of being overtaken by the sheer magnitude of the arsenal being directed at the Security Forces and us. But if we didn't resist, what the fuck would it be like? We concluded that Loyalists were left with only one option: for every team to carry on and try to improve its hit rate.

On 1 August, in response to a Parliamentary Question, the Attorney General published his answer regarding the file sent to the Director of Public Prosecutions for Northern Ireland by the police about Bloody Sunday. The conclusion: there would be no prosecutions against any member of the Security Forces. Charges against some of the people for riotous behaviour were also dropped. There was uproar over the decision and cries of a whitewash from the Catholic politicians, clergy and Republicans. It goes to show how much influence the MRF and the men further up the ranks, including Cabinet Ministers and, in all probability, the Prime Minister himself, had over the judicial system. We knew that was going to be the verdict, because Mike had said so from the word go. It made us realise that Mike had not been bullshitting us.

In Portadown a Catholic was found beaten to death in a drain, off Watson Street. Although no OOB was needed, we were told that a squad with a MRF contact carried out the opportunistic assault.

On 12 August, the body of a Catholic man was found in a stolen car parked in Jaffa Street, off the Crumlin Road. He had been picked up in the Durham Street area and taken to a romper room between the Shankill Road and Crumlin Road. He was severely beaten and tortured. One newspaper printed that he had been a victim of an execution squad which had been killing Catholics in the Oldpark and Crumlin districts over a couple of months. They were right, except for one small fact; there was more than one execution squad. There was an OOB in place at the time.

On 13 August, another gruesome murder occurred. A Catholic man had been abducted around nine o'clock on the Sunday night. He had been spotted leaving the Meeting of the Waters Bar and then being bundled into a car. From there he was transported to a romper room. Bound and gagged, he was stabbed 110 times, all over his body, before being taken to the Oldpark Road and shot. A witness heard someone screaming

'Kill me, Kill me'. Even before it filtered through the grapevine, the first name that sprang to mind was Lenny Murphy's. He led the Shankill Butcher gang and was to become one of the most notorious mass murderers in British criminal history.

A detective made a statement to the *Belfast Telegraph*: 'There doesn't seem to have been an apparent motive for either of the weekend killings, though this has been the pattern in this assassination campaign. There doesn't seem to have been any justification for picking Mr Madden. People may just be in the wrong place at the wrong time. There is something about these murders which we just haven't hit on yet.'

He was right. How could they possibly track down the men involved when part of the Security Forces was orchestrating the whole campaign? They were picking targets, passing information and keeping the way in and out clear to enable these acts of violence to take place. I intend no disrespect to the RUC, but it stands to reason their top men must have known something untoward was taking place and being sanctioned from the top.

The whole purpose of our module was to keep a low profile, a *very* low profile. To all intents and purposes, this worked. Although people were becoming aware of the existence of the group, no one ever knew the extent of the whole operation and, critically, the part we played in the overall plan. As far as I know, author Martin Dillon is the only one who got close to the whole truth, and even he didn't know about us.

Oh, there was a lot of speculation about soldiers being involved in murders and assassinations, but these operations weren't carried out by soldiers; they were carried out by people like us with protection from the MRF.

The following information will substantiate many of the facts contained in this book. While serving his life sentence, Ginger

Baker of the McCreedy/Baker gang gave an interview to a Member of Parliament, in which he alleged that the RUC and Military Intelligence had been involved in sectarian murders in the early 1970s. He claimed that a senior Army Intelligence officer controlled Tommy Herron and had been given guns, information and other help from RUC officers. He was almost right. Herron was one of the MRF-trained men, and the weapons and information came from them.

Although we all wore balaclavas when we were in Palace Barracks, I know the name of one of the men there who were being trained alongside. Tommy Herron broke all the rules and instructions we had received during our training. It was only when I saw him on television and recognised his voice that I realised he was one of the faces behind the woolly masks. He certainly wasn't keeping a low profile; in fact, quite the opposite. There was much speculation over who killed Herron; all I'm doing is throwing another name into the hat. As I emphasised earlier, if someone became a problem, kill him and the problem is resolved.

On 27 September, a 16-year-old Catholic boy left his home to go to a party. He was picked up and driven to an entry off the Springfield Road where he was killed by a gunshot to the head. This murder was another attempt to put the blame on the IRA; he had been abducted and killed in Catholic areas. No group ever claimed the murder. It was Loyalists. An OOB was in operation at the time.

The same day, John Kelly was shot near his home in Andersonstown by a soldier. This is a classic example of the outcome of the instructions given to certain soldiers, that is, to shoot anyone who even looked suspicious or, if they were fired on, anyone standing about. The soldier claimed he had accidentally discharged his weapon and had seen a man handing a parcel to a girl. After the soldier gave chase, the man grappled with him and the gun went off, fatally wounding Mr Kelly. Counsel for the Ministry of Home Affairs said at the inquest, 'All the evidence pointed to the fact that John Kelly was an entirely innocent person.'

Whenever the Army shot someone, it was always 'in disputed circumstances'. Only a handful of soldiers were ever charged with anything after these ambiguous incidents.

The IRA issued a statement after they attacked three different targets on 2 October, to the effect that they were Intelligence operations for the MRF. When we heard the statement, we confronted Mike about the circumstances of the attacks and asked if it compromised our side of the operation. He gave us a rough outline of the facts.

Seamus Wright and Kevin McKee, both IRA men, were abducted and became part of a group of people known as 'The Disappeared'. I learned later from Mike that both Wright and McKee were actually Freds and had spent time in the Palace Barracks compound. The operation was ingenious.

The laundry was picked up each week – it was cheap and efficient and a lot of people were using it. What they didn't know was that all washing was forensically tested for bloodstains, traces of lead particles, to establish if someone had been handling guns or explosives. He also said there was a hidden compartment in the laundry van's roof where two operatives observed and photographed known Republicans. He told us about two other operations being run by the MRF: the second one in offices above a massage parlour on the Antrim Road; a third in offices at College Square East in the city centre.

The name of the laundry firm was Four Square Laundry Service. The IRA had opened fire when the van was in Twinbrook, riddling it with machine-gun fire and hitting a soldier, Edward Stuart, five times. A woman helper escaped injury by diving to the ground and local people looked after her until help arrived. The men who fired were supposed to shoot into the roof of the van but they didn't; although they told their superiors they had.

The two other premises were attacked on the same day and at the same time, but no one else was killed. It was at that point the IRA discovered the existence of the MRF. But they never knew the whole set-up or the extent of MRF's sphere of activities. Until now.

The next time we saw Mike, I remember asking him what the fuck was going on: 'The Provos made a statement saying they had attacked three operations run by you. How did they find out about them and the MRF and, more importantly, what if they know all about this end of the operation?'

He replied, 'As far as we can tell two of our Freds are missing and we believe they were rumbled and were able to give information to the IRA about the operations.'

Billy said, 'That's all very well, but how could informers know about them? Somebody must have been talking out of school. How do we know our part of your scheme hasn't been compromised by the same bucket mouth?'

Mike responded, 'Because it's a highly classified operation. Believe me, very, very few people know anything about this element of the strategy. This is something we can't afford to become public. Therefore it's necessary for it to be kept under wraps. Not even other soldiers stationed in Palace Barracks know anything about what goes on in our compounds.'

In *The Dirty War* Dillon speculates that Brigadier Frank Kitson set up elite squads, which operated with an uncontrolled autonomy. The author was so near to the truth he took it for granted; it would be soldiers who made up the squads. That was why it was admitted that some operations were indeed carried out by soldiers, as it diverted attention away from the main operation. This was confirmed when the senior officer gave us the lecture on the overall strategy. The senior officer could have been Brigadier Kitson, but his name was not revealed and I have never seen a photograph.

In the final page of chapter two in his book, Dillon sums it up succinctly: 'The MRF had more than one objective and method of gaining intelligence and damaging the IRA.'

Leeson Street is the heart of Republicanism, as the Shankill is the heart of Loyalism. A lot of Republicans drank in a certain bar on Leeson Street and must have felt safe enough not to have security at the door to prevent attacks or at least give warning. We knew there was no security on the door; the only way we could have known was to have been informed by soldiers who passed it quite regularly. To be able to get in and out was something special. But when you have a guardian angel watching over you, it makes it a bit easier. A car bomb was placed outside the bar. As the men planting the bomb jumped out of the car, they forgot to put the handbrake on, and the vehicle rolled away from the bar. An OOB was in place at the time.

On 14 October, two Catholic men were working in an off-licence on Tates Avenue, close to the village area at the top of the Donegall Road. The two men were each shot a number of times and a third was seriously injured. Although the two gunmen robbed the till before making off, they were there to assassinate the three men. An OOB was in place at the time.

On the same day, an OOB was in place for Turf Lodge for an attack on a PIRA man who wasn't at home when the hit team arrived. As they were driving away a gun accidentally discharged when the car hit a hole in the road. The men were unaware that the bullet hit a young boy who tragically died a week later. The incident destroyed the man responsible and he stood down from operations. I heard that he tried to take his life a number of times.

On 16 October a new controversial tactic by the Security Forces emerged, one that was to continue for several years – the shoot-to-kill policy. Members of the IRA, usually unarmed at the time, were shot and killed under highly suspicious circumstances. Patrick Mullan and Hugh Herron, both IRA members, were shot dead by the Army at a VCP at Coagh, County Tyrone.

Widespread street riots broke out in Protestant areas all over Belfast. A 15-year-old boy, William Warnock, was killed when an APC was deliberately driven over him. A second man, John Clarke, also died when a Saracen mounted the pavement, crushing him against the wall.

On 17 October, serious rioting was taking place on the Shankill Road. The UDA had issued a statement that day which said: 'To hell with the British Army. To hell with the Whitelaw administration. The British Army and the British Government are now our enemies.' The UDA went on to say that unless their Parliament was restored they would back the Loyalist Vanguard movement's call for an independent state.

The Army shot and killed two more Protestants in the Shankill Road. Eleanor Cooke died outside her home in Bracken Street, while an off-duty UDR soldier, John Todd, was shot in Wilton Street. It got so bad that the UDA brought their guns out and opened fire on the British Army. I thought it was ironic that the Army had probably supplied some of the weaponry being used against their soldiers. We had been ordered to remain in the background, in case back-up was required. But we couldn't resist joining in the riots.

Then reports came in that an Army lorry was trapped in

a street not far away, and a lot of the crowd rushed towards it. When we arrived, the crowd was baying for blood. It was one of those canvas-topped trucks that transported troops from place to place. But the rear flaps were open, and stones and bricks were flying into the back. The soldiers were trying their best to protect themselves, and eventually one of the soldiers fired a burst of rounds over all our heads and we retreated far enough for the driver to get the lorry into reverse and roar backwards out of the street. As it turned, another salvo of bricks and stones pelted the soldiers in the back of the vehicle. As the trouble fizzled out we were stood down and went home.

On 29 October, a 16-year-old Catholic lad was shot dead while walking with a friend along Cliftonville Avenue. The gunmen fired four shots from a passing car, hitting him in the head and slightly wounding his friend. The car had been hijacked in the Shankill area and the driver told not to report it for an hour; his driving licence had been taken as insurance. After the shooting, as they made their getaway, their car crashed into another car, and they jumped out and made off on foot towards the Limestone Road, leading to the Loyalist Tiger's Bay district. Police responding quickly should have had time to intercept them, but they didn't. An OOB was in place at the time.

The Northern Ireland Office issued a discussion document entitled *The Future of Northern Ireland*. The paper stated Britain's commitment to the Union as long as the majority of people wished to remain part of the United Kingdom. It also introduced the ideas of a power-sharing Government in Northern Ireland and an Irish dimension. Of course, once something was mentioned with Irish in it, it was automatically viewed with scepticism and cynicism.

On 31 October, another regrettable incident took place. A

bomb was left in a car outside Benny's Bar at Ship Street. It was Hallowe'en, and children were out playing after a fancy dress competition. Two little girls aged six and four were having fun running round a bonfire. The time was just past eight o'clock when the bomb exploded, wrecking the bar and burying customers under piles of rubble. The force of the blast sent bits of car and debris in all directions. The two little girls were about 100 metres away and were struck by fragments. One died at the scene, the second died on the way to hospital.

On 8 November, a Catholic man was travelling home from work when his bus was flagged down by two men at the bottom of Castlereagh Street in the Mountpottinger area. The bus stopped and one of the men ran upstairs, while the second man stood with his hand over his face and produced the butt of a gun from inside his coat, shaking his head for the driver not to move. His accomplice, who had gone upstairs, shot the target six times before running off the bus. The two men disappeared down an entry. The driver drove to a nearby police and Army post, but the man was dead. This incident occurred about 200 metres from Mountpottinger RUC station. An OOB was in place.

On 11 November, a Catholic newsagent was in his shop on the Upper Crumlin Road. It had been the focus of numerous attacks in the past, including two bombings. The man had moved his family to a house on the Antrim Road at Newtownabbey for safety. It's hard to give up your livelihood and move, but when the odds are stacked against you, there comes a time when you must cut and run. Two gunmen walked into his shop, bought some sweets, pulled out their guns and cold-bloodedly shot him eight times. An OOB was in place at the time.

On 13 November, a Catholic man who lived in Longlands Park at Newtownabbey was getting out of his car after work at

Courtaulds factory when he was shot. He died of his injuries in hospital the following morning. His brother had been killed when a bomb he was handling exploded prematurely. Two other members of the IRA also died along with his brother. A close relative had been detained in Long Kesh for three months, so it was assumed that the entire family had Republican sympathies. It is possible MRF did get the target wrong, but knowing the way they worked, it wouldn't have mattered. An OOB was in place at the time.

On 15 November, a Catholic shop owner was sitting in the living room of his home in Sintonville Avenue in East Belfast when he heard a knock at the door. He looked out the window and didn't recognise the men who were there. He called to his wife not to open the door, as he didn't like the look of the callers. The man at the door shouted that a bomb had been left at his shop. He shouted back, 'Let the bomb take care of itself.' Thinking the man had left, he went into the hall, not knowing an accomplice had seen him leaving the living room and given the signal. A gunman fired three shots through the door, hitting him in the chest. He died before reaching the hospital. Another OOB operation.

That same day, Edward Heath issued a warning against Unilateral Declaration of Independence, which William Craig's Vanguard Party had suggested and the UDA were threatening to back. In a speech earlier in the month, at a meeting of right-wing Members of Parliament in Westminster, Mr Craig said that he could mobilise 80,000 men to oppose the British Government.

On 21 November, a Catholic man was shot at his home in the Orangefield district in East Belfast while trying to repair a washing machine in his kitchen. The gunmen went to the rear of the house and opened fire, shooting five times and hitting him in the stomach. He was dead by the time he reached the hospital. An OOB was in place at the time.

As a Catholic man from Finvoy, near Ballymoney, County Antrim, was walking along the road from his house to meet some friends he was shot. A hit team was waiting for him and pulled up beside him. He thought someone was stopping to give him a lift. As he approached the car, a gunman fired, and when he fell they fired more bullets into him. He survived the attack for ten days, dying on 1 December. An OOB was in place at the time. In 1979, four men were charged with his murder. Later, three of the men had the charges against them dropped. Enough said, the MRF was pulling strings. One of the team was sacrificed in order to secure the release of the others.

On 27 November, a Catholic schoolboy was killed 'by mistake' when gunmen fired on his father's car as he was being driven to school. The shooting took place in the Shankill Road area. Three gunmen opened fire on the vehicle, which was hit ten times. One son died shortly after he was shot; his father, a leading eye surgeon, was hit in the shoulder; another son was wounded in the arm and leg; a third boy escaped injury. While I describe this murder as 'by mistake', it is of course not strictly accurate. Our instructions were to instill fear into the Catholic community by any means possible. The MRF wasn't concerned if children were killed in the process, because that caused even more terror than adults being killed. An OOB was in place at the time.

On 29 November, a Catholic man from Ardoyne got into an Arkle taxi in Clifton Street, headed homewards. Two men asked to share the taxi with him and he agreed. When they reached the Mater Hospital one of the young lads said he felt ill and the cab pulled over. The two gunmen got out, walked to the front of the car and opened fire, killing the Catholic man and wounding the driver. A woman who worked in the taxi company and gave evidence at the murdered man's inquest was later killed by Loyalists. An OOB was in place at the time.

December started with the murder rate accelerating. On Friday 1 December, the Irish Government was debating new legislation on the introduction of special emergency powers to deal with terrorist incidents. The MRF knew there was a danger of the bill being defeated and arranged for two bombs to be planted in Dublin.

Two men died when an explosive device detonated in Sackville Place, off O'Connell Street, in the centre of Dublin. Another bomb had already exploded at Liberty Hall, about 20 minutes earlier. As well as the two dead, 127 were injured. At the time of the explosions the Irish Government were debating a contentious Offences against the State (Amendment) Bill. The opposition party, Fine Gael, was split, with a majority likely to vote against. After the bombings the Dail had a one-hour adjournment. When the politicians returned, Fine Gael dropped its opposition to the Bill and the House voted overwhelming for the Bill at four o'clock in the morning. We had succeeded.

The new legislation meant that suspected terrorists could be sentenced on the evidence of a senior police officer, in front of three judges. It was over a year later — when two English brothers, Keith and Kenneth Littlejohn, during a robbery trial, claimed they were British agents — that the penny dropped; that the explosions on 1 December may have been caused by the British in order to influence the debate.

On 2 December, the naked body of a Catholic man from the Short Strand was found in Crossley Street, just off Templemore

Avenue. He was another victim of the McCreery/Baker gang, and the most gruesome yet. The man had been on the Falls Road that evening and decided to walk home. His killers picked him up and took him to a romper room, in a club. He was brutally tortured, and his hands and feet had been burned. A cross and the letters IRA were branded on his back. The murder was described as depraved and savage. An OOB was in place at the time of the abduction.

On 14 December, the daughter of a Catholic publican was killed in a bomb attack on her father's bar in Killeter, a village near Castlederg, County Tyrone. Loyalists carried out the bombing to revenge the murder of an off-duty UDR soldier in the village on nine days earlier. The car bomb wrecked the bar. No one claimed responsibility. An OOB was in place at the time.

On 15 December, a 16-year-old Catholic youth was shot and killed while standing at the corner of Dandy Street and Shore Road at Greencastle with some friends. A motorbike came along the road, seemingly heading towards the city centre. It returned a short time later and went into Dandy Street, where it then turned into a cul-de-sac. Two of the young lads went to investigate, as the two men on the back looked suspicious. As they walked up the street, the bike came out of the cul-de-sac and moved towards them slowly. As it neared, the pillion passenger opened fire on the youths, wounding both of them slightly. As the motorbike sped up to the corner, another burst was fired at the rest of the group. Joseph Reynolds was hit twice and died later in hospital. According to a relation, Joseph had been threatened at the training college he attended. This probably had nothing to do with it. It could have been any one of them. An OOB was in place at the time.

On 16 December, a butcher (and IRA man) from Derrylin, County Fermanagh, was working late in his shop. Earlier, he had been seen talking to two well dressed men at the front door. The two men had posed as detectives, claiming to be investigating the theft of a vanload of meat. After looking at their false ID, he invited them into the shop to look around. One man pulled his gun and fired a number of times. They lifted his body and dumped it into the fridge. As they left, they locked the shop. He was a Republican whose name had been given to Loyalists by the MRF. An OOB was in place at the time.

On the same day, a Catholic off-licence owner was killed on York Road, North Belfast. Three armed, masked men walked into his shop and told the man and his niece to put their hands where they could see them. When the man grabbed his phone and called out to his brother-in-law, one of the gunmen hit him over the head with the butt of his gun and fired a shot into the ceiling. They made the man lie face down behind the counter, before bundling the niece and brother-in-law into a cupboard. After asking the man for money and being informed it had been taken away, they shot him a number of times before escaping. It was recorded as an armed robbery, but the intention from the outset was to execute him. Why else would they leave his niece and brother-in-law alive? An OOB was in place at the time.

William Johnston, an Ulster Unionist Councillor and member of the Police Authority, was abducted and found shot dead in Drumarg, Armagh, on 18 December.

Just five days before Christmas, eight men were to die. A Catholic man was gunned down as he waited for a lift to work. He had been seen frequently in the same spot at the same time and presented an easy target. In January 1973, four men were arrested for his murder and two other killings. When O.O.B.s are in place and the opertaives get away safely, the only way they'd be caught is by bragging about it and someone reporting what they hear to the police or if they made a confession of their own free will.

On 20 December, a Catholic man was shot from a passing car as he got off a bus, arriving home from work. He lived in Clintyclay, near Loughgall. He and his neighbour worked in a tyre factory in Portadown. A car drove slowly past them to confirm their identity, turned and came back up the road behind them. A burst of machine-gun fire was directed at them and one man died after being hit four times. His friend was hit in the face but survived. An OOB was in place at the time.

George Hamilton, an off-duty UDR soldier was shot and killed at his workplace, a building site at Kildoag, Claudy, County Londonderry.

Two armed men entered the Top of the Hill Bar, in the Waterside area of Londonderry, where they raked the bar indiscriminately with Sterling submachine-guns. Pandemonium broke out as customers tried to find safety. Five men died in the hail of bullets and another four were injured. The attack sent shockwaves through both Protestant and Catholic communities, but in Londonderry the first anniversary of Bloody Sunday was just over a month away. One of the men who died was a Protestant; all the others were Catholic. The assault was retaliation for George Hamilton's killing by the IRA earlier that day. An OOB was in place at the time.

On the same day, the report from the Diplock Committee was published. It made recommendations on the legal procedures for terrorist-related crimes. There was a need for change, as ordinary people picked for jury service could be easily intimidated. Witnesses could also have pressure brought to bear on them or, as in a case earlier in the year, be killed before testifying. The report recommended that these cases should be heard before a Judge of the High Court or a County Court Judge sitting alone. This system was implemented and became known as trial in a Diplock Court. It hastened the beginning of a corrupt judicial system, with higher authorities manipulating single judges and men having their charges dropped or released after witnesses testified against them.

On 28 December, Loyalists mounted a daring mission in the Irish Republic. Two Catholic teenagers, a 17-year-old lad and a 15-year-old girl, died in an explosion in Belturbet, in County Cavan. The bomb was in a car left outside the town's post office. The girl had just left a fish and chip shop and was walking back to her brother's car when the device went off. The young lad was in a phonebox trying to contact his mother, to tell her he would be staying in Belturbet as it was too late to travel home to County Clare. Twelve people were injured, three seriously, in the bombing.

This was the third bomb attack that night on towns in the Republic of Ireland, close to the Fermanagh border. One, in Clones, County Monaghan, caused quite a lot of damage to the town's shopping centre but only slight injuries to people. Another bomb went off in the town of Pettigo, County Donegal, outside a pub where no one was injured.

On the last day of the year, Martin McGuinness, a very active IRA volunteer, was arrested in the Republic, and held under the same legislation as Ruairi O'Bradaigh. We thought perhaps the Irish police were starting to take a stronger stance against Republicans. We were wrong. The arrests were trivial and it wasn't long before McGuinness was back in action.

1972 was over and I can't accurately describe the mixed emotions I felt. Sad, depressed, poignant on one hand; excited, elated, jubilant on the other. The sheer numbers of the dead weighed heavily on my mind. Almost 500 people had been killed in one year. What was worse, not only did I greet a lot of these deaths with a sense of achievement, of triumph, but I had contributed to the taking of some of those lives.

1972 Statistics

Deaths by status		Responsibility for deaths	
Protestant civilians	77	Republicans	281
Catholic civilians	174	Loyalists	121
RUC	15	Army	79
RUC/R	2	RUC/RUC/R	6
UDR/RIR	26	UDR/RIR	1
Army	108	Others	9
Republicans	74		
Loyalists	11		
Others	10		
Total	497		
Bombs	1,853		
Shootings	10,564		

1973 STEPPING BACK
FROM THE BRINK

THE NEW YEAR was to start the same way as the old one ended – another night raid into the Republic by Loyalists on 1 January, just after midnight, in the search for victims. It was only two hours old when the first fatalities were picked up and killed. Loyalists crossed the border from Londonderry into Donegal and waited on anyone leaving a New Year's Eve dance. When the man and woman came out to go home, they were snatched and taken away for questioning and interrogation. Both were found stabbed and shot a number of times, at Drumadooey near Burnfoot, about four miles from the border.

An 18-year-old lad from Londonderry was arrested and extradited to the Republic and charged with the two murders. During extradition proceedings he claimed the man killed was an IRA man and the crime was political, thus he was exempt from extradition. For that reason he was acquitted at the Special Criminal Court in Dublin. Unionist politicians called for an inquiry into the methods used by some RUC officers to extract a confession from an innocent man.

They had been under pressure from the Garda to catch the men responsible for the double murder. In his book, *It Was Murder*, Garda Chief Superintendent, John Courtney, criticised the initial level of co-operation by the RUC in the case. As it was a MRF-sanctioned job I can understand their reluctance in investigating the crime. All operations that had been carried out or were to take place in the South by Loyalists had Military Intelligence assistance, with or without the actual participants' knowledge, such was the depth of MRF involvement and subterfuge within Loyalist ranks. The war against the IRA had to be won, nothing less would do.

A week passed with no deaths. I started to relax a bit. Perhaps both sides were taking hold of their senses, realising that the slaughter was counter-productive and stepping back from the brink of civil war. Although the number of fatalities did drop during 1973, attacks on both sides were still being carried out, as the Security Forces gained more and more experience in preventing attacks on themselves.

On 29 January, a 15-year-old Catholic lad was killed in a drive-by shooting on the Falls Road, near the top of the Donegall Road. This road is split into two parts: the bottom half is Loyalist; the upper half is Republican. The teenager was standing outside his mother's shop with a number of friends when a car pulled up, firing five or six shots at the group. One of the lads was fatally wounded and died a short time later in the Royal Victoria Hospital. A second boy suffered a gunshot wound in the back, but survived. An OOB was in place at the time.

The IRA exacted their revenge later that night. They captured a leading Loyalist, Francis Smith (nicknamed 'Hatchet'), from the Donegall Road area and shot him a number of times in the head. His body was found just off the Falls Road.

The last day of the month saw two more killings by Loyalists.

The first to be abducted was a 14-year-old lad picked up

near his home in Andersonstown, about 9.30 p.m. To abduct someone in a Republican district, which is heavily patrolled by Security Forces day and night, takes some courage or a guarantee of passage in and out. The victim was taken to the Giant's Ring, a beauty spot at the top of the Malone Road, where he was hooded and made to kneel, before he was shot in the head. His parents reported him missing around 1 a.m., but the body had been found two hours earlier, after an anonymous phone call. An OOB was in place at the time.

The second victim was picked up on the Andersonstown Road while waiting for a taxi with his girlfriend. A car pulled up and a man got out with a gun. The girl grappled with the gunman, but he threatened to shoot her and she ran for help. Her boyfriend was dragged into the car and driven away. Once again, an OOB was in place. After the girl escaped, the men continued with the abduction. Normally, he would have been shot immediately, but the men must have known there was time to complete the operation. His girlfriend found an Army foot patrol close by, which went to the scene right away and couldn't find any trace of the young man. He was found the next morning lying on the grass verge beside the M1 motorway, not far from the Loyalist village area on the Donegall Road. He had been questioned before being shot and killed, then driven to the motorway where his body was discarded.

What struck me as strange was that two operations were allowed to take place in the same area on the same night. It must have been sanctioned with the knowledge that both teams could be in and out during the OOB; as one victim was being taken to the place where he would be killed, the other was being taken to a romper room for questioning. These murders were very likely in retaliation for the killing of Francis Smith. Loyalists had finished the month as they had started it.

Lieutenant General Frank King became General Officer Commanding of the British Army in Northern Ireland, replacing General Harry Tuzo, the officer known for his *faux pas* when talking about the war with the IRA: 'It wasn't a battle that the military can win, by conventional means.' On 2 February, a Catholic man was abducted from the Falls Road district some time after 6.30 p.m. Bundled into a car, his hands were tied behind his back. He had been drinking and wouldn't answer any questions; even as he was beaten he said nothing. A short time later, his body was found in the car, hooded and shot through the head, in Maurice Street, off the Springfield Road. An OOB was in place at the time.

The night of Saturday 3 February turned into a remarkable night for us. It began when a Catholic man was shot and killed in his café on York Road. Two men walked into the café, one armed with a machine-gun and the second with a handgun. The victim had run into the back room when he saw the men arrive and locked himself inside. One of the gunmen went to the back of the shop and fired four rounds through the closed door, killing the man instantly.

Coincidentally, one of our team was transporting a weapon to Glengormly that night and we had found the easiest and safest method was to do it by bus. I had never been on a bus that the Security Forces had stopped and searched. The team member was waiting at the bus stop facing the intended target's café when he spotted two men approaching the café. He thought he recognised one of the men. The next thing he knew, shots were fired and the men ran away. He went over and had a look, saw the man was dead and beat a hasty retreat This is another prime example of an OOB in force. York Road Police Station was only 200/300 metres away from the café. Needless to say, the men escaped.

Later that night, gunmen in a passing car shot two Republicans dead, James Sloan and James McCann, on the Antrim Road, outside Lynch's Bar. A witness standing about five metres from where the two men were shot said the attack was carried out with precision. He also said the car did a U-turn and came back up the road firing another burst at a Chinese restaurant, before driving off towards the Crumlin Road. The car was abandoned in Tennent Street.

If the shootings were random, then his group of friends would also have been attacked and killed. The two men who died were members of the Provisionals. They had been under surveillance the whole day, part of an operation to try to lure the IRA into a firefight.

What I know is that Mike had contacted Billy and told him he would be over that evening; there was 'something going down' and he would meet him at my house about nine o'clock. Billy was already in my home when the team member returned with the gun, after the killing on York Road. We took the gun from him and joked about the coincidence of him possessing a gun while the two men did a hit opposite where he was standing.

Mike arrived shortly after nine, telling us that two Provos had been closely watched all day and would be eliminated later that night. A team was in place and when the time was right they would take the Provos out. Our job would be to go up an entry behind Edlingham Street and fire shots towards the New Lodge Road, to convince the IRA they were under attack from the Loyalist Tiger's Bay area.

Unbeknown to the Provos, a new nightscope (the Starlight Scope), developed in America for use in Vietnam, had been distributed to British soldiers and was now on the streets of Belfast. This scope magnifies every available glimmer of light and intensifies it into a green image, giving a sniper the advantage of seeing in the dark. The Army wanted it to be tested in a hostile situation.

Mike had brought combat gear with him, which we duly put on. We blackened our faces and got the weapons out. We spent an hour stripping, cleaning, oiling and loading them while keeping our ears to Mike's radio, listening to reports on various situations around town. It was after 11 o'clock when a call was transmitted saying, 'Targets are now standing on the Antrim Road at the top of the New Lodge Road. The command is to go, go, go.' We trooped out the door and headed up the entry between Upper Canning Street and Copperfield Street towards Edlingham Street in single file.

Just as we were coming to the top of the entry, we heard the first burst of gunfire. It sounded as if it had come from the next street. About a minute had passed when a second burst of firing was heard. Mike said, 'The snipers are in the area and will be setting up their firing positions at the corner of Copperfield Street and Edlingham Street within the next five minutes. We'll start ours in two.'

Adrenaline flooded my body. My gun moved jerkily; my hand was responding too rapidly to the signals from my brain. I was conscious of the firmness of the trigger against the ball of my finger and every indentation of the grip against my palm. The sound of blood pumping in my ears was like a hand banging on a heavy door.

Those two minutes lasted an hour. 'Right! Now!' Mike shouted, and we moved out into the street. A volley of shots reverberated in our ears as we opened up, directing gunfire towards the New Lodge Road. People were coming out of their houses. As we were dressed as soldiers, no one was any the wiser. We then followed Mike to the corner of Copperfield Street where he spoke to the soldiers who were setting up sandbags to lie behind. One of the snipers had a General-Purpose Machine-Gun, which is able to fire 600 rounds per minute.

All we needed now was the IRA to react. We fired another salvo of shots up the street towards the New Lodge, to give the impression the Loyalists were still waiting on their reply. It wasn't long in coming. Fusillades of shots were returned, ricocheting and echoing off walls and lamp-posts. One of the snipers fired of a couple of rounds; a second sniper fired a short burst and we could hear the scream. The sniper put his index finger in the air − one down.

The battle continued for some time, with gunfire coming from a number of directions. Mike asked the guy with the SLR to let him have a look through the Starlight scope. Peering round the corner with the rifle, he fired a number of shots and returned the gun to its owner.

It might explain why one of the dead men had 17 gunshot wounds. Mike handed the soldier a handful of rounds from his pocket and said, 'That will make up for the rounds I fired. Enjoy the rest of your night.'

The following morning the news came in: six dead and a number injured. Rumour had it there had been more killed, but the bodies had been hidden and ferried across the border to be buried at a later date. The third Provo to die that night was Anthony Campbell, who was involved in the later shoot-out with the Army, along with three civilians, Ambrose Hardy, Brendan Maguire and James Loughran.

Two Loyalists had been picked up and, following a decision by the authorities to intern the two men arrested on Saturday, a plea for a general strike under the backing of the United Loyalist Council was announced. Although hundreds of Republicans had been interned since its introduction in August 1971, this was the first time Loyalists had been held under the Detention of Terrorists Order, and this ruling was to lead to a dramatic surge in Loyalist violence.

On 6 February, a number of moderate Unionist politicians called on people not to heed the call for a strike by the United Loyalist Council. But, by the evening, electricity power cuts began to hit Belfast. The strike wasn't supposed to begin until Wednesday 7 February. That day, a soldier was killed when the IRA fired a rocket-propelled grenade (RPG) at an APC off the Falls Road. It was becoming apparent the kind of weaponry Colonel Gadaafi had supplied.

On Wednesday 7 February, the United Loyalist Council, led by William Craig, leader of the Vanguard Party, took control of the one-day strike. In fact, the ULC was an umbrella group which included the UDA, the largest Loyalist paramilitary organisation, the Loyalist Association of Workers and a number of other smaller Loyalist factions. The aim of the strike was to reinstate Protestant control over the internal running of Northern Ireland, especially security policy. Much of the Province was affected by the power cuts and public transport was brought to a standstill; all of which had a knock-on effect with schools, shops and businesses having to close. Of course, the paramilitaries used gentle persuasion and/or intimidation to discourage many people from going to work.

Widespread violence exploded in many towns; the worst in Belfast. Practically every Loyalist district had some form of disturbance. A number of RUC stations came under sustained attack during the day. Four people were killed in separate shootings: Brian Douglas, a Protestant fireman, was shot while attending a blaze in Bradbury Place when Loyalists opened fire nearby; Andrew Petherbridge, a UDA man, was shot by the Army during disturbances on the Newtownards Road in East

Belfast; Robert Bennett, a member of the UVF, was shot by the Army on the Albertbridge Road, East Belfast; the fourth man to die was another UDA man, Glen Clarke. The IRA abducted him near Unity Flats and his body was found a short time later just off the Antrim Road, behind a bar close to the Tiger's Bay district.

Throughout the day four men died and many were injured. There had been eight explosions and 35 arson attacks. Many Unionists were deeply disturbed by the amount of violence that had taken place. We had been mobilised and kept in the background, in case the Security Forces overwhelmed the UDA. In the end, they seemed only to be interested in containing the violence and didn't make any attempt to mount an arrest operation.

Two more men were shot dead on 8 February. Hugh Connolly was killed by soldiers near his home; to all intent and purposes he was an innocent victim. Loyalists had been firing across the peace-line that separated the Shankill and Falls areas in an attempt to draw the IRA into a firefight with the Army. It worked, and the Provos brought the guns out, opening fire on the heavily fortified RUC barracks on the Springfield Road. The IRA had a heavy-calibre machine-gun firing tracer rounds at the police station. The shooting went on well into the night. The soldiers claimed hits, but no one was taken to hospital or the morgue.

Thursday 15 February brought shock and outrage to the Loyalist community. Albert Browne, a member of the UDA, was convicted of the murder of a RUC man in October 1972 and sentenced to death. There was uproar throughout the entire Province, especially since the IRA were killing Security Forces day and night. Intense pressure was brought to bear and his sentence was commuted to life imprisonment. The death penalty was later abolished, as part of the Emergency Provisions Act.

That evening, William Craig held a rally in the Ulster Hall in the centre of Belfast and gave another proclamation speech, announcing, 'Much though we wish to maintain the Union, we should all be seriously thinking of an independent dominion of Ulster.'

On 18 February, two Catholic postmen were shot at Divis Street, lower Falls, on their way home from work. The car used was hijacked on the Shankill Road by three armed men and driven straight to Divis Street. This would suggest the men were under surveillance and a team was ready, just waiting for the word to go. The car pulled up beside the men and two men jumped out of the car. The two victims were shot at close range. As they lay on the ground, one gunman stood over them, firing his machine-gun into their bodies. A man who witnessed the attack ran towards the gunmen, but had second thoughts when they threatened him with a gun. The gunmen got into their car and drove off up the Falls Road.

If this was a random attack, the men would not only have pointed their guns at the man who ran towards them; they would have shot him as well. The two postmen had been set up for some reason, followed and killed. Another MRF operation, with an OOB in place.

On 20 February, there was another bomb attack in the heart of Dublin. A man was killed as he was passing the car that exploded, in Sackville Place, off O'Connell Street. Around 17 people were injured in the blast. Once again, another MRF operation had been successful and the men were back safe across the border.

Each time there was a successful operation in the South we were elated. At one of our meetings in Palace Barracks shortly after that incident one of the men there posed the question, 'Could there not be an operation mounted across the border that would be a bit spectacular?'

I remember the answer well. 'That's not a bad idea. Leave it with us. If some time in the future we think the justification is important for such a mission, I don't see why not. I think if something like that were to take place, it would need to be when the world's media was already focusing on the situation in Northern Ireland, for maximum publicity . . .'

A terrible mistake by the IRA in the Creggan estate, Londonderry, killed a nine-year-old Catholic child, Gordon Gallagher. They had laid a booby-trap for soldiers in the back garden of his home, and when the boy had walked out into his back garden he inadvertently detonated the device.

When the Officials killed a young local lad, home on leave from the Army, there was widespread criticism, culminating with so much pressure on them they were forced to end their military campaign. As I mentioned earlier, the whole protest was orchestrated by the Provos. But PIRA had so much control now that murdering their own, even a child, didn't make an iota of difference. No one was brave enough to stand up against them.

The first day of March started with Loyalist killings. A Catholic taxi-driver ended up dead in the back of a hired car in mysterious circumstances. It looked like a set-up by the IRA, who had threatened him previously.

Later that night, a Catholic man was killed in the centre of Belfast. His name had been passed to Loyalists as a member of Sinn Féin, and he had been under observation by a MRF team who were watching as he went into a bar. When they were certain he would be in the bar for a while, another team that had been standing by, were sent for. A man from the second team went into the bar and engaged in small talk with the target. After he left the bar, the gunman who had befriended him followed. As the target walked down Linenhall Street a volley of shots rang out and he was hit in the head. The gunman ran down a side street where a car was waiting for him in Bedford Street. A joint Police and Army patrol were 100 metres away and heard the shots, but the gunman escaped.

On 2 March, a Catholic bus-driver was shot and killed when he stopped his bus on the Woodvale Road in Belfast. The gunmen approached and fired a number of shots into his cab, hitting him several times. Another bus-driver was slightly injured in the same attack. The gunmen escaped by running down Woodvale Avenue.

How did the men know the bus-driver was a Catholic and he would be driving on that particular route, that day? It was surprisingly easy to find out where people would be at a given time. Some information came from work colleagues and some from MRF contacts who had access to all sorts of personal details. Information would be passed to their contacts, who in turn relayed it to their own teams. It was a simple, foolproof way of targeting victims.

On Tuesday 20 March, a Government White Paper was published, proposing a devolved power-sharing, 78-member Assembly in Northern Ireland. It also proposed the setting up of a Council of Ireland. The election would be held in a different format to the usual democratic system whereby whomever gets the most votes wins. This Assembly's members would be elected by proportional representation, with Westminster retaining control of law and order issues. These proposals were the result of a paper issued back in October 1972. The Unionist politicians were divided on the suggestion of a power-sharing Assembly; those against it still had a preference for majority rule as the only basis for Government. No prizes for guessing who led this group. The very idea of closer links with the Irish Republic, through the Council of Ireland, was always going to be a non-starter for most Unionists.

On 20 March, a Catholic crowd was set up in a MRF operation on the Grosvenor Road. A barricade of barrels and rubbish had been constructed. An Army Saracen armoured car ploughed through it, scattering debris all over the place and leaving a gap wide enough for a car to get through. A couple of moments later, as people gathered to repair the damage, a car came through the gap. A passenger opened fire at the small crowd, killing one man and wounding a number of others. It had been timed to perfection; straight in, bang-bang, and straight out, before anyone could move; car dumped and straight home.

On 24 March, a Catholic man was shot and killed in Durham Street outside his family home. He had been out buying a takeaway for his mother when the gunman drove up to him, fired a long burst from a machine-gun, emptying the magazine and hitting him in the body a number of times. His brother was also seriously injured. An OOB was in place at the time.

On Tuesday 27 March, the ruling body of the Ulster Unionist Party, the Ulster Unionist Council, held a meeting to come to a decision on whether to accept or reject the new proposals. The Council voted 381 to 231 to accept them. Even though Brian Faulkner, the leader of the Unionist Party, had won and now had the authority to negotiate, there remained strong opposition to the proposals.

On Friday 30 March, William Craig and some other former members of the Ulster Unionist Party formed a new political party, the Vanguard Unionist Progressive Party (VUPP). From that moment, all the Unionist parties set the Loyalist cause on the slippery road to oblivion. While Catholics and Nationalists were bonding together, the Unionists were fighting and squabbling, driving a wedge ever deeper between the various factions. The VUPP was formed with the support of the UDA. It had close links with other Loyalist paramilitary groups, as well, and it was prepared to accept the formation of an independent Northern Ireland. Craig knew that, in an election, the inevitable Unionist majority of any new Government would have very little opposition. It had its own paramilitary grouping, which never really amounted to much, the Vanguard Service Corps.

On 10 April, the British Government introduced the Northern Ireland Assembly Bill in Parliament. This bill was to allow for an Assembly at Stormont, based on the proposals outlined in the White Paper.

On 17 April, soldiers shot Brendan Smyth as he stood at the corner of Etna Drive and Brompton Park in Ardoyne. He was an officer in A. Company of the IRA Belfast Brigade's 3rd Auxiliary Battalion. I include this incident as it illustrates the instructions given to soldiers regarding shooting unarmed civilians or known IRA men. The soldiers from the 3rd Battalion of the Parachute Regiment were involved in the killing. An Army spokesman gave their version of events that day: 'A patrol saw a group of armed men about to open fire. We opened fire first and hit three men, killing one and injuring two others. Fire was returned at us, obviously not by the three men. A crowd of hostile women gathered preventing the soldiers recovering the weapons.'

Statements from all soldiers involved said they had witnessed guns being passed amongst the group of men at the corner. An Ardoyne man named at the inquest was arrested and charged with being in possession of a gun. He was given bail. As he walked from the court, he was rearrested under the Special Powers Act and detained in Long Kesh. In May 1974 he was sentenced to eight years for having a gun.

In March 1976 a soldier from the Parachute Regiment confessed he had been ordered to lie in the case. Merlyn Rees the Northern Ireland Secretary ordered an appeal to be heard and the Court of Appeal ordered a retrial, although the Crown opposed this.

During the retrial the soldier gave evidence that the man was unarmed at the time. The judge warned him that what he may say could implicate him in other charges.

He replied, 'Unfortunately, that is the only way the truth will come out.' He told how he was ordered to fire by a captain and was later told by the officer to lie. Saying, the captain had identified members of the IRA standing at the corner and this was too good a chance to miss.

The Northern Ireland Assembly Act received its Royal Assent and became law on 3 May. The Act made provisions for a 78-member Assembly, elected by proportional representation.

A sniper using an Armalite rifle shot a 14-year-old who lived in Springhill Estate, Ballymurphy. The IRA used this make of rifle at that time. The MRF had procured a number of these weapons, as well as a few Thompson submachine-guns and M1. Carbines, so that the Provos would get the blame if anyone was hit or killed by a bullet fired from one of them, as in this case. The gunman had waited until an Army patrol was in the area before opening fire. The intention was to kill someone and blame it on the Provos. Unfortunately, two schoolgirls were in the vicinity and they were targeted.

On 14 May, James Callaghan, then Shadow Foreign Secretary, speaking in the House of Commons, said that Britain might reconsider its position with regard to Northern Ireland if the

Assembly was sabotaged. This statement did nothing but inflame an already volatile situation. At this point, we were becoming increasingly anxious about the possibility of Labour winning the next General Election.

On 21 June, the IRA abducted a 16-year-old Protestant boy, David Walker, from his workplace near Belvoir in South Belfast. He was described as educationally sub-normal and lived close to where he worked. He was taken back to West Belfast and his body was found lying in a street in the lower Falls district.

This killing provoked a number of retaliatory murders by incensed Loyalists who fired at any group of people they found standing about in a number of Republican areas.

True to form, on 23 June, Harold Wilson put his foot in his mouth with his remark that 'if the principles in the White Paper were rejected, it might be necessary to reconsider the relationship between Britain and Northern Ireland'.

1973 MURDER RATE
SLOWS DOWN

O N 25 JUNE, the bodies of SDLP member Paddy Wilson and a Protestant woman friend were found beside his red Mini at a quarry on the Hightown Road in North Belfast. Wilson had been shot; both victims had multiple stab wounds. (Wilson's name was on a MRF hit list due to his connections with known IRA men.) An OOB was in place at the time.

These savage murders were a milestone in the barbarity and sickened both communities. What the hell was happening to us? Were we setting ourselves up as gods – killing people of our own faith because they worked alongside Catholics, or be-friended Catholics?

Thursday 28 June was a significant day. For the first time, elections were held for seats in the new Northern Ireland Assembly, under the new proportional representation voting system. The turnout was high with 72.3 per cent of the electorate casting their vote. But it became a total fuck-up. The election gave the parties supporting the White Paper 52 seats, and those opposing it 26. However, a number of the candidates who were elected with the Pro-White Paper parties were themselves against the proposals, reducing the margin in the new Assembly. Ordinary folk had no idea who was who and were completely in the dark as who had actually won.

On 30 June, a Catholic man was sitting in his flat in Eglantine Avenue, which runs between the Lisburn Road and the Malone Road in South Belfast – a place called Student Land due to the high density of students in the area. (Queen's University is close by.) His wife (to whom he had been married only a week ago) opened the door to be confronted by gunmen who walked past her into the house.

The first gunman asked the man, 'Are you . . .' and said the man's name.

When the man confirmed his name, the gunman pulled out a pistol and shot him in the stomach. As the wounded man attempted to leave the room, he was hit twice more in the back. The gunman had used the man's full name, both his Christian names and his surname – which would indicate this wasn't a random sectarian murder. An OOB was in place at the time.

The brick system was working for the Army. In the whole of June two soldiers had been killed, both of them by booby-trap bombs. The Army was constantly putting new tactics into place.

The Catholic Primate of All Ireland, Cardinal Conway, issued a statement condemning recent murders: 'There have been twice as many assassinations of this type in the first six months of this year as in the corresponding period last year.'

On Wednesday 18 June, the Northern Ireland Constitution Act received its Royal Assent. After 50 years, the axe had come down on the Stormont Parliament.

During July, the new Taoiseach, Liam Cosgrave, flew to London for a meeting with Edward Heath. As usual, that sort of event always put the wind up us. We didn't trust anyone at all any more, especially English politicians.

Tuesday was the last day of the month and the first meeting of the Assembly. There was uproar; fighting and name-calling.

It became so bad the RUC were called in to restore calm and order. I think I recall a number of police being injured in the scuffles inside the Stormont buildings. It was ridiculous watching the antics on television. Two factions of Unionists getting stuck into each other – the Republicans must have been doubled up with laughter.

On 5 August, a Catholic man and his wife were both shot dead at their farmhouse, at Broughadoey, near Dungannon. A two-year-old son, wounded in the leg and covered in blood beside his parents' bodies, was discovered by his 17-year-old brother, who ran screaming to a neighbour. Around 20 spent 9mm cartridges from a Sterling submachine-gun were found at the scene. An OOB was in place at the time.

Tuesday 6 August brought a startling revelation in a Dublin courtroom. Two brothers, Keith and Kenneth Littlejohn, had been arrested for a bank robbery in the Republic. During the trial Kenneth Littlejohn claimed they had been working for British Intelligence (MI6) and their role was to infiltrate the OIRA. The British Government made no comment on the brothers' allegations, and they received 20 years' imprisonment for their troubles.

On 10 August, a Catholic man from Ballymurphy had been visiting a patient in Musgrave Park Hospital. He was walking home from the hospital with his pregnant wife and his mother-in-law. They had reached Kennedy Way when a car pulled up beside them. A gunman jumped from it, firing at the man as he tried to make a run for it. He was hit and fell to the ground. As his wife tried to shield him, the gunman went over and fired another round into his head at close range. An OOB was in place at the time.

Musgrave Park Hospital, although part of it was for civilian patients, contained a Military Wing for soldier's injured and wounded. This was in a secure part of the hospital and very easy for MRF to find out if any patients were of interest to them, or who came visiting. If you look at this operation it stands out like a sore thumb that this man was the target and not a random attack. As he was on foot and walking home, they would have known it would take more than half an hour for him to reach home. Once notified the hit team had plenty of time to hi-jack the taxi and reach the victim long before the man would get home. Plus it was a straight walk, nowhere to turn off until he would have reached the Andersonstown Road.

Upon hearing the news of his son's death, Joe Murphy, who had been released from hospital a few weeks earlier suffering from angina, collapsed and died. It is horrific to admit now, but we revelled in the fact two people had died instead of one. This now sounds appallingly callous and cold to me, but at the time it was the nature of the war. The emphasis of the obligation on us to kill was being drummed into our heads. I would go as far as to say, we were becoming brainwashed into cold-blooded, merciless people. The more horrible and brutal Loyalists could make each murder the greater the fear element on the Catholic community. . I feel so revolted now at my attitude to events at those times. It is no wonder I lost my faith in God.

Monday 24 August brought news that caused more anxiety to all Loyalists. Garret Fitzgerald, the Irish Foreign Minister, stated that the British and Irish Governments had agreed on the formation of an Executive for Northern Ireland, the re-form of the Royal Ulster Constabulary and the civil service, and the creation of a Council of Ireland. The general feeling was, what right has the Republic to have a say in the inter-nal running of our country and particularly in how the RUC should be reformed.

There had been a dramatic fall in the number of murders

in September and it was to be the same in October. We were starting to feel as though the corner had been turned and after the previous years bloodletting maybe everyone involved in this war had become sickened of the killings, the suffering and torment being heaped upon ordinary folk. I know the pressure my mates and I were under and I'm sure the same went for the majority of volunteers.

On 5 October, William Whitelaw chaired a succession of meetings at Stormont Castle on forming an Executive to govern Northern Ireland. These meetings involved members of the Ulster Unionist Party, the Alliance Party and the SDLP. The parties disagreed on issues related to internment, policing and the Council of Ireland, however, they made progress on other less contentious issues in the social and economic arena.

On 8 October, a group of Ulster Unionists who opposed the sharing of power with the SDLP demanded the resignation of their leader, Brian Faulkner. The next day, representatives of the three parties engaged in talks, finally announcing that they had come to an agreement on an economic and social programme.

On 29 October, a Catholic man from Banbridge was shot in his doorway by a man who went on to become one of the most notorious hit men for the UVF's Mid-Ulster Brigade. It is believed this was his first murder.

Over a period of 25 years this man and his Brigade of dedicated men committed a large number of murders in and around Portadown and further afield. His original nickname had been 'Jacko', but eventually he became known as 'The Jackal'. He was particularly ruthless. The Jackal attracted a lot of media attention, especially in the late 1980s when Republicans alleged he had contact with Military Intelligence. This is true – his nickname arose in a lot of conversations with Mike.

In 1980, two policemen who had connections with 'The Jackal' were charged with the murder of a man in Ahoghill, County Antrim, in 1977. One of the policemen named 'The Jackal' as the gunman.

The judge asked, 'Why is this man not before the court?'

The RUC man replied, 'For reasons of operational strategy.'

This case alone underlines that this book is plain fact. Why did the judge not pursue this answer? He was being told that a man called the 'Jackal' (the UVF's Robin Jackson) killed a man and turned a blind eye to it. Corruption at all levels.

November saw a slight increase in the murders over the previous two months. During this month the UVF called a ceasefire, which lasted for 43 days. It didn't stop UVF operations; they were claimed under the pseudonym Ulster Freedom Fighters, the UDA's military wing.

On 8 November, a booby-trap bomb left in his byre killed a Catholic farmer. Loyalists had planted it in an attempt to have the blame put on the IRA. Although the UFF claimed it, the UVF had carried out the job, with the help of a MRF-trained bomb maker.

Kathleen Feeny, a 14-year-old schoolgirl, was killed during a sniper attack on the Army in Londonderry. At the time, it was thought the soldiers were responsible for her death. The truth only came to light in 2005. An IRA sniper had shot her.

On 23 November, William Whitelaw announced the breakthrough to the House of Commons and gave details of the running of the Executive. I remember watching the television and wondering if this was the end of Northern Ireland. A lot of things were happening that seemed beyond our control or influence.

Even the MRF was unsure about its position. They had had no orders to stop their operations, and there was no reason for the Provos to discontinue their campaign of violence.

While all this political activity was taking place we continued to carry out small operations. Although there were no fatalities, there were many attempts to terrify the Catholic community; our war was still ongoing.

It was about this time an incident took place that was to effect change in our modus operandi. I arrived home one night to find my father nursing a swollen jaw. Asking what had happened, I was told my brother had been pushed about a bit by the UDA outside a club not far from our house. My father had decided to go up and find out what was going on. Their commander didn't take too kindly to his comments about attacking Protestants and hit him in the face, breaking his false teeth. My father was determined to phone the police.

I was angry and told him not to phone anyone; I would sort it out. I rushed out and called for a mate to come with me. We arrived at the club and a couple of guys we knew were at the door. I asked to speak to their commander. He duly appeared with about a dozen of his men.

'What's your fucking problem?' were his first words.

I thought diplomacy was required, no heroics, so I asked him jokingly, 'Did you really need to bring all these men with you? I only wanted to ask you why you hit my father and broke his dentures?'

'Your da was doing a bit of slobbering about getting the police and he got a dig in the jaw for it. Have you a problem with that?'

That made me furious. 'So you had to hit an old man for a bit of mouthing off? Is that what we're about here? I thought we were supposed to protect our community, not go around punching helpless old men.'

He was sharp. He picked up on the word 'we'. 'Why? Who are you connected with?'

'I never said I was connected to anything. I'm only interested in why you had to punch my old man.' I emphasised the word 'old'.

One of the guys who came out with him, whom we knew, jumped in at this point. 'They're with the OVs or the UVF. I don't know which, but it's somebody.'

I denied it.

The boss said, 'I've had enough of this. Now, fuck off or we'll give you the same.'

I held my hands up, 'OK. No problem. I only wanted to know what happened.'

With that, we turned and walked away. I could feel my blood pressure rising.

My friend felt the same.

I reassured him that it wasn't his problem; it was mine. He could walk away.

He stopped and stared at me. 'That fucker wasn't just talking to you, he was talking to both of us. Let's get the pieces now and show the cunt he's not dealing with fucking children.'

I asked him if he was sure; what about our families, any repercussions. But I knew his answer before he uttered it. 'If you think I'm going to let a wank stain like that get away with it, you can think again.'

We collected two guns and discussed our options. As we headed back up to the club, I was aware of the semi-automatic Browning in my pocket, enjoying its solidity, its power. We decided to wait until the commander was on his way home and then to tackle him. This would give him the chance of not being made to look like a wee boy in front of his men. And, if he was prepared to do something, our whole team could become involved.

We hid in an entry close to the club and watched as the men slowly dispersed homewards. When our target came out, he stood talking with a number of men for about ten minutes, before walking off. As he approached the entry, we made our move and grabbed him. I remember the shock on his face in the streetlight, before the shadows concealed it.

'I think we have some unfinished business, you fucking wanker,' said my mate, sticking the barrel of his gun against the side of his head. 'On your fucking knees now.'

The man collapsed to the ground, pleading, 'Don't shoot me, lads. I'll sort it out for you. Please don't kill me.'

I hunkered down so his face was level with mine. 'I want you to listen very carefully. First rule in this game; don't mess with anybody when you don't know a thing about them. I tried to warn you earlier when I said "we". You sussed it, but you thought you could be the big man and push the issue. We aren't like you. We joined up to defend our people and do whatever it takes to stop these Republican bastards winning the war. Now we're going to spare your miserable life on a few conditions.

'Firstly, in the morning you will go to my parents' house and apologise for whacking my da. Secondly, you'll hand him a couple of hundred pounds to fix his dentures and any discomfort you have caused him. Thirdly, we're doing it this way in order to save you embarrassment in front of your men. If you say nothing about it, no one needs to know. Fourthly, if anything happens to our families, or us, men you don't know will come and kill you. The beauty of this is that we know you, and you can be sure we'll be telling them all about this little talk. But you don't know them, and that makes it very easy for them to get to you. Any problems with that?'

He stammered, 'No, none at all.'

Sure enough, he turned up first thing the next day. I answered the door and shouted for my father, 'Da, there's someone here to see you.'

When my father came to the door, he got the money and the apology.

I said, 'That's it over as far as I'm concerned. It's up to you now, if you want to take it any further.'

He replied, 'No, that's fine. Thanks.'

The following Sunday two men called at my door and asked if I would come with them; someone would like to speak to me. I knew one of them from way back. He told me not to worry; it was just to clear up a small matter. I went to get my coat and slipped a gun into my waistband behind my back. I wasn't taking any chances. When I came out, one of them was at my mate's door. I assumed he was being asked to do the same. The four of us climbed into their car and they drove us up to The Park Bar in Tiger's Bay. We followed them through the bar and out the back. An alarm bell was going off in my head and I was glad I'd brought something with me. We went out into the backyard and were taken through another door into a yard where we climbed up a ladder fixed to the wall. At the top of the ladder, a door opened into a large room, where half a dozen men were sitting about. You would never have suspected it existed from outside. I recognised some of them from the area and nodded at them. We were told to take a seat on the other side facing them.

The commander was sitting in the middle. 'Put your minds at ease, lads. You're here just to clear up a small matter that's been brought to our attention. First off, who are you?'

Before I could say a word, my mate said, 'Before we say anything, we'd like to know who's asking the questions.'

I had an inkling what the answer was going to be.

'We're from the third battalion UVF and I'm the CO. Who are you connected with?'

I was right. 'We're with a team from the Shankill.'

He asked, 'Who's this team from the Shankill, and what are you doing in our area?'

I said, 'Because we live here.'

'I take it you're the team operating in and around this area?'

I looked him in the eye and said, 'We might have done a couple of operations, yeah.'

He looked straight back and said, 'I think it's been more than a couple. We want to know who authorised your operations.'

My mate replied, 'We're working with the USSF.' He then mentioned the names of the two brothers who were in charge.

I said, 'They give us the go-ahead to operate when and where and when we want.'

The three men at the table looked at each other. One of them said, 'Fuck me, we should have guessed. It could only be them who would allow this sort of action to take place without anyone else's permission. They're a fucking law unto themselves.'

The CO said, 'OK. Now we know who's been operating in our district, we'll have a talk with Brigade Staff and the CO of the USSF, and sort something out. You'll understand, loose cannons could jeopardise our men if they're on an operation at the same time. And vice versa. We wondered who would have the balls to leave the UDA's commander lying on the ground.'

I explained what had happened and why we took the action we did.

He said, 'You'll hear no more about it, I can assure you. Give us a couple of days and we'll get back to you, hopefully to let you know what arrangement we can put in place to accommodate you to our mutual satisfaction.'

We were then offered a lift back home, which we declined. We headed to Billy's house and told him about the encounter.

He got in touch with his contacts up the road and let them know what was going on, so there would be no surprises.

A couple of days later, Billy asked me to come to his house after work. Jim was coming over to see us.

Entering the parlour, I said, 'Well, Jim, I hope it's not bad news.'

He started to laugh. 'No, it's not too bad. They want you to choose which battalion you would like to join, as there are men from both areas in your team. It can be the third battalion based in Tiger's Bay or the East Antrim Brigade from Rathcoole and Monkstown. You can vote and pick whichever one you choose. That's the official position.

'Our opinion is, unofficially, to let you carry on what you're doing and if you're questioned about an operation, just deny everything.'

Billy and I agreed; it sounded like an ideal set-up.

Jim confirmed that the CO from the Bay would be in touch in a day or so.

A few nights later, at a meeting of our team, it was put to the vote; it went in East Antrim's favour. Some weeks later, we all went down to the Farm, Rathcoole's base, which was in the process of being renovated into a club. It must have been the largest UVF swearing-in ceremony ever. Twenty-five of us recited the oath of allegiance.

On 3 December, Francis Pym replaced William Whitelaw as Secretary of State for Northern Ireland. This came as a complete surprise to us all, especially to politicians, given that talks concerning the Council of Ireland had reached a crucial stage and were scheduled to start in three days. It was widely believed that Francis Pym knew very little about Northern Ireland.

Meanwhile, Harry West and other unpledged Unionists announced the setting up of a new party, the Ulster Unionist

Assembly Party. Confusion reigned: new Unionist parties were springing up every other day. I could picture some wee woman from the back streets of Belfast who had voted Unionist all her life going into the polling booth and being confronted by a ballot paper with half a dozen Unionist parties on it – *and* trying to cope with proportional representation.

Francis Pym held a meeting with the Reverend Ian Paisley and informed him that Loyalists would not be invited to the Sunningdale Conference, but that they could come and put their point of view. Predictably, the Big Man stormed out of the meeting.

More fun and games took place on 5 December. At a meeting of the Assembly, pro-Executive Unionist members were attacked by the DUP and Vanguard members. Again, it got so heated, the RUC had to be called in to break it up. I wondered what the world media made of it all.

The leaders of the three opposition parties, Harry West (UUAP), Ian Paisley (DUP) and William Craig (Vanguard) held a joint rally in the Ulster Hall and formed yet another Unionist body. It was called the United Ulster Unionist Council (UUUC). It opposed power sharing and aimed to bring down the Executive. About 600 Ulster Unionist Party delegates attended the rally. The rift was becoming deeper.

The big day had arrived, 6 December. The Civil Service Staff College at Sunningdale in England hosted the meeting of all pro-Agreement parties. They were there to resolve the remaining obstacles to completing the setting up of the Executive. It was the first time that the British and Irish Prime Ministers and the Northern Ireland Government (designate) had attended talks on the future of Northern Ireland since 1925.

As well as the Prime Ministers and senior ministers, representatives of the three parties engaged in the destruction of our Province attended Sunningdale. The collaborators, as we saw them, discussed a number of matters, but the main stumbling block, regarding the unresolved issue of the Council of Ireland, remained. This was to become known as the 'Irish Dimension'. Suggestions for this 'Irish Dimension' were finally agreed in the form of a proposed Council of Ireland. The elements of the Council would consist of a Council of Ministers and a Consultative Assembly. The Council of Ministers was to be comprised of seven members of the Northern Ireland Executive and seven members of the Irish Government. This Council would have executive and co-ordinating objectives, and a consultative role. The Consultative Assembly was to be made up of 30 members of the Northern Ireland Assembly and the same from the Dail. It was to have advisory and review functions.

We watched the political scene unfold. We were on 'ceasefire' and had cut military operations, in order to give the impression we were actually observing it.

On 9 December, a communiqué was issued announcing an agreed outcome – it would be known as the 'Sunningdale Agreement'.

The following day, the 10th Loyalists formed the Ulster Army Council (UAC) – which comprised all paramilitary groups, including the two main ones, the UVF and the UDA/UFF – to resist the proposed Council of Ireland.

We were called to a meeting on 11 December and told that plans were being drawn up to bring down the 'Sunningdale Agreement'. All UVF volunteers would be required to participate in whatever action was deemed necessary to achieve this objective. If that scenario included engaging the Army, with whatever means and weaponry available, then it was expected that every man would do his duty.

Everyone present that night cheered. From what looked like a Doomsday situation, emerged hope. We were going to be like Lord Carson's old Ulster Volunteer Force, prepared to fight to remain part of the United Kingdom. We were told to prepare for a declaration of an independent Ulster; to go for it alone, if necessary, before being forced into a United Ireland. We left the meeting hyped-up, feeling positive; knowing that something was going to be planned to defeat this sell-out. All it needed was the support of the Loyalist people, as in 1912, when all the Protestant population united against Home Rule. I confess we relished the challenge.

We took a back seat for the rest of the month, awaiting orders. With Christmas approaching, no one was really interested in operating. After seeing so much sorrow, none of us wanted to inflict any grief on anyone. Terrorists with a conscience? Wishful thinking on my part.

The murders had dropped by almost half from the previous year, as well as the number of shootings. Bombings had dropped as well, although not significantly but a drop never the less. Maybe the trend would continue and before too long everybody would wise up and see the senselessness of all this suffering.

1973 Statistics

Deaths by year and status		Responsibility for deaths	
Protestant civilians	48	Republicans	137
Catholics civilians	80	Loyalists	90
RUC	9	Army	29
RUC/R	4	RUC/RUC/R	1
UDR/RIR	8	UDR/RIR	2
Army	59	Others	4
Republicans	38		
Loyalists	13		
Others	4		
TOTAL	263		
Bombs	1,520		
Shootings	5,018		

1974 CIVIL DISOBEDIENCE

THE FIRST OF January 1974 was the date the Northern Ireland Executive officially took over the running of Northern Ireland. Only certain powers had been devolved to the Executive and the Assembly; the British Government and the Northern Ireland Office retained power over security and certain economic issues.

New Year's Day brought no respite from the killing. John Whyte, a Catholic civilian, was shot dead during a IRA sniper attack on soldiers just off the Ormeau Road, Belfast.

On 4 January, the Ulster Unionist Council, the policy-making body of the Ulster Unionists, voted to reject the Council of Ireland. The ballot result was 427 to 374.

On 5 January, the first Loyalist killing that year took place in East Belfast. A Catholic man was shot in the chest when he answered a knock at the door. The gunmen asked if his son was in; when they found he wasn't, they fired at the father who died later in hospital. An OOB was in place at the time.

On 7 January, Brian Faulkner resigned as leader of the Ulster Unionist Party, although he retained his position as Chief Executive in the Assembly. He travelled to Dublin for a meeting with the Taoiseach. The High Court in Dublin had made a ruling that implied that the reunification of Ireland did not need the consent of the majority of people in Northern Ireland. We all greeted this ruling with the contempt it deserved. The following day, an Assembly member of the SDLP, Hugh Logue, gave a speech at Trinity College, Dublin, in which he said that the Council of Ireland was the vehicle that would trundle Unionists into a United Ireland.

Even my parents, who were very moderate in their views, were taken aback by these comments. When reasonable folk are upset and baying for blood, you realise the writing is on the wall. Preparations were being made for the 'Protestant backlash' that politicians and commentators had harped on and on about.

A strange murder took place on 30 January. A Protestant, Thomas Walker, was shot dead by Loyalists at his home near Donegall Pass. It was suspected he was an informer. Normally, these people would be picked up and subjected to an in-depth grilling to find out how much information they had actually passed to their handlers.

On 31 January, two Catholic men who worked for the Northern Ireland Electricity Service were shot dead as they laid cables at Rush Park, part of the Protestant Rathcoole estate on the outskirts of North Belfast. During their lunch break all the workmen were playing cards, when two armed and masked gunmen burst into the hut. Twelve men were in the hut at the time. At first, everyone thought it was a robbery, as the men were asked for their wage packets.

The gunmen told the Protestant workers to leave and ordered the Catholics to move to the back of the hut. They knew exactly who was Catholic and who was Protestant. They shot the two Catholic men with a burst of Sterling submachine-gun fire and left the scene. An OOB was in place at the time. The UVF carried out the killing; not the UFF as was reported. This was one of the operations done under the 'ceasefire' and claimed under the pseudonym.

On 7 February, the Ulster Protestants received the worst news possible. Edward Heath had called for a General Election to be held on 28 February. Francis Pym argued strongly for a later date, believing that the Executive would not survive the outcome. We began preparing for all-out war. Heath's Government was bad enough, having tried to force us into accepting a power-sharing Executive and Council of Ireland that no one wanted. What if, God forbid, Harold Wilson and his party actually won? Once again, we were in a predicament.

On 21 February, a Catholic man was killed in another bomb attack on a Catholic bar, the Spa Inn, in the heart of the Republican New Lodge Road district. The bomb had been spotted and all the people evacuated, but a man sitting in the upstairs lounge bar had been overlooked. The lounge bar and much of the ground floor were completely wrecked. It was ironic that before the Troubles started, my mates and I used to drink there after football training on a Monday night, and knew the layout of the pub quite well. At that time a lot of Protestants lived in the streets close to the New Lodge Road and there had never been any problems at all.

When these attacks happened in my own area, I felt sickened. I had a conscience then. When you watched men breaking into Catholic houses, wrecking and ransacking them, then setting alight furniture and bedding – places where people had spent years building up a home for themselves – it felt wrong. Luckily, the residents had already fled the area; I think, if they had stayed, they would have been in grave danger.

Yet, when it happened to a friend of mine, any sense of compassion evaporated. He lived close to the New Lodge and got a call from his wife saying the Catholics were giving her a hard time, and she was very frightened. We worked at the same timber company and he asked if I could give him a lift home.

He had contacted his brother, who was on his way there with a lorry to salvage their belongings. By the time we got there his brother was loading the lorry with a couple of other guys. A hostile crowd had gathered and was hurling abuse.

When we had loaded the lorry with as much as we could, my friend wanted to wreck the house completely, to prevent a Catholic family from moving in. So, we set about destroying what we could, taking a sledgehammer to the walls, pulling the fireplace out, and smashing all the windows. We were about to set fire to it, when the crowd realised and edged closer. As we tore off, I remember my friend's parting words: 'You can have it now you, Fenian bastards.'

On Saturday 23 February, black-taxi drivers, who ran a shuttle service on the Shankill Road with the help of the paramilitaries, hijacked some buses and used them to block roads in and around the Shankill district. They were protesting against Army harassment. VCPs had been set up on the roads, and the processing of all drivers and passengers, which involved taking their names and addresses, and doing a P check on them all, was delaying the cabs for up to thirty minutes every time. A P check involved the soldiers radioing your name and address into headquarters to check if you were suspected of being involved in paramilitary activities. You can imagine the frustration felt by the taxi-drivers, stopped on the way up the Shankill, then again on the way down.

I should explain the history of the service provided by black taxis. Whenever street disturbances took place, when either side would take on the Army in riots, the first casualties were the buses as they made great burning barricades. Once trouble flared and the hijacking started, the bus service to those areas were suspended and the passengers complained.

The IRA decided this was a way to make some money. They

allowed members and non-members to buy black taxis and put on a transport service. Each driver paid the Provos a fee so they could operate without fear of being hijacked. Their route went from Castle Street in the city centre up to the Falls Road, ending in Twinbrook or Polglass estates. When Loyalists cottoned on, they did exactly the same. Their route went from North Street in the city centre up the Shankill Road, and finished at Glencairn. The fares were far cheaper than those on the buses so even when there was no trouble, people would use a black taxi, rather than the buses.

However, the taxis' insurance didn't permit customers to be picked up at bus stops. But, eventually, to avoid alienating much of the community, they changed the law to make the practice legal. They're still operating today.

Widespread rioting continued in Protestant districts on 25 February.

The General Election went ahead on Thursday 28 February, and over 30,000 Security Forces personnel were on duty throughout the Province. There were a number of shooting and bombing incidents, and some rioting. The election in Northern Ireland was fought like a referendum. The Loyalist people had two choices: a pro-Agreement candidate or an anti-Agreement candidate. A pact had been formed amongst those opposed to the Agreement. Under the umbrella group, the UUUC, each of the three parties – the DUP (under Paisley), the Official Unionists (West) and Vanguard (Craig) – agreed they would put forward one candidate in each constituency. Their campaign slogan was, 'Dublin is just a Sunningdale away.'

It was an overwhelming defeat for the pro-Agreement parties, with the parties under the UUUC taking 11 out of the 12 seats. The SDLP held onto Catholic West Belfast, with 51 per cent of the vote. We celebrated our victory, only to be plunged into despair again when all the counting was completed. The Labour Party had defeated the Conservatives and returned Harold Wilson back to power, albeit with a minority.

That night, ten bombs exploded within an hour of each other in Belfast city centre. The sole fatality resulted from a Loyalist attack on the Red Star Bar, near the docks area. The man killed was a Protestant, and a woman lost both her legs in the blast. The bomb had been spotted, and everyone had tried to run past it. The two casualties were passing it as it detonated. There were several OOBs in place at the time.

Now that the IRA had begun to bomb and kill on the mainland, many people wanted the troops pulled out of Northern Ireland and to let us sort out our problems. Was a situation similar to that in 1912 approaching? In 1912, they hadn't had a vicious Republican campaign raging at the same time.

Meetings were called to discuss the situation. Firstly, if the British Government tried to force the Sunningdale Agreement upon us, we would have to fight the Army to prevent it being implemented. They in turn would have to use force against the Protestant population to enforce the rule of the new Assembly and the Council of Ireland. That would mean the entire population of the Province, both sides, fighting the Army for two entirely different reasons. The soldiers would be stuck in the middle. That scenario would give the British Government a reason to disengage the troops within Ireland altogether, leaving us to fight it out with the Republicans for a United Ireland or an independent Ulster. It would also pave the way for the Republic to send their Army across the border to quash any Loyalist uprising.

The Republic wouldn't want to go down that road, because their economy couldn't withstand the terrorist onslaught we were suffering. We would become a terrorist organisation, doing exactly the same to the Republic as the Provos were doing in the North, only we would be fighting to achieve an independent Ulster.

Secondly, we could just go ahead and declare an Independent Ulster. Heath had already warned us about proclaiming a Unilateral Declaration of Independence, on 15 November 1972, yet, on 18 September 1973, he threatened that if the Northern Ireland Assembly failed to form a power-sharing Executive by March 1974, the best alternative would be to integrate Northern Ireland fully into the United Kingdom. This would have put the Province in a stronger position than we were before the Troubles began. But with Wilson and the Labour Party now in government, it was a whole new ball game. They would never entertain the idea of integration. It would be more convenient for them if we went ahead and pronounced our independence, because Wilson could then wash his hands of the problem and let us fight it out with Republicans. To the victor, the spoils.

It was at one of these meetings that a suggestion for an all-out strike by everyone was put forward. This seemed an excellent idea. The first day-long strike back in February 1973 had been reasonably well supported and, if a bit more pressure could be put on the people to help embrace the protest until the issue was resolved, it could be made to work. A man stood up and said the key to making a strike work was to encourage the power station's workers to back the proposed stoppage, because if that could be done, without electricity, firms would have to close anyway, which would cut down the need for widespread intimidation. An important aspect of taking this path was to make sure the violence against the Security Forces that occurred during the previous strike, didn't happen, as it would give them the excuse to try and break it with heavy-handed tactics. This idea was greeted with a chorus of approval.

The men at the top said they would put the suggestion forward and it seemed as if we had a solution.

We left the meeting that night with a spring in our step. If this suggestion were accepted, then we would be in for an exciting time. Trying to imagine a whole country going on strike in support of a single aim seemed impossible, but if it did come to pass, it would be heralded as a fantastic achievement.

Monday 4 March saw those Unionists who were in favour of the Assembly and the Executive decide that the Sunningdale Agreement should not be ratified unless Articles 2 and 3 of the Irish Constitution were repealed. The SDLP argued that there could be no watering down of the Agreement. It's marvellous how history repeats itself. These politicians had signed up to a power-sharing Assembly. Now, they realised they should have fought for something else during negotiations – exactly the same as with the Good Friday Agreement.

On 5 March, Harold Wilson announced the appointment of Merlyn Rees as the new Secretary of State for Northern Ireland. Due to Labour's small majority, Rees had to spend a lot more time at Westminster instead of Stormont Castle. As a result, he was out of touch with developments on the ground in Northern Ireland. It was established later, through Mike, that they were keeping a lot of information from the Labour Government and wanted it to fail.

On Saturday 9 March, the UUUC organised a protest march to Stormont calling for the termination of the Executive. We were all there with our Ulster flags and Union Jacks, although the latter seemed to be in the minority. It was easy to understand how masses of people could get carried away by dramatic speeches. You felt part of something special; you were on the same side as thousands of fellow men and women. Better to support what was taking place, than stand against it.

We were exhilarated at being a part of this momentous occasion. Excitement bubbled in my veins. We had been involved with acts of violence and feared no one. It's hard to explain, but it had reached a stage where we felt almost godlike, able to kill at the drop of a hat. Somehow, I didn't fear death, only the pain and agony that could accompany it, before the sinking into oblivion. Some of those poor victims who suffered so horribly would have welcomed the peace death offered them.

On 10 March, two Catholic teenagers, Michael Gallagher (18) and Michael McCreesh (15), were both killed in a boo-by-trap bomb left in an abandoned car near Forkhill, County Armagh. It had been intended for soldiers on foot patrol. I'm ashamed to say it felt good when one of the IRA's operations killed their own.

The same day, Liam Cosgrave stated in a speech to the Dail that the position of Northern Ireland within the United Kingdom could not be changed without the consent of the majority of the people of Northern Ireland. It took courage to say that. The Provos hadn't the intelligence at the time to realise that, while it felt good to be part of the struggle for their cause, to get the British out of Ireland, we the Loyalists would have destroyed the economy of the Free State completely. Ireland would have been washed down the proverbial plughole.

The only mistake Cosgrave made in that comment was that he needed not only the consent of the majority, but the consent of every single person within the Province. The IRA was working with approximately 400–500 active volunteers – I'm being generous with that figure – and others as back-up. The Loyalists could muster 20,000-plus. What sort of damage could we have wreaked on them?

On 16 March, a Catholic man was shot by two gunmen on the way home from a bar in Cromac Street with his sister. The man's name and his movements were passed on to Loyalists by the MRF. He was hit twice in the head and died at the scene. His sister tried to protect him, before passing out. An OOB was in place at the time.

On 19 March, an off-duty RUC man, Frederick Robinson, was killed by a car bomb at his home in Greenisland, County Antrim. The RUC made a terrible blunder the following day. Two undercover soldiers (MRF), Michael Herbert and Michael Cotton, were sitting in a civilian van at Mowhan, near Markethill, County Armagh, when a RUC patrol mistook them for terrorists and opened fire, killing both. Reports at the time suggested they were on an undercover operation – we were told they were – but Merlyn Rees denied it. Maybe he wasn't aware of it; I got the distinct impression from Mike that the Intelligence Services were withholding a lot of information.

On 21 March, a Catholic man who worked for a timber company close to the docks was murdered. Workers who had to travel towards the city centre were given a lift on one of the company's lorries. About 20 men, mostly Catholics, were sitting in the trailer as it pulled out of the yard. A masked gunman opened fire, killing one man and wounding five others. An OOB was in place at the time.

Around this time a new Loyalist group was formed, the Ulster Workers Council (UWC), which was an umbrella group for all Loyalist paramilitaries and all Unionist dissident parties. They issued a statement demanding new elections for the Northern Ireland Executive. They threatened civil disobedience unless the present Executive was disbanded. Word had filtered down through the chain of command that the idea of a complete all-out stoppage was being discussed in detail by all interested groups. It was looking good. Some had doubts that it would be supported Province-wide. If it were to succeed, it would only work with 100 per cent co-operation and backing of the Protestant population. Things were getting exciting. I could feel a prickling of the hairs on the back of my neck every time the subject was raised.

On 1 April, key UVF man James Hanna was shot in the head. The motive for his murder was a complete mystery. A number of reasons have been considered: 1) that he informed on a bomb-making factory close to where he lived; 2) he was seen in the town of Portadown shortly before a UDA officer was injured in a booby-trap bomb attack; 3) it was due to an internal UVF power struggle; 4) he was part of a delegation that went to Dublin to talk to the PIRA and to Monaghan to meet the OIRA. At that time, hardliners would not have appreciated anyone attempting to bring about a truce, none more so than the MRF.

If a truce had come about, it would have given the IRA a free hand to increase their attacks on Security Forces personnel, and would have meant they could carry on their campaign without fear of reprisals.

So who killed James Hanna?

The UVF denied any involvement, stating, 'He played a prominent role in the UVF's military campaign against the PIRA.' If they had done it, because he was thought to be an informer, it would have been announced as a warning to other informers.

If it had been done by the UDA, there would have been retaliation killings. My reasoning, for what it's worth, is that he was taken out by hardliners, sanctioned and assisted by the MRF, to prevent any more meetings with Republicans. The Top Brass would have frowned upon any activity of that nature. Too much time and money had been spent in trying to

defeat the IRA to let someone interfere with the overall strategy now.

I asked Mike about it, but he was non-committal: 'I don't
honestly know, but if anybody tries to rock the boat, then they
must pay the penalty.'

I still wonder if that was a subtle hint to me that the same
end would be meted out to any of us who 'rocked the boat'.
We all knew the consequences if anyone stepped out of line.
But Mike's comment sent shivers up and down my spine.

On 4 April 1974, Merlyn Rees announced that he was going
to de-proscribe (remove the illegal status) from the UVF and
Sinn Féin, and in another massive concession to Republicans,
began the phasing out of internment. Despite the fact that
there were some Loyalists internees, the vast majority was
Republican. His statement was regarded as a major appeasement to Nationalists.

As I mentioned in the Prologue, the UVF had actually co-
erced and negotiated the Government into this concession, on
the pretext that it would help the Security Forces to concentrate
on Republican violence. A meeting between Government officials and UVF representatives was organised. The Government
had been stalling and was apprehensive about lifting the ban, so
the UVF arranged for a couple of explosions in the vicinity to
emphasise how hard it was to control their hardliners.

It worked. The UVF became legal. This was a critical moment. From being a secretive organisation, they started to let
any Tom, Dick or Harry join. People who would normally not
have stood a chance began to swell the ranks, with their black
leather jackets, black polo-necks, black corduroy trousers and
black boots becoming the order of the day. This standard UVF
uniform earned them the nickname of 'black necks'.

Whenever you walked into any bar or Loyalist club they stood out like sore thumbs. The RUC Special Branch became more able to recruit informers, and it really was the downfall of the UVF as an elite force of loyal men dedicated to Ulster's cause. Before this, anybody refused entry into the UVF joined the UDA, who admitted anybody and everybody. That is not to say there were no good men in the UDA, there were – I knew and still know quite a few of them – but they admitted anyone willing to take up a stick, man a barricade or generally do any shitty job that needed to be done. As a result, they picked up a few derogatory nicknames through the years: 'Stick men', 'The Hair Bear Bunch', 'The Ant Hill Mob' and, more recently, 'The Wombles'.

Many petty criminals seized the opportunity, seeing it as an easy way to expand their activities and make money. The good men at the top soon tried to put a stop to it, but it was difficult as some of the gangsters were very high up in the organisation.

On Monday 8 April, Merlyn Rees met with representatives of the UWC. The meeting did not reach an agreement. At that time, the Council was not seen as a serious threat to the Executive. This was due to earlier failures of a smaller organisation, the Loyalist Association of Workers, who had tried to organise previous stoppages and had low turnouts during demonstrations against the Sunningdale Agreement.

On 14 April, Sinn Féin supporters captured Captain Anthony Pollen, a member of the MRF on plain-clothes duty, at a march in Londonderry. Although by then the MRF was becoming known as 14th Intelligence Company, I will continue to use the initials MRF when referring to them. Pollen was seized while photographing a Republican Easter Commemoration Parade. He and a Corporal were challenged by a number of men and decided to run away. The Corporal escaped, but the Captain was caught, beaten, tortured and murdered. Mike and others were furious that there was no back-up for the men on the ground.

On 16 April, a RUC officer, Thomas McCall, was shot and killed by a sniper outside Newtownhamilton RUC barracks, County Armagh. Also on that day, another leading UVF man was killed in an explosion at his house. Ronald Joseph Neill was said by the Army to have been killed while working on the bomb. The UVF issued a statement saying the device had been left there while the man was out. It seems to be substantiated by the sister of the woman who lived in the house. She said that when she answered the door earlier some men claimed they had something for Joseph Neill. When told he wasn't at home, they left a bag in the kitchen. The woman said that, after her sister had left, she heard Neill come in and go into the kitchen. Then she heard him exclaim, 'What the hell is this?' Going towards the kitchen, she saw him leaning over something. A bright flash and two bangs knocked her down and she found herself lying in the hallway. Was that version or the Army's true? We can reflect on their account of the bomb at McGurk's Bar on 4 December 1971.

It appeared to me the three murders of George Hyde, James Hanna and Joseph Neill were somehow connected. I asked questions, but no answer was ever forthcoming. I got the distinct impression there was more to these killings than was being made known. Perhaps it was better to let sleeping dogs lie. Someone might consider you too nosy for your own good.

On 18 April, while Harold Wilson was visiting the Province, he made the following statement: 'There is no alternative to the Sunningdale Agreement.' We could like it or lump it. He didn't know that, with that single message, he was drawing the battle lines. That obnoxious little man was telling us to do as we're told, or else, he would rap our knuckles, using the Army to do it. I genuinely believe he hadn't a clue about the situation or the resolve of the Ulster people. He certainly didn't get any information or feedback from Her Majesty's Intelligence Services; they knew exactly what was in the pipeline for the coming weeks.

Mike was over visiting Billy one night and told him he thought the suggestion put forward about an all-out strike was a sound idea and, if it could be pulled off, it would go down in history as a momentous achievement. Billy wondered how he knew about that. He smiled and said there were some very important men at the top, whose ears they had for directing events in the political arena.

He added that steps were being taken to remove Labour from Government and the more often Harold Wilson was left with egg all over his face, the better and easier it would be to get him voted out at the next election. He said, 'Believe me, there are very important people within the top echelons of power that don't like what's going on with Northern Ireland and will be doing everything within their power to help you to defeat this Executive.'

Billy rushed over to tell me what Mike had said. I was stunned. We were all only pawns in a very large and complex game of chess. We thought our little actions were helping to attain our objective, but they were nothing compared to the overall game, the bigger picture being played in the corridors of power. As we sat and talked over a bottle of Scotch, we grew more disillusioned with the whole scenario. Everybody involved – all Loyalist paramilitaries, the MRF, the Army, the police, even our leaders and politicians – was being used by shadowy figures in the background who were directing and manipulating events to suit any circumstances that arose.

What the fuck was going on? How could it be possible for

someone to talk about bringing a government down? It didn't seem possible when I heard it, but the proof of the pudding is in the eating. The Conservatives replaced Labour in Government in 1979, and Margaret Thatcher became the first woman prime minister of the United Kingdom. Was it a fluke or did these powerful men accomplish their objective? I believe the latter.

On 21 April, James Murphy became the first (probably) Sinn Féin member to be murdered in this campaign. He owned a garage on the Enniskillen–Derrylin Road at Thompson's Bridge, near Kinawley. His name had been passed to Loyalists by the MRF and put on their death list. No organisation claimed responsibility for the murder, which was done deliberately to cause confusion amongst Republicans. When it's not claimed, doubt arises? Was it Loyalists, soldiers, MRF or maybe the Officials? I know there was an OOB in place at the time.

The last person to be murdered that month, on 22 April, was an easy target. Muhammed Khalid, a civilian employed by the Army, was found dead in his car, after being shot by the Provos at Silverbridge, near Crossmaglen, County Armagh.

Three days later, we were summoned to a meeting. We were told to prepare for action in the coming weeks and to make sure all weapons were cleaned and ready. A proposal for an all-out campaign of civil disobedience would be made and then a walk-out of workplaces, leading to a complete closure of all businesses. Strike action would be implemented. People would be given 48 hours to make up their minds up whether they would support the shutdown voluntarily and, if not, they would be given some friendly persuasion. Failing that, they would be given some not so friendly persuasion.

The man who had put forward the advice regarding electricity workers got to his feet again and asked if the power-station workers had been approached for their support. We were told that they were expected to back the strike 100 per cent. But it wasn't a matter of just pulling the plug and switching off the generators. They would have to run them down slowly, in order not to permanently damage them. I asked if the Army be put into the stations and take over the running of the generators, or could the Government bring in power-station workers from England to get them working again? It was thought that the Army would not have the technology to operate the generators, but they would be told in no uncertain terms if there were any outside interference, the generators would be sabotaged, which would cost millions to repair. All possible circumstances had been assessed in detail; we were sure all bases were covered. We were told to report to our battalion commanders for further instructions.

Our cynicism vanished, and the expectation of what was ahead gave us a buzz. Risk is a narcotic. While there is still an element of fear in the back of your mind, it is a good thing; it keeps you on your toes. Those without fear tend to make mistakes.

Our whole team was on a high. None of us knew what was going to happen, but the idea of the whole population, the Loyalists anyway, taking part in industrial action gave us all a sense of adventure. Another aspect was that whatever happened, the Catholic community would suffer with the power cuts and anything else we were prepared to put up with. They would have no choice in the matter; they would have to endure the hardship as well.

Our commanders had ordered weapons to be prepared, so they were either getting geared up in case the Government would use the Army to put us down or they were just being organised to cover all possibilities. The question on all our minds was what actions the Provos would be prepared to take if the strike was a success. If so many Loyalists were on the streets would they be terrified of an all-out assault on their districts? Would they use the strike to step up their campaign on the Security Forces, who were going to be stuck between a rock and a hard place? There were no answers to these questions; it was going to be a case of dealing with each situation as it arose. Plans could be drawn up, but ultimately it was anybody's guess which actions would be necessary to accomplish our goal.

May 1974. No one knew that this month would go down in history. It was a turning-point in our resistance against repression and concessions. It was a time when those two words passed down to all Protestants by our forefathers ruled our thoughts and actions, rang in our ears, echoed in our songs of battles past – *No Surrender*. They had first been uttered in the siege of Londonderry in 1689 by the Reverend George Walker, the governor of Londonderry at the time.

May was two days old when the first killings took place. A bomb attack on the Rose and Crown Bar on the Ormeau Road killed six Catholic men and injured about 18 more. A device left at the front door exploded within seconds of being lit. Five died at the scene, and a sixth man died nine days later. An OOB was in place at the time.

Sad to say, we were disappointed the death toll wasn't as high as that at McGurk's Bar, but a gauntlet was being thrown down to the IRA and the British Government: this was what they could expect if they messed us about.

Also on 2 May, the Irish Government interfered again in the internal affairs of Northern Ireland. They brought a case of torture against the British Government to the European Commission on Human Rights. The case concerned the treatment of internees held in Northern Ireland. Something needed to be done to stop their unwelcome meddling in events outside their jurisdiction.

On Sunday 5 May, the pro-Assembly Unionists held a meeting in Portstewart, a small seaside resort on the north coast. They announced the reformation of the group and that they would be known as the Unionist Party. Yet another Unionist Party, it was becoming a joke. What happened to the old saying, 'United we stand, divided we fall'. All the Unionist parties should have put their differences aside and shown Republicans they were prepared to stand together, no matter what. When Sinn Féin/IRA saw the divisions within Unionism, they were able to cash in on the propaganda side of the conflict.

The Ulster Workers Council released a statement demanding the abolition of the present Assembly and fresh elections for a new Northern Ireland Assembly, to be held as soon as possible.

We were summoned to a meeting and told there would be a debate the next day, Tuesday 14 May, at Stormont, where a motion would be tabled condemning power-sharing and the Council of Ireland. If the motion was defeated, a general strike would be called, to begin on Wednesday 15 May. We had to report to our battalion commanders on Tuesday night for instructions, as it was expected the proposal would be dismissed and thrown out by pro-Agreement parties.

Sure enough, the following day, the motion was defeated by 44 votes to 28. At six o'clock, following the winding up of the day's business, Harry Murray announced to a group of journalists that a general strike was to start the next day. The organisation named as being responsible for the strike was the UWC.

Absurd as it may seem, legislation to legalise the UVF and Sinn Féin was passed at Westminster the same day.

Another piece of good news filtered through the grapevine

to us. Two more IRA men had been caught trying to plant a land mine near Newry, County Down. Shortly after, soldiers had captured Colman Rowntree and Martin McAlinden; both men were shot and killed by the Army in suspicious circumstances.

The initial response to the strike wasn't great. People just didn't know what was expected of them. They were apprehensive about staying off work to support it, only to find that the rest of their workmates had turned up, and the risk of being dismissed for not going to work. Many people did go to work that morning. Once in their places of employment, meetings were called and votes taken on what action should be taken. People started to leave their workplaces in increasing numbers throughout the morning and at lunchtime.

By the end of the day, the port of Larne was, to all intents and purposes, sealed off. With the power cuts being rotated on a four-hourly basis, many firms had to close and send their workers home. Many roads were blocked with hijacked vehicles. In rural towns and villages, trees were cut down to obstruct access in and out. There was no violence from any Loyalist paramilitaries. It was like a cat-and-mouse game; when police moved in and cleared one barricade, and left the scene, ten minutes later the road would be blocked again. They were run ragged with these tactics.

A statement from the UWC was released saying that all essential services would be maintained. A meeting of the leaders of the Loyalist groups advocating the strike with the Minister of State, Stanley Orme, took place at the Northern Ireland Office. They reaffirmed their demands and left again, with nothing gained.

Support for the strike was strengthened on day two, with many of the major engineering companies (who had mainly Protestant workforces) – Harland & Wolfe, the ship builders, Short Brothers & Harland, the aircraft builders, Sirocco Engineering Company and Mackie's Foundry – having to shut down. Although most of the workers did back the strike, the firms just couldn't continue without power; and each power cut was lasting longer than the previous one. Intimidating gangs of Loyalist volunteers were stationed at different spots around each district. No one in their right mind would attempt to pass any of these groups early in the morning. Even if you had to go out for an entirely different reason, many wouldn't, in case they were suspected of going to work.

The strike began to have an effect on the farming community. Perishable dairy produce had to be dumped. It came to the stage where farmers brought their milk and other dairy products to different groups to give out to the people in each area. It was great fun driving around estates in a small flat-topped truck with churns of milk, telling folk to bring containers and dishing out ladles of milk. Men would accompany the truck and call at the houses of pensioners, then fetch and carry the milk for them. It was a magic feeling when women came up to you, saying 'God bless you, son' or 'Oh, you're a life saver' or just plain 'Thank you'. Comments like that made you feel good.

I remember a couple of elderly ladies coming up to a group of us, saying that so-and-so had increased the price of everything in his shop and it had been hard enough to survive on the pension before, without paying his exorbitant prices. We walked round to the man's shop and burst through the door. There were about a dozen customers at the time. The guy turned white when he was confronted with about ten of us in balaclavas, suddenly appearing at the counter. Some of the men went round the shop lifting items off the shelves and brought them up to the counter. We could see where he had stickered higher prices on top of the normal ones.

I asked him, 'Would you mind explaining to us why every-thing in your shop has become more expensive all of a sud-den, since the strike began? To me, it appears you're prepared to milk the situation and take advantage of ordinary, decent, working-class people of this community for your own ends. For a quick buck.

'You see these good people standing around here? They come into your shop probably every day of the week and keep you in business throughout the year. Now their reward for loy-alty to you is being fleeced by you in Ulster's darkest hour. I would describe that as treason, wouldn't you?'

One of the men hit him on the nose and mouth saying, 'I don't think that's very nice.'

The man slammed into the wall behind him, blood running down his face.

The customers just stood there, mesmerised, until one wee woman said, 'That's right, mister. He's taking us on. Look at the price of a tin of beans. It's nearly double what it used to be.'

My mate made to hit the shop-keeper again but I grabbed him by the arm, saying, 'Now, now. We can't hit such an up-standing man of the community, especially since he's just told me that, as a special favour to all his loyal customers, he's pre-pared to have a closing down sale and everything must go for ten pence an item.' Turning to him, I continued, 'Isn't that right?'

At that stage, I felt a bit sorry for him. He was scared shit-less; he had gone as pale as the moon, and blood was pouring from his nose. He nodded his head frantically in agreement. Some of the men were sent out to find as many pensioners and one-parent families as they could and bring them down to the shop, before everyone got wind of it. We left a couple of men there to make sure it was done and told them to empty the storeroom as well. Although I did have a pang of remorse, it passed quickly as I thought of his greed, particularly concerning pensioners.

The UWC released a list of essential services and instructions on how people involved could get a pass to allow them through the barricades. Bars and clubs were told to close. Their reckoning was that if they were allowed to remain open, drunken men coming out onto the streets would be a recipe for trouble.

The strike was discussed at length during Northern Ireland Question Time at Westminster. Paddy Devlin, a member of the SDLP and in charge of Social Services at the time of the strike, threatened to resign over internment. I didn't understand his reasoning; the Secretary of State had already stated that he would phase out internment. Merlyn Rees met with Loyalist leaders and stated categorically that he would under no circumstances sit down and negotiate with the UWC.

During the stoppage everybody claimed they were entitled to unemployment benefit, including people like myself who were paid monthly. Although I wasn't working, through no fault of my own, my wages still continued. When the strike finished, Devlin made the decision to pay everybody's claim without any assessment being carried out. There were thousands and thousands of claims, and it would have taken about five years to sort out.

Republicans had begun to complain bitterly about the operational stance of the Army, in relation to the reopening of roads. It appeared that the Army had no real desire to get bogged down in the quagmire of the political implications taking place. As long as there was no violence being directed at anyone, then the Army's presence wasn't needed. The soldiers had been bearing the brunt of the Provos' onslaught for a number of years, with many casualties; it was only natural they didn't want to engage in open warfare with a community who whole-heartedly supported them.

The same day, a Catholic woman was standing talking to a friend at the corner of Edlingham Street and Stratheden Street, close to the New Lodge Road. A gunman was standing at the corner of Edlingham Street and Duncairn Gardens on the Tiger's Bay side.

A witness said, 'He pulled out his pistol and began shooting from the hip. I heard about six or eight shots and the last one hit Maureen in the head.'

Another witness said, 'There is no doubt she was picked out by the gunman for his target.'

I would like to offer an alternative perspective. Handguns can be very accurate over a short distance, depending on the person who is using it. The distance from the gunman to the target was roughly 200 metres. A man firing from the hip would have had to be Clint Eastwood in *Dirty Harry* to hit a target at that range. If the witnesses were correct in their description of his stance during the shooting, then it was an extremely 'lucky' shot on his part.

The gunman wasn't alone; there were two men involved. One of them was firing from the corner seen by the witnesses and not from the hip. A second gunman was at the opposite corner and wouldn't have been seen by the witnesses. He was in a better position to fire, as he was on the same side as the women and needed only to fire parallel with the street to have a much better chance of hitting anyone from that range. It would seem to me to have been done just for the hell of it. There was no OOB in place, as the Security Forces were being kept busy throughout the six counties. The weapons were back in their safe hiding place within a couple of minutes.

The third day of the strike was the day Billy and me had been waiting for. Plans had been made to give the Irish Republic a taste of what would happen if they tried to interfere in the internal workings of Northern Ireland, during the UWC strike and afterwards.

Mike had informed us a few days before that the Free State was going to be hit with something spectacular that day. He said it had been suggested at one of our meetings in Palace Barracks and the time was now, with the world's press focused on Northern Ireland. We waited all day, listening to every news report.

Then the news broke. The TV programme being broadcast was interrupted – a number of bombs had exploded in the centre of Dublin, and reports indicated there were a number of dead and injured. More details would follow on the six o'clock news bulletin.

We were all in our base at the Farm, on the O'Neill's Road. Only Billy and I knew something was to happen that day, but the excitement felt by all of us in the large clubroom was palpable.

We couldn't wait for the six o'clock news. When the news came on, you could have heard a pin drop. We were glued to the scenes of devastation. Everybody was running about in utter panic. No one had any idea of how many people were dead or injured. Ambulances were flying all over the place; the Fire Brigade were trying to douse the areas with water. The police seemed totally out of their depth.

It brought back memories of Bloody Friday. We had no compassion whatsoever for those people. All we felt was jubilation and anticipation that the Republic's Army would try to invade the North. This was it. Those who wanted to join the South would be forced to go and live there. Fuck them, no one was making them stay here. We honestly thought this was the start of the Protestant backlash the media and politicians kept warning us was just around the corner. All it needed was for someone to say the word and Civil War would have engulfed the country.

Three car bombs had gone off, one in Parnell Street, one in Talbot Street and the third in South Leinster Street. The damning evidence: the MRF was involved, either in working with the teams from Belfast and Mid-Ulster Brigades, or in training the men in making highly accurate timing devices, or supplying explosives and knowledge. The three bombs exploded almost simultaneously and that required the expertise of Technical Army men. The men were able to take their cars over the border without discovery, and then return back again safely. OOBs again, and avoiding the Garda patrols. Although Loyalists carried out the attacks, MRF men were in the background, encouraging and synchronising the mission.

We listened to every news bulletin as the death count rose progressively, and then more news sent us all crazy again. Another bomb had just exploded in Church Square, Monaghan, with more death and destruction heaped upon the innocent people of the South. Now they would understand what it was like for everyone in the North, suffering these sorts of atrocities daily. The bombings had two outcomes: 1) they caused the Irish Government to increase border patrols (troops were brought home from United Nations peacekeeping duties in the Middle East to aid police in the border areas); 2) it sent a clear message to the Dublin Government that, if they tried to force the issue of a United Ireland, the Republic would suffer in the same way we were suffering at the hands of the IRA.

Ever since these bombs detonated there have been many reports on collusion between Military Intelligence and Loyalists to cause this atrocity. As you have just read, we knew something was about to take place in the South that day. What I have just described to you is the truth. I wrote this account long before I had access to the internet, so it's only now that I am able to read reports made to the Irish Government that the explosives were provided by the Army (MRF) to carry out the attacks.

I discovered an article printed in the *Sunday Times* on 12 January 2003. An inquiry held by a retired judge, Mr Justice Henry Barron, had to be repeatedly postponed because the British authorities had been slow to give him vital information. Perhaps this book will finally help to get the truth out of the British Government at last.

The press report went on to say that Loyalists did not have the expertise to produce and prime these bombs in such an efficient manner and must have had help from experts. Yet, experts in all aspects of guerrilla warfare trained Loyalist men. They keep saying that only a small number of men, all British soldiers, had the knowledge and level of access to Loyalist paramilitaries to carry out these bombings. Why do the explosives have to have been captured from the IRA? Could these experts not have shown other men the process the IRA was using to produce the explosives?

The *Sunday Times* article mentions a bomb that exploded at a pub in Silverbridge in County Armagh, close to Crossmaglen, in December 1975. I will outline what I know about this attack in the next chapter, and I can assure you that the man who made the bomb was trained in the art of bomb making and was not a British soldier.

The final body count was 33: the highest number of people killed in one day in all the years of conflict. The number of injured was almost 200.

Reductions in the power supply were causing major problems for many businesses in industry and commerce, and for the domestic population. Distribution of petrol had become difficult and filling stations were only operating during the hours when their district had power. Eventually, the Army took over certain petrol stations in order to keep them open without fear of intimidation. With so many vehicles being hijacked and used as barricades, very few people were driving anywhere.

Postal services were stopped after Royal Mail workers were intimidated. As many Catholics were unemployed they relied on their welfare benefits being posted to them. Stopping the mail was a ploy to prevent payments reaching them. Our attitude was, fuck them; they might as well suffer a bit of hardship like the Loyalists did. After an outcry from Nationalists, the Northern Ireland Executive made alternative arrangements to ensure all people on benefits would receive their money.

William Craig condemned Merlyn Rees for refusing to enter into negotiations with members of the UWC.

Farmers were finding it increasingly difficult to get their produce into shops and many came to us for help. Vans and cars were sent out to farms to collect whatever the farmer wanted, and their containers were then returned. Our distribution system delivered to the most needy, before anybody else. I loved that bit. It made us look good in the minds of the people; we were giving them a helping hand. I asked one of the farmers how he was going to survive. He told me not to worry about it, as he had already spoken to the Department of Agriculture and they had told him to dump the stuff. When the strike was over, he would be able to claim compensation for his loss. The people were getting it for free and the farmer was going to be paid for it anyway, so, rather than dump it, he got us to hand it out to people in need. It was announced that day that milk, dairy produce and bread suppliers would be added to the list of essential services and their vehicles would be allowed free passage in and out of Loyalist districts.

In my view, that's one of the most important reasons why the strike was so successful, because the spirit of the people was strong and everybody was pulling together. I remember communal fires being lit and people cooking for maybe half the street. Everyone had all pitched in with grub and sat around the fire enjoying the banter. Many times, women would call us over and give us a bit of whatever had been cooked. It was beginning to look more and more like one huge street party. There was no way the British Government, or anybody else for that matter, could have beaten the feeling of camaraderie that was growing in strength each day the strike continued. It was a wonderful experience, one that I will never forget.

On 18 May, the fourth day of the strike, the UWC condemned the Secretary of State for Northern Ireland for refusing point-blank to enter into talks with them. They called for a complete stoppage to start at midnight on Sunday 19 May. The Northern Ireland Labour Party tried to get negotiations started, but, as they were another Nationalist Party, no one was interested in talking to them. The Northern Ireland Executive called for the Army to be put into the power stations to keep them going. They were told the Army hadn't the technology to man the stations on their own.

The Executive still felt that the strike could fail, as they were under the impression that many middle-class workers – lawyers, managers, doctors, teachers and self-employed businessmen – didn't want the strike and would continue to work.

Then, one of the worst imaginable things that could have happened happened. Joseph Shaw was shot dead that day. His murder almost sparked a full-scale war between the UVF and the UDA. A volunteer in the UVF, Shaw was standing in a bar in North Belfast with some mates. The bar should have been shut in accordance with UWC orders. A UDA patrol had come across the open bar and entered it to evict the men drinking there. The men in the bar had gathered a large quantity of glasses and bottles together in case such an event arose. Being fairly intoxicated, a battle ensued and the UDA men were ejected from the bar. Having had their pride dented, they returned with a shotgun to frighten the customers, in particular volunteer Shaw and companions. In the mêlée, a shot was discharged that killed Joseph Shaw.

News spread like wildfire and all units of the UVF were put on stand-by. Weapons were collected from arms dumps, and all it needed was the word to go, and there would have been a bloodbath throughout Loyalist areas that night. There were quite a few minor incidents where houses were shot up, and you could cut the tension with a blunt knife. UVF and UDA commanders promptly set up a meeting in a bid to resolve the situation before it went beyond the point of no return.

As we sat in the Loyalist Club on the Shore Road, poised to go into action, I looked around; every table was covered in weapons of all kinds. If the Security Forces had raided the club there would have been carnage.

Two UDA men, whom the UVF said were involved in the murder, were exonerated in a statement from the UDA saying they were nowhere near the scene of the shooting. The commanders agreed the death was a tragic accident and that no further action would take place. They also agreed that ill-feeling existed and violence would in all likelihood erupt. Each commander subsequently issued an order instructing their men that if violence did occur because of the hostility, under no circumstances were any weapons to be used. Fisticuffs would be allowed on a man-to-man basis.

All units stood down. Thank God, it was one thing fighting the enemy, but to become embroiled in a confrontation with fellow Loyalists was something entirely different. It would be like doing the IRA's work for them.

There were a number of fights involving the two UDA men and UVF personnel in which the two UDA men proved the better each time. Because they could hold their own, they were earmarked for death when the opportunity arose. Some time later, the two men were drinking in the Alexander Bar on York Road, when two masked and armed UVF men walked in and shot them both dead. There were no recriminations over the murders. I think it had been accepted it was inevitable it was going to happen. The two men should have quit while they were ahead and left the country.

Sunday 19 May saw the fifth day of the strike – a relatively quiet day. We used it to get some well earned sleep, as we had been kipping down in the club at night, before going out on patrols through the estates every couple of hours. Merlyn Rees declared a State of Emergency under Section 40 of the Northern Ireland Constitution Act of 1973. He then flew to Chequers for talks on the worsening situation. The United Ulster Unionists met and jumped on the bandwagon. They didn't get involved until they were sure the strike was going to be a success. A statement was issued by them announcing they were giving total commitment and support to the UWC.

Reports were coming in from many shops that people were panic-buying and stocking up on essential items. It was getting so bad the UWC called off its appeal for an all-out stoppage at midnight.

Monday 20 May was the sixth day of the stoppage and action was stepped up a couple of gears. We had all stayed at the club on Sunday night and were awakened at 6 a.m. We headed to the Alpha, the UDA's meeting place, to take part in a joint operation to seal off all roads in the area with barricades. Only this time it was a bit more serious; all the vehicles stolen or hijacked were set alight. We had gone down to the Shore Road at the bottom of Rathcoole, where there was a used-car sales compound. The padlock was easily snapped off. Cars were pushed out from the compound and the road was blocked. Just as we were getting ready to torch the barricade, a car came round the bend from the direction of the city centre. The passenger saw what was happening and pulled into the side.

The road was blocked from footpath to footpath, jammed solid with cars. One of the lads waved at the guy to come on up, and I watched in surprise as he started towards us. Picture the scene facing this man. The road was totally impassable, about 50 men were standing with balaclavas covering their faces and he drove up to the barricade. Anyone with half a brain would have disappeared in a cloud of smoke from their burning tyres.

He pulled up in front of us and he was even more naïve than I thought; as the lad that had waved him forward bent down to talk to him, he rolled his window down. The young lad asked him where he was going and he said he was going home to Rush Park. To my amazement, he added that he was coming from work.

Three or four men yanked the driver's door open and hauled him from the car, yelling in his face, 'Fucking *work*! Don't you fucking know there's a fucking *strike* on?'

The man was in his fifties, shaking like a leaf and getting paler by the second. He stammered nervously, 'I'm sorry, I didn't know.'

I just stood there shaking my head. Why on earth did he drive up to the barricade in the first place? The road was blocked and masked men were milling around. More importantly, what possessed him to say he was returning from work? All he had to say was that he'd received a phone call from his elderly mother, who was feeling ill, and he was rushing down to see her, or some other excuse like that, and we would have cleared a passage through the barricade for him.

I jumped into the car and drove it straight into the cars across the road, about ten metres away, with very little speed. I then got out of the car and shouted, 'Right, torch those cars,' pointing to the ones that had already been doused with petrol. The man had been given a kick in the arse and sent back the way he came. I shouted loud enough for him to hear, 'OK, lads, move it quickly. We have other roads to block, before the peelers are alerted.'

Petrol bombs were lit and thrown into a couple of the cars across the road. As the flames took hold, we made our way back through the estate towards the Doagh Road.

I had been trying to help the man. His car was only slightly damaged; the keys were still in the ignition; he had heard me shouting we were leaving. All he had to do was run back to the car, put it in reverse and get the hell out of there. We had been walking for about five minutes when the first of the petrol tanks in the cars exploded, so he had time to recover the car. I never knew if he did or not.

During the sixth day, the worst incident was a Loyalist abduction of a Catholic man. His body was later found at the side of the road at Shaw's Bridge, South Belfast.

There was a co-ordinated operation across the Province and many roads were impassable. I remember watching news reports and being amazed at the number of places that were blocked. The mid-Ulster Brigade had brought Portadown to a standstill. Lorries across the roads were causing congestion on the M1 motorway. More trees had been felled and many villages were completely sealed.

Electricity levels were now down to about 33 per cent of normal supplies. The telephone system was under pressure and the public had been advised to use their phones only in an emergency.

Another 500 troops were arriving in the Province to help with the state of affairs. *The Newsletter*, a Protestant morning newspaper, carried an advertisement inserted by Unionist politicians urging people to come out in full support of the strike.

Stanley Orme reaffirmed the Government's stance of not negotiating with the UWC. The country was slowly grinding to a halt. More importantly, the Ulster people were beginning to throw their weight behind the actions taking place on the ground.

On the seventh day of the strike, everything was going better than expected. The Trade Union Council, headed by General Secretary Len Murray, tried to lead a back-to-work march to the Belfast shipyard and other industries in East Belfast. Other trade union officials backed it, but only 100–200 people turned up. RUC officers and soldiers protected the marchers. Even with this protection, an intimidating crowd still managed to attack some of the men trying to return to work. A revised list of emergency services was released by the UWC, which outlined who would be allowed through the barricades. New opening hours for shops were also announced.

Then, our infamous Prime Minister launched into a tirade of condemnation: '[The strike] was a sectarian strike, being done for sectarian purposes, having no relation to this century, but only to the 17th century.'

When everyone heard that, it was greeted with the contempt it deserved. We could see he was rattled.

The eighth day of the strike saw many roads still barricaded. As the Security Forces cleared one road and moved off to clear

another one, we just hid until they were gone, then went out
and sealed them off again. At no time did we confront them
or give them a reason to try any heavy-handed tactics, so the
British Government couldn't order the soldiers to quell the uprising with force. No force was being used against them. There
was an attempt by the Northern Ireland Executive to placate
and the UWC by watering down the Sunningdale Agreement.
They offered to postpone specified elements of the Agreement
until 1977 and to decrease the size of the Council of Ireland.

Loyalist paramilitary leaders rejected the offer immediately. It
showed us that the Executive were coming under pressure, and
it gave everyone a sense that victory was close. TV and radio
interviews with members of the public indicated 99 per cent
of the ordinary folk backed the strike and were determined
to continue to the bitter end. I remember watching an elderly
lady sitting beside a fire, while other women were cooking a
meal for a crowd of people standing around. She was asked if
she minded the hardship everybody was suffering because of
the strike.

Her reply has stuck in my mind ever since. 'Hardship? You've
got to be joking. I haven't enjoyed myself like this for years. Do
you see all these people standing round here? Well, the strike
has brought whole communities together. We all muck in and
help whoever needs help. No one will go hungry or have to do
without, the men are seeing to that. I hope it never ends.'

The reporter was visibly gobsmacked and turned to the
camera saying, 'There you have it. Instead of the stoppage causing the resolve of the people to wane, it is having the opposite
effect. The determination to see it through to the end is actually strengthening.'

A huge cheer went up from all of us sitting in the club.
When we heard words like that, it gave us a lift. Your spirits

rose and you could sense the Loyalist population becoming more and more steadfast, no matter how long it took. The British Government emphasised its intransigence by not meeting or negotiating with the leaders of the UWC. John Hume, a member of the SDLP, who was Minister of Commerce in the Executive, mooted a 'fuel oil plan', as supplies of petrol were becoming depleted.

Thursday 23 May, the ninth day of the strike. There was one place in our area of operations, the Michelin tyre factory at Mallusk, on the fringe of Glengormly, which remained open. The early shift was just finishing that afternoon when about 200 of us arrived at the gate. The workers had to pass through the crowd outside the gate, and they came under a lot of verbal abuse. If any of them dared to answer back they received a few digs in the head or a couple of kicks round the groin. Suddenly, a shout rang out, 'Fuck off, you bastards.' Then another one, 'That's that fucker from Bawnmore.' (Bawnmore was a Republican district, just off the Shore Road, close to the Rathcoole Estate.)

The man who had shouted was knocked to the ground, and those beside him started kicking the shit out of him. A guy standing on top of the entrance gate pillar jumped onto this guy's head, knocking him out. Then half a dozen men dragged him across the road to a ditch; I thought they were going to nut him (shoot him in the head), but they eventually left him lying there. He was a very lucky man to escape with his life.

Some schools had tried to remain open, mostly Catholic ones; the kids were enjoying the extra holidays and were in no hurry to return. Reports said that GCE examinations were being hit by the lack of attendance at schools. Gerry Fitt, leader of the SDLP and Deputy Chief Executive, demanded the British Government send soldiers into the power stations and oil refineries. Once again Northern Ireland Question Time in the House of Commons was dominated by the strike. Merlyn Rees told the Prime Minister that British soldiers would be needed to implement the fuel oil plan being drawn up by John Hume.

That evening, more pressure was brought to bear when Loyalists set fire to the barricades. People with old bangers – and there were quite a lot in those days as no MOT certificates were required – would contact us and arrange for their cars to be taken away and burned at a barricade. They planned to claim compensation after the strike was over and hopefully receive more than the car was worth. Saracen Armoured Cars were used to punch a way through these barriers, leaving behind a gap for anyone who wanted to take a chance. However, they risked being hijacked or getting a puncture, which would make them an easy target for squads of men patrolling the district.

On Friday 24 May, the tenth day of the strike, things began to happen on the political front. Talks were held at Chequers between Harold Wilson, Merlyn Rees, Brian Faulkner, Gerry Fitt and Oliver Napier (Alliance Party, Legal Minister and head of the Office of Law Reform in the Executive). After many hours, the best they could offer was a brief statement about there being no negotiations with those who operated outside constitutional politics. All that talking and they came out with the same bullshit they had been preaching since the strike began. Did Harold Wilson not sit and talk with the IRA when he was Opposition Leader? Were these murderers operating 'inside constitutional politics'?

Later that day, the British Cabinet agreed that Merlyn Rees could put soldiers into the power stations, if he deemed it necessary. Senior Army officers disagreed, fearing that a comparatively peaceful protest might escalate into a bloodbath, with civilian deaths or injuries. This was similar to the stance taken by British officers in 1912, when they refused to fight the loyal subjects of Ulster to implement the Home Rule Bill.

There had been two murders in the Province during the strike. Unfortunately, that number was to double on Saturday night. Reports had reached us that a lot of pubs and businesses were remaining open in and around Ballymena. A squad of men from the two Loyalist organisations in Rathcoole were sent out to persuade them it would be in their best interests to close. After wrecking three bars in Ballymena, they came across the Wayside Inn at Tannaghmore, County Antrim, owned by two Catholic brothers. They proceeded to smash up the pub. As they were leaving, the brothers caught one of the raiders and were giving him a good hiding. One of the squad spotted what was happening, drew his legal weapon – he was in the UDR – and opened fire, hitting one brother three times and the other twice at close range. Both men died from their wounds.

As the men drove off towards the village of Doagh they didn't spot a police car following them. When they eventually noticed it, bottles, hoods and cudgels were seen by the police officers being thrown from one of the minibuses. A roadblock was set up and 30 men were detained. One of our team was present and charged with causing criminal damage. He told us about what happened at the roadblock.

The police had lined everyone up to be searched had taken his gloves from him.

The cop had walked away about ten paces before returning and saying, 'These are your gloves, aren't they?'

Quick as lightning, he looked at the gloves and replied, 'No, sorry. I've never seen them before in my life.'

The cop looked a bit peeved before shouting, 'I'm only after taking them from you. Now are these your gloves?'

This guy, who was as cool as a cucumber, said, 'I've already told you they're not mine. I don't own any gloves, never mind those ones. They must be someone else's.'

The policeman walked away in disgust.

Billy had a word with Mike about the guy's predicament. This was a test of what Mike had told us at the start; as long as you don't plead guilty, he might be able to help. A week later we were all in Crusader's Football Club having a drink, when in walks the mate.

We all asked, 'How in hell did you get out?'

He replied, 'I don't know. They just came to me and told me to get my stuff – I was free to go, all charges had been dropped. So here I am.'

Billy and I were flabbergasted. This seemed to prove the MRF held sway over the police and/or the Director of Public Prosecutions. Definitive proof came some time later, and it wasn't just the RUC and the DPP; its power went as high as it possibly could.

On 25 May, the 11th day of the strike, Harold Wilson made a speech on BBC television and radio at 10.15 p.m. – the most dim-witted and ill-advised illustration speech ever made by any Prime Minister. It became a nationwide joke amongst the Protestant population. He referred to the UWC and their supporters as 'spongers' – at that stage, 90 per cent of the Protestant population! I couldn't understand his rationale. This was a workers' strike, but he was implying very few of us worked and drew dole money; that we were reliant on the British Government subsidising us so heavily we were 'sponging' off the British tax-payer.

Many people took to wearing small pieces of sponge on their lapels. The accusation was an insult to us all.

During that night a Catholic man was picked up and brutally

murdered. He was known as a harmless wino and he hung about the city centre with others of his ilk. He was very drunk and must have stumbled into a Loyalist district by mistake. He was spotted almost immediately, taken away and plied with more drink. When he was virtually unconscious, he was brought to Glencairn where he was beaten to death with stones.

Sunday 26 May, the twelfth day of the strike. The UWC announced that support and offers of help were increasing daily, and their system of permits was working efficiently to maintain essential services. The Army raided Protestant areas and detained 30 men. Areas looked like ghost towns with very little traffic on the roads. People took the time to rest. We did the same. Children played around the burnt-out cars and barricades.

Throughout the Troubles, scrap metal merchants cashed in on the street violence. As dawn broke, they would be out scouring the areas that had seen disturbances for wrecked cars, which they would load onto their lorries. Often the police would inform a person their stolen or hijacked car was at such and such a place, only for the owner to arrive to find it gone and have to drive round the various scrap dealers to locate it, so that they could claim the insurance money.

On Monday 27 May, the 13th day of the strike, there was increased activity on the political front and on the ground. Gas suppliers, who had previously been able to maintain a reasonable service, announced that Belfast and rural areas were going to be hit hard by a drop in the pressure. They advised all customers to turn off their gas at the mains. The Army moved into 21 petrol stations all over the country. Anyone who required petrol for essential services could apply to the Ministry of Commerce for permits and use them at those 21 stations.

The UWC hit back, saying that the British Army would have to start supplying all essential services, including the delivery of milk and bread throughout the six counties. They also called on people who worked in essential services to stop maintaining these amenities. The jewel in the crown was kept to the last. They announced that the main power station at Ballylumford, at Islandmagee, would shut down completely at midnight.

This was the news we had been waiting for, since the beginning of the strike. Without power nothing could open, no one could work. The end was in sight.

On the 14th day of the strike, 28 May, victory was ours. For two weeks the Protestant population had held steadfast. Chief Executive Brian Faulkner asked Merlyn Rees to meet with the leaders of the UWC. Rees refused to do so and Faulkner's Unionist Ministers resigned with him. This marked the end of the Northern Ireland Executive and the Assembly.

A large demonstration, organised beforehand, was taking place in the grounds of Stormont. Farmers and their tractors had blocked the entrance to the Parliament buildings and much of the Upper Newtownards Road. It wasn't long before news of the resignations and the collapse of the Executive filtered through to the masses gathered at Stormont.

Huge cheers rang out and there was jubilation in Loyalist districts across the country. Then something occurred that made me see red. Some of the politicians who had supported the strike came out onto a small balcony and the crowd cheered them, waving their Ulster flags and roaring their approval of what was being said. Always a shrewd politician, Brian Faulkner suddenly came into view. He was allowed to speak and waffled on about how he had listened to the voice of the people and come to the decision, for the good of the country, to resign. The crowd actually cheered, instead of lynching him – this treacherous man who was quite prepared to send us up the proverbial river without a paddle.

I felt frustrated at the failure of our leaders to capitalise on the support of the whole Loyalist population. The purpose of the strike was to bring down the Sunningdale Agreement, and it had done so magnificently, but we had had the British Government on the run and should have upped our demands for *everything* we sought – to return the running of our country to a democratically elected parliament and the removal of direct rule.

On Wednesday 29 May, a general return to work was announced by the UWC. The strike was officially over. The following day, the Northern Ireland Assembly was suspended for four months. On 31 May, Merlyn Rees fired the first shot across the Loyalists' bows. He said: 'The Ulster Workers Council strike has demonstrated a rise in "Ulster Nationalism" which would be taken into account by the Westminster Government.'

During the strike, the IRA campaign was suspended. On 2 May, they had killed a UDR woman; on 10 May, they had killed two RUC men; and, of course, their mistake on 31 August

Loyalists were responsible for 49 deaths throughout May, including the 33 killed in the Republic of Ireland bombings. While the strike was taking place, the Provos had taken a back seat to watch the events unfold. If they had continued their campaign, the consequences would have been devastating, but it would have given Harold Wilson's Government an excuse to pull out of Northern Ireland. The Provos would have been one step closer to their United Ireland.

There comes a time when the pressure of what you're doing begins to take effect. Some felt it within days; others took a bit longer, months or years. It depended on your ability to sublimate your conscience, your belief of what is right and what is wrong. Then there was a tiny majority who were different; who were capable of killing time and time again, without remorse: for example, Lenny 'The Little General' Murphy, Dominic

'Mad Dog' McGlinchey, Robin 'The Jackal' Jackson and Billy 'King Rat'Wright. Others would break down; their self-image and view of other human beings inalterably changed. Some cursed God.

We lived in a culture of pain and death. It was part of the norm, part of our souls. It was only a matter of time before we produced someone who saw the Ulster cause as an altar on which to slaughter all Catholics. Tragically, the Loyalist community didn't produce just one, we helped spawn several, from within a small population.

Lenny Murphy had a special effect on people. There was an aura of potential violence around him at all times. It was like an odour, a message to others' subconscious. As Professor Oppenheimer said after the first atomic bomb test in 1945: 'I have become death, the destroyer of worlds.' And, as the Bhagavad-Gita says, 'I have become death.' Maybe that's what he was – pure Death.

Although you knew that you were pretty certain to escape, when you went out on a mission, there was still an enormous amount of mental stress. Every operation weighed on your mind.

It emerged later to what degree the Military and the Government were working to achieve 'an acceptable level of violence'. They were prepared to tolerate a level of killing and bombing within reason. If they could reduce the number of soldiers being sent home in boxes, then anyone else who happened to die . . . well, that was tolerable. As long as it was Loyalists killing Catholics or vice versa, then the British public wouldn't object too much to what was going on in Northern Ireland.

Each man had his own way to relieve the tension after an operation. Men from other teams would often arrive at a certain bar or club and surround themselves with other members, slapping their backs and getting them drink and having a good laugh. You might describe it as a need for a bit of hero worship from mates. Maybe it helped to reduce the gnawing guilt and justify your actions. But the social situation also left you in a position of vulnerability, as you could be eavesdropped or observed by informers. These touts weren't necessarily connected to any paramilitary group; they might be an alcoholic, in fact, anybody who needed a few quid, picked up the gist of what had happened and was willing to contact the police and sell information.

When I was arrested and held in a RUC station, I remember a detective arriving from York Road, RUC Barracks (I was from their area). After a couple of questions, which I had replied in the negative, he urged me to come clean as all he needed to do was go down York Road, pay a couple of pounds and he could find out what I had for breakfast.

After we had completed a job, it was straight to one of our houses where clothes went into the washing machine, a shower or bath was take and bottles of drink were opened. We then proceeded to get pissed out of our minds listening to music; the louder, the better. It blasted the tension and tremors out of your body. Temporarily, anyway. Heavy rock was my choice, head-banging stuff. I just lay back and absorbed it, the beat pushing everything else out. Alcohol and nicotine were my way of coping. Drugs were taboo in 1970s Belfast. In today's organisations they not only allow you to use narcotics, they're up to their neck in supplying them.

Maire Drumm, Vice President of Sinn Féin, announced that they were prepared to meet with leaders of the UWC. Andy Tyrie, Leader of the UDA, had previously said he wanted a dialogue with the Republicans. There were a number of common issues between the two groups, for example, internment and prisoners. The Government released a White Paper which set out plans to hold elections for a Constitutional Convention where a political settlement to the Northern Ireland conflict would be discussed. Contained within the new Paper were many elements present in the old Sunningdale Agreement, including power-sharing and a provision for an Irish dimension. The talks took place in Oxford on 6 July, attended by members of the dismantled Executive together with Northern Ireland Office Ministers and Harry Murray, Chairman of the UWC. On 9 July, Merlyn Rees announced that internment would be gradually phased out.

On the night of 11 July and into the early morning, the usual festivities took place throughout the Province. John Beattie, a UDA man, was watching a bonfire burning itself out when shots were heard off Duncairn Gardens. He was hit and died at the scene. That same night, a young Catholic man who meant no harm had gone out to watch the fires in Bangor, County Down. Bangor is a quiet seaside town and, although there were a few incidents in the town, they were few and far between. Unfortunately, he was spotted by someone who knew he was Catholic. He was picked up and taken to Castle grounds, where he was shot and killed by Loyalists.

On 20 July, a Catholic man who lived in Strabane, County Tyrone, was the victim of another attempt to make out an IRA punishment had gone wrong. The man was dragged from his bed into his back garden, then hit on the head with a crowbar. He died on the spot where he fell. The two Republican groups both denied involvement. An OOB was in place at the time.

On 24 July, a Catholic man, a Nationalist councillor on Omagh District Council, went missing after working at the

Corner Bar in Trillick, County Fermanagh. Bloodstains, shirt buttons and empty cartridge cases were found near his home. A search of the area revealed nothing. On 10 August, his body was found floating in Lough Erne. The man had become a thorn in the flesh; he had been an active member of the civil rights movement and asked awkward questions. His name had been on the MRF's list.

The same day, Ann Ogilby went missing. Her murder must rate as one of the most sickening and cowardly murders to take place during the Troubles. Men would have queued up to kill the perpetrators. No matter how hard-hearted we had become, every so often a certain killing would make us question our sanity.

It was at this point I lost my faith in any kind or merciful God.

Ann Ogilby, a Protestant single mother originally from Sion Mills, had been living in a YWCA hostel on the Malone Road. The motive for her murder was never clear. She had been picked up and taken to a UDA club in Sandy Row, along with her six-year-old daughter. The woman was taken into a room, where about a dozen women were waiting. Her daughter was held in an adjoining room. The women tied her to a chair and beat her with a variety of weapons, including a large brick. During this frenzied attack, they stopped for a cigarette break before continuing their onslaught. Meanwhile, her daughter was banging on the door, screaming for her mother. Paying no attention to the girl's pleas, they battered Ann Ogilby until she was dead.

This notorious incident lost the UDA much of their support within the Protestant community. I knew men who walked away from the organisation there and then, because they felt so disgusted by that murder. The repercussions of this atrocity reverberated throughout the whole nation and were universally condemned. Eleven women and one man received jail sentences for their part in the act.

On 19 September, Patrick McGreevy was shot and killed as he stood outside a café in Clifton Street near Carlisle Circus. The gunman knew his target – a photograph had been given to the MRF – and was aware he belonged to the Fianna na Eireann. At the time of the shooting, a group of teenagers were standing near McGreevy when the gunman struck. He fired six shots at the target. This was not a random shooting. Because of the accuracy, the original claim was that the IRA shot him for passing information to the RUC. They denied it and the effort to provoke another feud between the Republican groups failed. An OOB was in place at the time.

Due to bombings in Guildford in early October, Loyalists encouraged by the MRF stepped up their attacks. On 8 October, Loyalists attacked workmen arriving at the Belfast City Hospital, acting on information provided by the MRF. A gunman opened up with a long burst of automatic fire from a Sterling submachine-gun. Two Catholic men were hit and taken to hospital; one man recovered, the other died on Christmas Eve. His mother-in-law died of a heart attack a few days before him, when she was told he wasn't going to survive. An OOB was in place at the time.

On 10 October, a Catholic man was shot dead while visiting a woman friend at her house in the mainly Protestant Ballyduff estate in Newtownabbey. He was from Ardoyne but information of his movements and whom he visited in the estate had been passed to Loyalists. Two men pushed past the woman as she answered the door, went straight into the living room and shot him three times. This murder was significant, as it was one of the first murders claimed by the Protestant Action Force

(PAF), which we had been told to use as a cover name for the UVF. An OOB was in place at the time.

The next day, a talented Catholic footballer was shot dead, the second killing in two days claimed by the PAF. The gunman had waited for him coming down Brougham Street, close to the Tiger's Bay district, on his way to work at 8 a.m. He was well known to Loyalists and considered an easy target. An OOB was in place at the time.

The following day, a relative of Gerry Adams was abducted from the Cliftonville Road. After being trailed into a car, he was taken away for questioning. His badly beaten body was found near the quarry where Paddy Wilson and his friend had been discovered. He had six gunshot wounds. The man had been under surveillance by the MRF. He had become the fourth Catholic to die in as many days. An OOB was in place at the time.

A few hours later, IRA gunmen burst into a shop not far from where the young man's body was found. They shot two leading Loyalists; one had been a former UDA Chairman and the other a former Chairman of the Loyalist Association of Workers. Both men lived to talk about it.

The Ministry of Defence announced that the names of British soldiers who died during the troubles would not be added to war memorials, as 'the conflict in Northern Ireland was not classified as a war situation'. This was seen as a terrible snub to all the men and women who had made the ultimate sacrifice for Queen and Country. We still felt very proud of our soldiers, thrown in at the deep end to sink or swim. They were sent to Northern Ireland like lambs to the slaughter, with no training or experience in guerrilla warfare.

On 9 November, two Catholic men were shot dead in a garage on the Seven Mile Straight near Aldergrove Airport. A colleague had heard a man say, 'This is a hold-up. Kneel down.' One man was shot in the head and the second man, who tried to run away, was hit ten times with a burst of Sterling Machine-gun fire. An OOB was in place at the time.

On 20 December 1974, the IRA announced that a ceasefire would take place at midnight on 22 December to last until midnight on 2 January 1975. The Protestant population wondered what was happening. We felt there had to be something else going on. Then, a man in charge of security at Harrods issued a challenge to the bombers, declaring that there was no way they would be able to plant a bomb in his shop. It was like waving a red flag at a bull.

We held our breath. It would be satisfying to end the conflict, but the fundamental question was 'Peace at what price?' After what our victory in the workers' strike, which had left the Labour Government with egg all over its face, they would be out for revenge. We would need to watch events closely, for any sign of betrayal.

By the end of 1974, my country was deeply entrenched in hate and suspicion. Where had that innocent, peaceful man I had been gone? I had become skilled in death and destruction, revelling in others' demise. Not even animals behaved this way.

1974 Statistics

Deaths by year and status		*Responsibility for deaths*	
Protestant civilians	51	Republicans	150
Catholic civilians	123	Loyalists	131
RUC	12	Army	15
RUC/R	3	RUC/RUC/R	2
UDR/RIR	7	UDR/RIR	0
Army	45	Others	6
Republicans	24		
Loyalists	6		
Others	33		
TOTAL	304		
Bombs	1,113		
Shootings	3,206		
Incendiary bombs	270		

1975 APPREHENDED

THE NEW YEAR started with more worrying news. On 2 January, the IRA proclaimed they were extending the ceasefire until 17 January. Alarm bells were ringing; bells the size of Big Ben. At Westminster, secret talks between Northern Ireland Office representatives and members of the PIRA led to a truce between the IRA and the Security Forces, for as long as the talks continued.

Mike kept us informed of developments, assuring us that the MRF and other senior Intelligence officers were opposed to what was taking place behind closed doors. Billy then passed the information to those in charge. (Mike told us at a later date that the room being used for these talks was bugged: everything discussed was taped, so anything that might threaten the position of Northern Ireland within the United Kingdom could be sabotaged immediately. It was good to hear those words of defiance from a man who had never let us down in the past.

On 7 January, Ian Paisley led a delegation from the DUP to a meeting with Merlyn Rees. The meeting ended in a shambles, with the DUP walking out because of arguments about the secret talks with Government officials and the IRA. We knew there was something in the air when Rees wouldn't give the Big Man straight answers. We prepared ourselves for any scenario that would come out of these negotiations.

Then, on January 9/10, Loyalists carried out a successful

operation in conjunction with Robert Nairac, one of the most courageous undercover agents within Military Intelligence. John Francis Green was described in death notices as an IRA staff captain. The Lurgan man was in the North Armagh second battalion of the Provisionals. He became an icon within the ranks of the IRA after pulling off a sensational escape from Long Kesh. His brother, who was a priest, went to the prison to say Mass. He was overpowered by men and tied up, and his brother walked nonchalantly out of prison, wearing his brother's clothes. There has been much speculation over the years about whether or not Military Intelligence played any part in Green's death.

Who supplied the intelligence to the Loyalists about where he was living? If he had lived somewhere in the North, there would have been a number of ways his address could have been obtained. Since it was in the Republic, it would have been impossible for Loyalist gunmen to ascertain in which isolated house he stayed – the house belonged to an elderly Republican sympathiser – without external help. The information must have come from an intelligence agency, and the MRF had the capability and the means to collect this type information.

I shall relate what Mike told us. Captain Robert Nairac visited Palace Barracks on a Saturday before Christmas 1974 and congratulated the men assembled there on the campaign we were waging. The message was getting across to the Catholic community and, more importantly, to the hierarchy of the Catholic Church, who had helped the Republicans arm themselves. He stressed the need to continue our onslaught as hard as possible in the coming months and concluded with encouraging news that people were in place within the IRA to provide them with high-grade operational data about where top men were staying. It was hoped that some important people would be targeted in the not too distant future.

Mike filled us in on some more details after the New Year. He said that Nairac had done a 'reccie' (reconnaissance mission) across the border and found out where John Francis Green was living. He was in the process of organising a team to cross the border and assassinate him, adding that he might take them over himself or simple provide them with a map of the area and directions to the house. The team would be from the Mid-Ulster area and the operation would take place very soon. It was never confirmed that Nairac did in fact take them over, but the general feeling amongst the MRF was that he did.

This seems to be confirmed in a book by Nicky Curtis, *Faith and Duty*. Curtis was a regular soldier who had done a number of tours in Northern Ireland, before becoming involved in undercover work, and he states that he saw the Captain take two men across the border on the night Green was killed, and that he brought them back again. He thought the two men were SAS soldiers but, they were loyalists.

Robert Nairac was a dark-haired, good-looking guy with an air of confidence about him. His nose gave the impression he had done a bit of boxing in his time. While a bit arrogant, he was very much a man at ease with his own abilities. He believed passionately that to weaken the IRA they needed to hit where it hurt by going after them into their strongholds and eliminating them. Nairac was like a modern-day Lawrence of Arabia to me. His speciality was deep-cover penetration, as he was highly skilled at mixing with people, adopting different disguises and talking in several Irish dialects to pass himself off as a local, whilst gathering information. This was an extremely dangerous game to play; one slip could blow your cover and lead to capture, torture and death.

On 16 January, negotiations broke down and the IRA announced their ceasefire would end from midnight. Relief flooded through us; the status quo was resumed for the time being. Merlyn Rees said he would not be influenced by opinions backed up by the bomb and the gun.

Only three days later, a seven-year-old Catholic boy, Patrick Toner, was killed by a booby-trap bomb meant for soldiers, which detonated in a field close to his home in Forkhill, County Armagh. The next day, the Army shot dead IRA man Kevin Coen while he was attempting to hijack a bus in Kinawley, County Fermanagh.

There were a number of bomb attacks in and around Belfast on 21 January, and two members of the Provos, John Kelly and John Stone, died when the device they were transporting exploded prematurely while they were driving along Victoria Street.

A world-weary fatigue swept over me. I couldn't seem to think clearly. Fear was creeping up on me – a gradually mounting terror of what I would become if this cycle of violence went on for much longer. Everything seemed to be slipping away from me: job security, self-confidence and sanity.

On 30 January, the Gardiner Report was published. The report had been commissioned to examine strategies to deal with terrorism within the perspectives of human rights and civil liberties. It recommended that Special Category status for paramilitary prisoners should be ended and detention without trial should be held in reserve, under the control of the Secretary of State for Northern Ireland.

Signs of a sell-out and deals done with Sinn Féin/IRA behind Protestants' backs came to light in February. Loyalist killings were on the increase and a feud started between members of OIRA and INLA, in which we took great pleasure.

On 5 February, the British Government issued a discussion paper on power-sharing for the Province. The paper was called *The Government of Northern Ireland: A Society Divided.* They must have been living on a different planet. Did they not understand there had been a strike in May 1974 supported by practically every Protestant in Ulster *against* a power-sharing Government? On the same day, Merlyn Rees ominously revealed that plans were in place to build new accommodation blocks in the Maze Prison (previously Long Kesh and still referred to as that) –when the building of a new prison at Maghaberry was completed. It implied the Government was under the impression that the Troubles weren't going to be over for a long time; why else go to all this expense?

Around this time an internal IRA leadership feud emerged between Seamus Twoomey and the much younger Gerry Adams.

When it got too hot for the men to stay in A-Wing, an incident was fabricated which led to the Provos being locked up and the two men being taken into protective custody. At their trial they were found not guilty – a foregone conclusion.

After the men were acquitted and released, the leadership of the IRA in Crumlin Road Prison sent word out for the two young men to be executed. The old leadership, still in charge at this point, refused, declaring that the confessions had been forced out of them. Heatherington was killed some time after, as was the other young lad.

The killing started in early February with a Catholic woman in Larne. On 8 February, a Catholic man was killed when gunmen called at his house in Ligoniel. After answering a knock at his door, he was shot once and fell backwards into the hall. The gunman stepped over him and fired more bullets into him. In an attempt to stop him, his wife was shot and wounded. The man was an ex-Republican internee and had been detained in Long Kesh; another case of inside information being passed to MRF. There was an OOB in place at the time.

On 9 February, two Catholics lads were shot and killed as they left St Bride's Chapel, close to the Malone Road. The gunmen walked calmly towards the two 18-year-old students who were the first out of the chapel and fired a number of times. A man ran at the gunmen before the gun could be re-aimed properly and hit one of them a blow that deflected the bullet. There was a UDR barracks close by, but an OOB was in place at the time and they escaped easily.

On the same day, came the bombshell that we were dreading. The IRA issued a statement saying that it was re-establishing its ceasefire for an indeterminate period, from 6 p.m. on 10 February. We were all convinced: Ulster was about to be sold out. After we had made a mockery of the Labour Government's policies and defeated them, we were sure they would jump at the chance to stab us in the back.

In the leadership challenge the old Brigade would seem to have won; they had called the ceasefire. In fact many in the IRA were opposed to the ceasefire. In *The Provisional IRA* by Eamonn Mallie, the Provos admitted that the ceasefire was their darkest hour, bringing it very close to 'collapse and defeat'. The MRF, with all its units up and running, almost achieved their objective of 'the eradication of the IRA'.

On 10 February, a Catholic man was killed while sweeping the streets near his home on the Ormeau Road. He was shot a number of times. An OOB was in place at the time.

That same day, two Catholic men were enjoying a drink in Hayden's Bar, near Pomeroy, County Tyrone. A gunman burst into the bar and sprayed it with Sterling submachine-gun fire, killing the two men. These two murders brought the number of Catholics murdered in the Dungannon/Pomeroy area to 11. An OOB was in place at the time.

As planned, the IRA ceasefire began. The British Government and the Northern Ireland Office vehemently refuted claims that there had been any arrangement or deal done with Sinn Féin/IRA. Of course, no one believed a word of it. We were used to their treachery. Sometimes I wondered if our fervent aspirations to remain part of the United Kingdom were worth the effort. When I saw the way the Loyalist population had been treated, I wondered if an independent Ulster might actually be worse than what we had.

On 11 February, so much for their ceasefire. A Protestant milkman, Christopher Mein, was shot dead by the IRA while on his milk round in Cappagh, County Tyrone. He was covering for the regular milkman who had been the target. The truce was between the IRA and the Security Forces by the look of it, and didn't include Protestants. Because of the ceasefire it enabled the IRA to concentrate on the genuinely sectarian aspect of their war, in which they kept denying they were involved.

The following day, proof of what seemed like a pact with the Provos was emerging; seven incident centres were set up in Republican districts across Northern Ireland. The centres were to be manned by Sinn Féin members who liaised with the Northern Ireland Office. They were to monitor the ceasefire between the IRA and the Army. It was laughable. Throughout the truce the Government and the Northern Ireland Office denied that a deal had been done. Mike assured us that the situation was well in hand, and they were carefully scrutinising developments. If they felt the Government was about to betray the Ulster people, it would be immediately wrecked.

Meanwhile, the Provos and Sinn Féin consistently emphasised that they had agreed a 12-point plan with the British.

Some of these points were quite evident on the ground: the establishment of incident centres and the reduction of Security Forces patrolling in Republican districts were a slight giveaway. Who were we supposed to believe?

On 19 February, James Breen, a brother-in-law of a well known Nationalist politician, was shot at his front door. He had IRA links. Death notices in the paper said he was killed as a result of 'an accident'! In the sense of a Loyalist gunman getting to him, it was an accident. The information was passed on to Loyalists and they had got him. There was an OOB in place at the time.

Mike reassured us that, although a deal was done behind everybody's backs, they were still carefully monitoring the situation: Sinn Féin's incident centres were being bugged and the phones tapped, as were NIO officials' offices and home numbers. This seemed to prove the rumours that the intelligence agencies were working to bring down the Labour Government.

On 18 February, Airey Neave, a hardliner and supporter of the Union, was appointed as the Conservative Party's spokesman on Northern Ireland. He would have become Secretary of State for Northern Ireland when the party came to power in 1979. However, the INLA breached security at the House of Commons – probably before Neave entered the Westminster underground car park – and placed a bomb under his car. A mercury-tilt switch triggered the device as he drove up the ramp out of the car park, killing him instantly.

Throughout the conflict the INLA had been used to eliminate high-profile targets. There were numerous occasions on which this organisation was responsible for murders that appear to have been beneficial to Military Intelligence.

Airey Neave believed passionately in the Union and would

have taken a much tougher stance if the Conservatives came to power. He would no doubt have demanded to see what was in place and, most significantly, what the Intelligence Agencies were up to. Thus Military Intelligence would have lost the power Heath gave them – the last thing they would have wanted. They were running the whole show and didn't want that to change.

On 20 February, a Catholic man was killed when a bomb in a duffle bag exploded in the Railway Bar at Greencastle, North Belfast. This bar was close to Conway's Bar, which had been attacked on a number of occasions. Twenty-five people were injured in the bombing. An OOB was in place at the time.

This launched the feud between the two Republican factions, bringing great satisfaction to all Loyalists. Hugh Ferguson, the chairman of Whiterock IRSP was gunned down where he worked in Ballymurphy. The OIRA was blamed. There were a number of retaliatory murders before the feud ended in June. As usual, Mike kept us informed of events before and after they happened. He had already told us there had been a plan to cause a feud between the two organisations. It was a master plan by the MRF; one worth looking at in detail.

We were pleased with the result; the more they killed, the more we would revel in the feud. Knowing what I know now makes me wonder: just how much had the MRF achieved in terms of infiltrating the Republican groups at a high level and, in later years, Loyalist groups so they could control both sides? (Martin Ingram, an ex-FRU agent and joint author of the book *Stakeknife* claimed they never recruited Loyalist informers.)

On the same day, a Catholic man was fatally wounded in a Loyalist gun and bomb attack on the Bush Bar in Leeson Street, off the Falls Road. MRF information indicated that Cathal Goulding, the OIRA's chief of staff, was in the bar. A team was sent out to assassinate him. Luckily for Goulding he left the bar just before the attack. Two men were shot, one dying immediately and the other three months later. The bomb failed to explode and the Army defused it. As I mentioned earlier, Leeson Street was the heart and soul of Republicanism; information about anything happening thereabouts could only come from Military Intelligence. An OOB was in place at the time.

On 8 March, a Catholic man was killed as he opened his door at Clifton Drive, off the Cliftonville Road, North Belfast. He was shot by one of two gunmen; one was dressed for a wedding, right down to wearing a flower in his buttonhole. (The man's brother was getting married in a few hours.) They then fired at his wife who had run into the hall when she heard the shots, wounding her three times. Some inside information was passed to Loyalists who knew the man's brother was due to get married. An OOB was in place at the time.

The Provos retaliated four days later when they shot dead a 51-year-old Protestant man, Raymond Carrothers, at his home in Orient Gardens, off the Cliftonville Road, Belfast.

The execution of John Fulton and Stephen Goatley on 15 March in the Alexandra Bar on York Street was part of a feud between the UVF and the UDA, which started when UVF volunteer Joseph Shaw was killed during the Loyalist strike on 18 May 1974. The UVF had insisted that Fulton and Goatley were among the gang that killed their volunteer.

In November later that year tensions hit at an all-time high between the two Loyalist organisations when UVF men wrecked two UDA bars in the York Road area. The following night, a mob of UDA men surrounded a UVF bar in Tiger's Bay and threw bottles and bricks. A UDA man, Thomas Haddock, fired a shot into the bar from the doorway, although he managed to miss everyone inside. A UVF man returned fire and hit Haddock who later died in hospital.

The feud resulted in another UDA man's death on 30 January 1976. Samuel Hollywood was drinking in the North Star Bar, the same bar where Joseph Shaw was shot. He provoked an argument with two senior UVF men by alleging that the UVF was harassing his family and promising that he would get the UVF members responsible. In the assault that ensued, he was stabbed in the heart and died as a result of his injuries. Two UVF men were charged with his murder, but were found not guilty and released due to MRF intervention.

On 23 March, a 15-year-old member of the Fianna Na hEireann was discovered lying in his house, close to the New Lodge Road. A bullet fired into his head had ended his life. Detectives arriving at the scene were attacked by a crowd and had to return later with Army back-up. The police concluded he was shot accidentally. They were wrong. He was a suspected IRA member and Loyalists had been given his name and address. They had gone to his house where they found the door open. The young lad spotted them and tried to run to the back door, where he was shot in the head. A neighbour found him; his head in the kitchen and the rest of his body stretched out into the yard. The woman called an ambulance, but he died in hospital.

If he had been shot accidentally, then whoever was with him must have left him lying there; if help had been called right away, he might have survived. That he shot himself accidentally is highly improbable, as the gun would have been lying beside him. His death was the result of a MRF/Loyalist hit team's co-operation. An OOB was in place at the time.

On 25 March, Harold Wilson paid a visit to Stormont where he announced that an election of members to the new Constitutional Convention would take place on 1 May.

April was a bad month. Reminiscent of the earlier years when the killings were out of control, sectarian murders rose dramatically. Out of 34 dead, Loyalists were responsible for 21, and three were due to the internal feud between the OIRA and the INLA. As there was a ceasefire between the IRA and the Security Forces, all the dead were civilians.

On 1 April, Protestant-born Dorothy Trainer was walking home with her Catholic husband after a night out. As they made their way across a park beside the Garvaghy Road in Portadown – to become one of the most infamous roads throughout the country during the latter part of the conflict – two gunmen approached them. They killed Dorothy Trainer and badly wounded her husband who survived. I was not aware of an OOB in place at the time.

On the same date, an Indian man who had lived in Carrickfergus for about six years was killed. He was married to a Catholic woman from Ardoyne. Word came through that, due to his wife's connections, he was thought to be a Republican. He had stood for election to the Council in the Greenisland area as a NILP candidate, but failed to get elected. At the time his party was associated with Republicanism so this may be why MRF intelligence gatherers knew him, and his name was on a list of targets.

A detail which struck me as odd was why he would open his door at 4.30 a.m. without establishing who was at the door. Was he used to men calling at odd hours? When he opened the door, the gunman hit him on the head with the gun. He was forced into the living room where he was questioned about the IRA until his wife arrived on the scene. The gunman shot him and then fired at his wife, missing, as she ran out of the room, before fleeing. An OOB was in place at the time.

Saturday 5 April was a major killing day: eight men lost their lives in three attacks. A crowd of Catholic men were watching the Grand National in a packed McLaughlin's Bar at the top of the New Lodge Road. A bomb was planted in the doorway by Loyalists and exploded without warning, killing two and injuring seven others. An OOB was in place at the time.

Five hours after the bombing, the IRA got their revenge. A bomb went off at the Mountainview Tavern, at the corner of Cambria Street and the Shankill Road. Two men walked into the bar; one had an automatic pistol and fired shots at the people there. As people dived for cover, the other man left a box just inside the door. A few seconds later it exploded, killing five men, William Andrews (UDA), Alan Madden, Albert Fletcher, Nathaniel Adams and Joseph Bell, and injuring many more.

After that attack a Loyalist operation was swiftly put together, and men were despatched to search for a victim. A Catholic and his wife had visited a social club in Ardoyne, when they heard about the attack at the Mountainview Tavern. They decided to leave early, in case there would be any more trouble. When they reached their house, their grandchildren weren't in and they had no key. As they went to look for them upon, two men approached and shot the man dead.

A soldier at the inquest recalled observing two men in Etna Drive just before the shooting. Shop lighting had apparently blinded his night sight as he heard shots being fired. The two men ran down an entry, and as the soldier swung his sight around he noticed the man lying on the ground. Those shop lights were very convenient, allowing a hasty OOB order to take place.

The following day, the Provos were equally quick to retaliate. William Archer was standing outside a Loyalist club on Alliance Road, on the Protestant side of Ardoyne, when he was killed by the IRA. And as part of the feud between the two Republican movements, Daniel Loughran (a member of the INLA) was shot and killed while walking along Albert Street, lower Falls Road.

On the morning of 7 April, Gerard McLaughlin took the same route as usual to his work at Campbell's Mill, Newtownabbey. Two men and a woman were with him that morning and noticed a car drive slowly past them. A man jumped out and fired six shots at Gerard McLaughlin, killing him instantly. I was not aware of an OOB in place, but it bears all the hallmarks of a MRF-backed operation as only one man was targeted.

Hugh McVeigh and David Douglas both belonged to the UDA. McVeigh was a commander of North Down and a member of the UDA's ruling body, the Inner Council. The two men disappeared on the same day while making furniture deliveries on the Shankill Road. Later that day, their vehicle was found on the Antrim Road, with the furniture still in it. The IRA was the first group to be suspected of their kidnapping. There was no trace of the men and no one ever claimed the abduction. The case baffled everybody, none more so than the UDA.

Why had no Republican organisation claimed responsibility for the seizure and subsequent murders? McVeigh would be a feather in their cap and a great propaganda victory.

Almost five months after they vanished, a dramatic turn of events led to the discovery of their bodies in a shallow grave at an isolated spot at the Gobbins, in Islandmagee. Locals in the area had noticed a man going to the place and praying. They didn't realise at the time it was a grave he was visiting. The man had recently come under suspicion within his own organisation; he had been acting strangely and was thought to be a tout. He was picked up for questioning and taken to the Orange Hall in Carrickfergus. When he realised what was about to happen, he asked to use the toilet. He jumped out of the toilet window and made a run for the police station. He made it to the station, where he banged on the wire fence, begging to be let in.

Once inside he told them everything he knew; names, locations of graves and information about other murders. He squealed on 26 men in total. It was like a supergrass trial, which was a tactic to be used by police in later years. He described two of the men at the burial site; one was an 'intelligence officer' from Brigade staff; the other was a 'commander of the USSF, a special services unit in the UVF' that very few people knew about. The 26 men in the dock were jailed for almost 700 years between them. Eight of them were given life sentences.

People were starting to complain about the number of murders happening in the Mid-Ulster district and the fact that no one had been arrested or charged with any of them. Allegations followed, that at least one Loyalist hit squad was operating in the area with Security Forces' help.

Little did they realise how close to the truth those accusations actually were ... until now.

On 11 April, the Army came across a gun and bomb attack being carried out by Loyalists at the Jubilee Arms Bar off the Ormeau Road, South Belfast. They opened fire, killing Robert Wadsworth as he tried to escape from the scene. There was no OOB in place at the time.

On 12 April, there was yet another feud-related death – we loved every minute of it. Paul Crawford, an OIRA man, was shot dead by the INLA while selling copies of the newspaper, *The United Irishman* outside a bar on the Falls Road. Our feeling at the time, I am not proud to say, was that it couldn't happen to nicer people.

That same day, the 12th Loyalists reaped terrible revenge with a bomb attack on the Strand Bar in Anderson Street, Short Strand district, of East Belfast. This case proves the influence the MRF had over the judicial system. Just before 8.15 p.m., a Loyalist team arrived at the bar. They put a length of wood through the door handles to prevent anyone escaping and left a bomb in the doorway before escaping. An OOB was in place at the time.

Michael Mulligan was in the bar and, realising what was happening, threw a chair through the door's glass window. Before anyone could get out, the device exploded. It killed one man and four women, and fatally injured Michael Mulligan who died a week later on 19 April. It was alleged that a Catholic, Seamus Brendan O'Brien, was involved in the attack. He had joined forces with Loyalists when the IRA killed a family member. The IRA killed him in January 1976. A self-confessed UVF man was charged with the murder of Michael Mulligan in September 1975. Four months later, he was also charged with the other Strand Bar murders.

A son of one of the victims, who sat at one of the hearings, walked up and punched him in the face.

A month earlier, the man's 11-year-old brother had been doused in petrol and set alight. Incredibly, the child wasn't seriously injured, but it was condemned as a sectarian attack. Enter the MRF. During the man's trial a heavily disguised prosecution witness appeared and told the court, pointing at the defendant, 'That is the person I saw driving the car that night.'

When the accused came to the stand he admitted being a member of the UVF but denied the murder accusations. When the trial ended, the accused was acquitted of all charges. While the judge paid tribute to the bravery of 'Mr X' in testifying, he said, 'I think the possibility that he may be mistaken exists, and therefore the certainty required for conviction is missing.' You can see the pattern emerging very clearly in many similar cases described in one book, *Lost Lives*.

Twenty minutes after the Strand Bar bomb blast, a Protestant, Stafford Mateer, was fatally wounded as he sat in his van at traffic lights at the junction of Albertbridge Road and Woodstock Road. The IRA hadn't waited long to retaliate, firing from the Short Strand and hitting Mateer. He died in hospital on 14 April.

At 10 a.m. on 13 April, a paperboy found Robert Kennedy's body. Kennedy, a Protestant, had been walking home from a club along York Street to where he lived just off the Shore Road, in Northwood Drive. He was set upon by three Catholic teenagers who said in court that they had been angry about the people killed in the bomb attack in the Short Strand and had decided to 'beat him up'.

A police doctor said that Mr Kennedy's skull was 'pulverised', and the injuries were the worst he have ever seen. In summing up, the judge said, 'I do not propose to describe any further your actions that night. The facts speak with an eloquence I cannot approach.'

All three got life sentences. One of them, who had only one arm, had repeatedly beaten the man over the head with his artificial limb. When he was dead, they robbed him of three pounds. It would appear the teenagers didn't belong to the IRA, yet they were able to inflict on an innocent man injuries incomparable to anything the police doctor had seen and then lower themselves to search his pockets and steal three lousy pounds. Could anyone sink lower? In Northern Ireland we were proving it could be done time and time again.

On 17 April, three members of a family were killed in a booby-trap bomb explosion in a cottage at Killyliss, between Dungannon and Ballygawley. Marion Teresa Bowen had bought the cottage, and her two brothers, Seamus and Michael McKenna, were renovating it for her, her husband and their unborn baby which was due to be born in a month's time. She had made a last-minute decision to visit the cottage to see how the work was coming along. The three went inside together and triggered a bomb hidden in the hot press. Debris was blown over 150 metres away; all three adults died of multiple injuries. A master bomber (trained by the MRF) had placed a specialised bomb in the hot press, to be set off when the door was opened.

On 25 April, the Provos killed a Protestant man, Samuel Johnston, as he walked near his home in Portadown, County Armagh, in a drive-by shooting.

Two days later, Loyalists were in action again in Mid-Ulster. Three Catholic men were killed and another man seriously injured when Loyalists attacked a darts club near Bleary, Portadown, mainly frequented by Catholics. The gunmen sprayed the bar before escaping. An OOB was in place at the time.

The man nicknamed 'The Jackal' – connected with the Mid-Ulster Brigade of the UVF – was becoming increasingly notorious in the Portadown area. All Loyalist paramilitary members admired his team. He carried out his murder campaign with a ruthlessness and conviction only surpassed by another Mid-Ulster man, Billy 'King Rat' Wright. The body bags of Catholics piled high as a result of these two men's reign of terror.

The month of May and a return to what the Government called 'an acceptable level of violence'. On 1 May the election for the new Constitution Convention took place, held under the proportional representation system. There were 78 seats contested throughout the Province. The UUUC won 47 seats, with 54.8 per cent of the first preference votes; the SDLP won 17 seats; the Alliance Party won eight seats, the Unionist Party of Northern Ireland (UPNI), Brian Faulkner's new party, won five seats, with the remaining seat going to the NILP. As the UUUC held the majority of seats and were fundamentally opposed to a power-sharing Government, the whole thing was doomed from the start. Any chance of a constitutional agreement was, at best, remote.

On 18 May, Francis Anthony Rice's name appeared on a MRF list given to Loyalists, describing him as an IRA member. A Loyalist team picked him up in Castlewellan after midnight. A honey trap was used to lure him to a quiet spot where he was interrogated for some time. After he gave a number of names, he was finished off with a flurry of stab wounds to his chest, before his body was dumped. A caller to the *Sunday News* said he was the first of three OIRA men they were planning to kill in the area. An OOB was in place at the time of the abduction and killing.

On 22 May, Gerald D'Eath discovered a booby-trap bomb on a building site at Hightown Road, Glengormly. The bomb was created with MRF expertise, hidden in a thermos flask and left on a pile of bricks at the weekend. As the majority of the workforce was Catholic, the chances of one of them picking it up were very high. It sat on those bricks until Thursday, when Gerald D'Eath picked it up. It killed him instantly.

On 1 June, Margaret Kilfedder, a 61-year-old Protestant pensioner, was killed when a bomb went off at her home in Garrison, County Fermanagh. The house she was living in had belonged to a UDR soldier who was the intended target.

Two days later the IRA murdered three Protestant men. David Thompson was found shot to death in his car in Killeen, County Armagh. Two other men were also found dead in Thompson's car. One of them, Alfred Doyle, was probably the intended target; he was an off-duty UDR soldier. The other man, John Presha, was a Protestant.

Merlyn Rees announced another concession on 24 July,

which really put the wind up Loyalists. He revealed that all internees held without trial would be released by Christmas. Ulster, it seemed, was going to be scuppered and the Irish Republic was taking control.

Mike had dropped a hint that something big was being planned for the next month or two. I had completely forgotten about it. He had mentioned something about the Mid-Ulster Brigade and Robert Nairac throwing a spanner in the works.

On 31 July, reports came through that a show band's minibus had been destroyed in an explosion and a number of men had been killed. I still hadn't made the connection until more facts were released. Apparently, the minibus driver had stopped at what he thought was a Security Forces roadblock. The Miami Show Band members had been ordered out of the van while it was being searched. Two men had boarded the vehicle, when it suddenly exploded. The members of the band were being held in a line, facing away from the road, with a man covering them with a machine-gun. When the man standing behind them realised the operation had gone wrong, he opened fire, killing three members, Fran O'Toole, Brian McCoy and Tony Geraghty, while a fourth dived into a ditch and survived. Early reports suggested the band was carrying the bomb when it went off prematurely.

It was only when I heard the two men in the van had been identified as UVF volunteers – a severed arm had been found with a UVF tattoo on it – did it all start to fall into place. As more details emerged I knew this was the operation Mike had hinted at. One of the team had been knocked unconscious by the blast and was helped away from the scene. The man wore very strong prescription glasses, which had come off during the explosion. When the two men killed were identified, Harris Boyle and Wesley Sommerfield, from the Mid-Ulster area, it wasn't long before the police traced the owner of the spectacles.

Eventually, two men were charged with the murder and causing an explosion. We knew, if found guilty, they would face a long time in prison, but the length of their sentences stunned us all. They were both sentenced to life and would serve a minimum of 35 years before being considered for release. While I was in Long Kesh both men arrived in my compound and I found them to be two of the most genuine pleasant men I have ever met.

An incident took place on 1 August that almost certainly led to a revenge attack at the end of the year. Two Catholic men, Joseph Toland and James Marks, died when Loyalist gunmen opened fire on their minibus as it travelled back from bingo. The IRA waited, before killing three people in the same district. (Detailed later.)

On 10 August, a serious gun battle between the Army and the IRA in West Belfast saw two Catholic children, Siobhan McCabe (4) and Patrick Crawford (15) killed in the crossfire. We could see the ceasefire crumbling slowly before our very eyes.

On 13 August, five people lost their lives in a gun and bomb attack on the Bayardo Bar: William Gracy, Samuel Gunning, Hugh Harris, Joanne McDowell and Linda Boyle.

Samuel Llewellyn, a 29-year-old Protestant, was delivering hardboard to the Central Citizens Defence Committee's premises in the lower Falls Road on 15 August when an IRA gang abducted and shot him. The wood was to board up windows blown in by an explosion. This senseless death became known as the Good Samaritan murder.

Retaliation for the bombing on the Shankill Road Bar wasn't long in coming. On 22 August, a Loyalist device exploded after a gun attack on McGleenan's Bar, Upper English Street, Armagh. John McGleenan, Patrick Hughes and Thomas Morris all died in the attack. An OOB was in place at the time.

Two days later, the PAF abducted and shot two more Catholics, Colm McCartney and Sean Farmer, in the Newtownhamilton area, County Armagh. An OOB was in place at the time.

On 1 September, there was an IRA reprisal for the murders just over a week earlier in County Armagh. Five Protestant middle-aged and elderly people were attending a meeting in Tullyvallen Orange Hall, Newtownhamilton. James McKee, Ronald McKee, John Johnston, Nevin McConnell and William Herron all died in an indiscriminate shooting. Seven other people were injured in the attack. The PIRA tried to distance themselves from these murders by claiming it had been carried out by the South Armagh Republican Action Force (SARAF), but everybody knew PIRA were responsible.

On 3 September, a Catholic father, William Hamilton, and his daughter, Patricia McGrenaghan, were shot dead his house on the Hightown Road, Glengormly. An OOB was in place at the time.

On the political scene, a rather puzzling event happened, which made us wonder if the strain of being in the spotlight all the time made some men go crazy. On 8 September, at a meeting of the UUUC, William Craig of the Vanguard Party voted for a voluntary coalition with the SDLP, the only member to do so. This was the man who made the speech about how we might have to kill our enemies and who had supported the Loyalist Workers Strike. Fucking insane.

Four Catholic workers, Marie McGrattan, Frances Donnelly, Gerard Grogan and Thomas Osborne, all died on 2 October when a UVF hit team burst into their workplace at Casey's bottling plant, Millfield, Belfast, at the bottom of the Shankill. The

UVF also killed Thomas Murphy in a booby-trap bomb attack at his photographer's shop on Antrim Road, North Belfast, and John Stewart in a gun and bomb attack on McKenna's Bar, Ballyainaiff, near Aldergrove Airport, County Antrim. The UVF also killed a Protestant woman, Irene Nicholson, by accident, when a bomb exploded in the Anchor Bar, Catherine Street, Killyleagh, County Down. There were OOBs in place for them all except the bomb attack on the Antrim Road.

Also on that day, Ronald Winters, Samuel Swanson, Mark Dodd and Robert Freeman died when the bomb they were transporting exploded prematurely at Farrenlester, near Coleraine, County Londonderry.

This day marked the ending of the UVF being a legal organisation. It was officially proscribed on 3 October.

Another bomb in London, at Green Park Tube Station, killed one person, Graham Tuck, and injured 20 more on 9 October. After William Craig's voting for a voluntary coalition with the SDLP in September, a meeting of the UUUC on 12 October decided to expel him. Nine more people were to lose their lives before the end of the month, including a Catholic man, Peter McKearney, and his wife, Jane, who were shot dead by the Mid-Ulster Brigade of the UVF in their home at Listamlet, near Moy, County Tyrone. An OOB was in place at the time.

On 23 October, there was another bomb attack in England, which left Gordon Hamilton-Fairley dead. A bomb attached to the car owned by Conservative MP Hugh Fraser exploded prematurely as he was passing. Rumour had it that he saw the package and was poking at it with his umbrella, which set it off.

As a sign of these brutal times there was great delight in the events between 29 October and 12 November. The OIRA and the PIRA had a bloody feud. In all, 11 members of the two Republican groups were shot and killed in those couple of weeks. Most of those killed were OIRA members.

On 4 November, Merlyn Rees announced the ending of Special Category status for anyone convicted of terrorist crimes, to take effect from 1 March 1976.

On 7 November came a report from the UUUC proposing a return to the 'majority rule' system and a series of all-party committees to scrutinise the work of the departments.

Given that the incident centres had been set up during the truce to monitor IRA and Army activities and investigate complaints from both sides, it was amusing to us when the IRA bombed the Londonderry incident centre on 10 November. The man then in charge of the Londonderry Brigade is, of course, now at the heart of a devolved Assembly in helping to govern Northern Ireland.

This is very interesting when you can remember what I have described in chapter four. It was the comment made to us by Mike, just after Bloody Sunday. It concerned the refererence to Martin McGuinness and how the MRF needed the first shot to be fired by him to get the ball rolling. Now when I think of Mike's threat to sabotage anything that would harm Ulster's position within the United Kingdom, I have realised it was the Londonderry IRA who dealt the blow that would bring the ceasefire down. Was he carrying out something the MRF wanted? Or were the MRF simply counting on his "hot-headness" to aid their plans? The question arises again was he or was he not, one of the highly placed informers that was talked about.

In London, on 12 November, a bomb was thrown into Scott's Restaurant, in Mount Street, Mayfair, killing John Batey. Merlyn Rees declared that the remaining incident centres would be closed.

On 15 November, the ongoing feud between the UVF and

the UDA in North Belfast resulted in Thomas Haddock being shot dead in the Park Bar (as mentioned previously).

In London, Audrey Edgson and Theodore Williams died when a bomb was thrown into Walton's Restaurant in Chelsea on 18 November; 23 were injured.

Four soldiers lost their lives on 21 and 22 November. Simon Francis died when he picked up an abandoned rifle, which was booby-trapped, close to a crashed car. James Duncan, Peter McDonald and Michael Sampson died in a gun attack on an observation post in Drmmuckavall, near Crossmaglen, County Armagh. The IRA must have used very powerful weapons as the OPs were very well protected with sandbags and could withstand a sustained assault.

The Shankill Butchers burst onto the headlines of the *Belfast Telegraph* on 26 November – SLAUGHTER IN BACK ALLEY – after the body of Francis Crossan was discovered lying in an entry off Wimbledon Street, in the Shankill district. His throat had been cut so deeply, his head was almost severed from his body. No one realised this would be the start of a prolonged killing spree by the most depraved and merciless gang ever spawned in this conflict.

When the gang was eventually arrested, it emerged that Crossan had been abducted then bundled into a black taxi where he was severely beaten with a wheel brace. Apparently, Murphy kept yelling at his victim, 'I'm going to kill you, you bastard.' When they arrived at the Wimbledon Street entry, the victim was carried up it, until they were out of sight from the main road. Murphy produced a butcher's knife and began the gruesome task of hacking off the man's head.

At the time, very few details about the ferocity of the attack and the injuries sustained by Mr Crossan were released by the RUC. The state pathologist, Dr Thomas Marshall, reported that death was caused by a cut to the man's throat, which started at the left side and came across the front of the neck, under the chin and then to the right side to the nape of his neck. The severing of the jugular vein caused substantial bleeding, which resulted in his death.

There were seven linear wounds on Crossan's head inflicted by the wheel brace. Glass was embedded in a wound over his right eyebrow – from a beer glass being pushed into his face – and there were two depressed fractures in his skull. Multiple abrasions and bruises on his face, right shoulder, the left hip and the backs of his wrists and hands indicated the intensity of his assault.

Years later, when most of the gang were jailed and Murphy had been killed by the PIRA, a friend of mine asked me what I thought of him, knowing I had come across him. Did I really think he could have done those brutal murders? I had no hesitation in confirming it.

Ross McWhirter, who along with his brother started the *Guinness Book of Records*, had the nerve to offer a reward for anyone who was prepared to give information leading to the identity, capture and conviction of the London-based bombers. He probably didn't realise how dangerous this was. He was shot at his home in Village Road, Enfield, on 27 November; another 'soft' target for the IRA in England.

A bomb attack carried out by Loyalists at Dublin Airport resulted in the death of airport employee John Hayes when the device exploded in the toilets of the arrivals lounge. The MRF controlled the operation.

On 19 December, the UVF and RHC mounted two strikes in the heart of IRA territory. A car bomb exploded outside Kay's Tavern, Crowe Street, Dundalk, in the Republic, killing two men. Dundalk was close to the border and frequently used by PIRA men on the run to hide out. A lot of attacks on the North originated there.

The second attack was more daring. It took place near Crossmaglen, in the heart of what became known as Bandit Country, where security personnel had to be helicoptered in and out due to bomb traps. The IRA unit in this area was second to none. They could operate openly, as they knew they had complete support from the close-knit community.

At the Silverbridge Inn, not far from Crossmaglen, a gun and bomb attack left three men dead. While I was inside in jail, I met a man who described an attack his team had carried out in that area. It bore all the hallmarks of a MRF operation. The men who carried out the mission knew they had very little time as there were would be armed IRA men on the door, watching for such an attack. The bomb could only have seconds on the fuse.

The account I was told went as follows. When they arrived the car was swung round to face in the direction of their escape route. Two men jumped out and opened fire at the doorway, to ensure anyone on guard dived for cover. A third man lit the fuse and hurled the device through the door. Then they threw themselves back into the car, burning rubber as they sped away. The bomb exploded instantly and caught the rear end of the car, causing the boot to fly up. They had succeeded and made good their escape. From this description and the origin of the team, I was convinced the MRF were involved.

On the 22 December, the US police foiled an attempt by Republicans to send weapons to Ireland. A heartening Christmas present for us all.

I should make clear that I had been arrested in the latter part of 1975 for a very foolish act. I was caught leaving the scene. The operation was not one sanctioned by the MRF – it was a UVF one – and I was sentenced to a number of years in prison.

For obvious reasons I will not go into any details as it would comprise other men, which I'm not prepared to do. I was released on bail and the thought of facing Mike and Billy troubled me. Billy and some other mates picked me up and took me to his house for a drink (after stopping off to let my parents know I was all right) – a large drink.

Did I receive any stick about it? A lot of fucking stick. They all had a good laugh at my expense, but they had every right to. After all, wasn't I their senior colleague? When the rest of the men left, Billy and I continued talking for a while.

He told me about Mike's reaction to my little escapade. Apparently, he'd gone 'absolutely crackers' when he heard I had made a statement admitting it. He had gone on and on about how could I have been so naïve to get involved in a fuck-up like that after all the training and instructions I had been given.

As I lay on my bed later, I decided to discuss things with Mike and Billy, thinking, believe it or not, that it might be better to do a bit of time and get my head straightened out. I reflected on the time I had spent waiting for my bail application to be heard when I'd actually felt a weight being lifted off my shoulders. A couple of years without stress could be the answer. I had made a stupid blunder and an error of judgement that still troubles me today. I lost sleep over it; running through the whole operation from start to finish again and again, saying to myself, if I had done this or done that, it would have turned out differently.

I had allowed myself to be used for a job that was doomed to fail. Perhaps it was fate.

In the morning, Billy mentioned that Mike was coming to see me.

I said, 'Thanks for keeping the good news to the end.'

He appeared on Sunday at Billy's house. I got ready and headed over for the showdown.

He just stopped dead on seeing me and shook his head. 'What in the name of fuck were you thinking about? Have all my efforts been wasted? Tell me you didn't go against my instructions and make a statement of admission? . . . Are you going fucking nuts?'

I answered, 'No idea to the first one and yes to the last three.'

He sat down. 'Tell me all the grisly details.'

I went over everything that had taken place. He sat facing me in silence, still shaking his head. When I had finished, he stared at me with a look of incredulity. 'I find it extremely hard to take that in. You've got a logical mind. You can step back and see the whole picture before taking anything on. I can only put it down to a lapse of intelligence and a moment of madness. It's the only explanation.'

I could only nod.

Before he left, he said that he would see what he could do, but no promises. Because I had admitted carrying out the job, it might not be able to get the charges dropped, but a lenient sentence *might* be an option.

Billy and I went up to the Brennan Street Club in Agnes Street and got completely legless; we hadn't to put our hands in our pockets once. While listening to Mike I had decided it wasn't the best time to broach the subject of packing it all in. I would wait and see what transpired.

Even though I was out on bail and wanting out of it all, I still carried on doing what was required, right up until my trial. Mike had kept us up to date with the usual sitreps on OOBs in place and anything else he thought we should know.

I spent most of the month before the trial in limbo. I lazed around the house before going to some pub or club and re-turning legless. I spent a lot of time reflecting on the last five years. It became a nightmare: images of things I had done and witnessed flashed through my mind; the horror, the sadness, the depression, the excitement, the adrenaline rush, the pain, the anguish, the sorrow.

Mike appeared a few days before my trial and we met in Billy's parlour. He said, 'I hate to tell you this, but the picture's looking bleak. The powers-to-be are taking a dim view of the case, as it wasn't a sanctioned job, and what you did doesn't come under our radar. They aren't prepared to set a precedent, in case it starts a free-for-all. They would be inundated with silly, botched operations, and that's not what we are about. A quiet word might be whispered in the judge's ear, advising a lenient sentence, but they're not prepared to bring the full weight of their influence to bear, even taking into account the extenuating circumstances.'

I told him not to worry and confirmed that I had decided to plead guilty. After making a statement admitting it, I didn't have much choice. I continued, 'Come what may at the trial, it's time for me to call it a day. During the couple of months I've been on bail, I've had time to think. This is my one and only chance to try and redeem myself, before it's too late. We joined up with you because we were going to go on the offen-sive anyway, with the USSF as members of the UVF. We chose to go down this path because what you were offering was the genuine article. Back then, for us, it made sense and it was the most logical course to take.

'To cover ourselves, we contacted men from the Shankill and told them the score.'

He interrupted me, 'Oh, thanks very much, and here was me thinking we were good friends!' Before we could butt in, he held up his hand. 'Only kidding. I knew you were sensible men from the start. What you did showed brains. That's why I still can't understand why you did what you did. It just doesn't make sense.'

I continued, 'The men on the Road thought what you were offering was too good to be true until you proved it with the McGurk's operation. They've been using the OOB system through Billy and the teams, though we never mentioned that to you before ...'

He interrupted again, 'Don't worry. I knew that. It was a clever idea and it took me a while to work out what was going on. We didn't mind at all, in fact we hoped other men would employ the same strategy. Well done, it worked remarkably well. When both the teams helped out, when some of the country units needed a job done, where masks couldn't be used, and local men couldn't do it for fear of being recognised. It was ingenious. Those guys from the USSF team don't take many fucking prisoners.'

Billy said, 'How the fuck do you know all that? We were completely sure we'd covered all our tracks!'

He answered, 'It was quite easy really. First, I wondered why you were operating so much out of your area. Whenever you, Billy, gave me the location of a job you never asked to make sure if the OOB covered you from your area to the target and back again. There had to be a second team involved. Second, we had men like you, Billy, within different units in Mid-Ulster and around the Province who put OOBs in place for their missions. When we asked how certain jobs could be done without the men being recognised, we were told that men from groups in Belfast were being used.

We heard a few names and we were able to work out the teams involved. It was down to The Jackal's cunning that such operations took place. He's one of the most efficient operators there is.'

I said, 'Remember, Mike, this was when the Army was using the softly, softly approach, playing by the book. Except the Provos were using a different book. You can't play by the rules if your enemy isn't. At this point enter the MRF and Loyalist paramilitaries – the Government's illegal or maybe legal tools, judging how you can manipulate the judicial system.'

Mike jumped in, 'Listen to me. We're a necessary evil, but don't ever get cocky. We're extra legal, unsupervised, unregulated. Sometimes *I* don't even feel safe knowing we're around. Every one of us praised the ingenuity of the tactics. Believe me when I say very little goes down that we don't know about, and that includes the IRA. We've now got a couple of very highly placed Freds within the ranks of the Provos and their feedback is turning out to be second to none.'

I replied, 'Yes, I agree with everything you say, but I have a feeling this Labour Government knows very little about this whole set-up. I can't see them putting up with all this, when they seem to be bending over backwards to appease the rebels every chance they get. So, tell us, Mike, when is all this going to end?'

'When is what going to end?'

I answered, 'Terrorism. The taking of innocent lives to make a political statement. The sacrifice of people on the opposite side . . . and your own side. When is it going to end?'

He replied, 'When there are no more people in the world who feel oppressed enough to pick up a gun or a bomb. When there are no more religious or ethnic zealots. When there are no more maniacs who get their kicks by shedding blood.'

I answered, 'So . . . I guess the answer is never. It will never end.'

He paused for a moment. 'Zealots fought the Roman occupation of the Promised Land using terrorism. It's hardly a new phenomenon.'

I said, 'When Loyalists entered the fight, they were normal young men. They liked a drink, chasing women, watching and playing football; in fact there was nothing special about them. But because the Provos decided to embark on their campaign of violence when they were at a vulnerable age, they were drawn into the affray. What we're forgetting is the psychological and emotional effect it has on us all. Death in its most shocking form has affected people's every waking moment, victim and perpretator. When someone takes a life, the dead man follows him. He takes his meals with him, shares his bed. Every waking moment. When that happens, it's time to get out, because a man who sees ghosts can no longer behave like a professional. I'm afraid I reached that point some time ago.'

Billy said, 'Amen to that. Mike, I've learned perseverance, discipline, sacrifice and the importance of offensive, defence of a cause, for all our people. I have fought for the land, hunted the enemy, done my duty with the other combatants, trained, refined and murdered . . . for what? Am I going to end up like one of those post-traumatic guys from Vietnam who jump whenever they hear a car backfiring or a firework going off?'

Mike replied, 'I know what your problem is. You believe Loyalists are the great unsung fucking heroes. That's the unshakeable conviction that's enabled Loyalists to endure years of tension so brutal any lesser men would have cracked long ago.'

Billy said, 'Maybe, but only because of your dehumanising training. There comes a time when you have to step back and stop, take a break at least, before the pressure breaks you. If I killed a man and, in my head, I know I didn't do it deliberately, there would still be that fraction of doubt niggling, eating away at my brain. Perhaps I'd let my training take over and used excessive force in subduing him, resulting in his death. Maybe my reflexes just kicked into gear. That's something I don't think I'll ever know.'

I continued, 'We've have spent too long looking at death. Personally, I don't want to force myself to look at it any more. We can at least try to put our ghosts behind us. I'm no longer what I once was, but maybe I can still step back, before I lose myself for ever. I can't go back, even if I wanted to. Like most rebels we fail to see how much we've come to resemble the very thing we loathe. It's true. Some Loyalists are exactly the same as the IRA now, killing innocent people for "a cause".'

Mike could hear the emotion in our voices as we spoke. He hadn't offered any answers, just sat and listened. Eventually, he said, 'What about all the deaths? Were they all for nothing?'

Billy answered, 'No, it wasn't for nothing. Bullets and bombs killed them. Other people wanted them killed; Loyalists were just the weapons. We're not responsible for their deaths, the Provos' leadership, the Irish Republic's Government in 1969, and, more importantly, the Holy Catholic fucking Church. They'll be held accountable for all the deaths that have occurred since August 1969, and any more in the future. Loyalists are not hired hands. They did this because they believed in it. Hoping they'd make a difference. But it hasn't. How can killing all those people make a difference? You can't kill them all.'

Mike replied, 'It shows we're serious. It sends out a message to the murdering bastards that we're not going down without a fight.'

I said, 'But the problem with that is the majority of people dying are *innocent* Catholics, set up by you, to be sure there's a sectarian slant to these murders. The IRA doesn't give two fucks how many of them die, because so many Catholics have been killed by them, in mistakes, caught in crossfire or whatever. By the look of it, the Catholic community is prepared to accept those mistakes willingly, or else they're powerless to stop it. Until actual IRA or Sinn Féin men are being killed day in and day out, nothing will change.

'All those men who have been murdered in the name of our cause, even if they did deserve to die . . . if what they got was no more than they deserved . . . it was not for Loyalists to act as judge and executioner. In the next life, if there is such a thing, we'll get justice. In this one we have the law. In the last minutes of their lives, there was no law for them.'

Mike answered, 'I understand, but it's still necessary to draw attention to the Provos' disregard for all human life in their pursuit of an all-Ireland Republic. What I don't understand is, why the change of heart? You both revelled in the action. You enjoyed sitting in my car listening to the reports of operations going down. The buzz was, to quote you both, "fucking magic".'

I answered, 'Yes, you're right. I'll be the first in line with my hand in the air to admit it. It *was* magic. Risk is a narcotic; it makes you feel excited, on a high. But I'm tired. Those who have to struggle will always have to pay the price eventually. The human mind can only take in so much, and I am way beyond my capacity.

'What frightens me most is what all this killing is doing to everybody involved. My whole personality has changed so much, it terrifies me. Bear with me, and I'll tell you a story. Maybe you know it, but indulge me . . .

'It's the story of the scorpion and the frog at the river's edge. The scorpion asks the frog to take him to the other side. The frog is reluctant and refuses because he's afraid the scorpion might sting him. The scorpion assures the frog that he won't sting him. To do so would be foolish, because both of them would drown. The frog sees the logic of this and agrees to take the scorpion to the other side. When they reach the middle of the river, the scorpion stings the frog.

"'Now we'll both drown," the frog cries, as his body goes numb with the scorpion's venom. "Why did you do that?"

'The scorpion smiles and says, "Because that's my nature and I can't change that."

'That story sums up the existence of men involved in killing, the more the killings go on, the harder they get. There's so little compassion or mercy left in our souls now it will be impossible to stop. If we keep going, how far down will we sink into the bowels of hell? There are men who take pleasure in the torture and suffering they inflict on fellow human beings. What are they becoming? Death. Pure death.'

We all sat in silence for a few minutes before Mike asked, 'So, what are you going to do with the rest of your life, assuming you get off lightly?'

I replied, 'Develop a drinking problem. I have one at the minute; it's the only way I can cope with the bloodshed.'

We sat and talked for a while longer before Mike left. He said he would be there on Monday to see how I got on and wished me all the best. When I left Billy's house, I felt 20 years older than I was; shoulders hunched, hands thrust deep in my pockets, head down. I remembered the death of the first soldier killed in the Troubles, Gunner Robert Curtis, who died in an attack only 50 metres from where I was standing and all the other unfortunate troops who had died to keep Ulster free, and a message I had read once jumped into my mind.

It was from a headstone of a young officer who went down with the *Titanic* on 15 April 1912 – 'Each man stood his post as the weaker ones went by, and showed once more how Englishmen should die.'

And I thought that epitaph summed up the fate of young soldiers, some still in their teens or younger than me, who were sent like lambs to the slaughter by uncaring politicians into a conflict they knew nothing about and died wondering why.

1975 Statistics

Deaths by year and status		*Responsibility for deaths*	
Protestant civilians	62	Republicans	130
Catholics civilians	100	Loyalists	121
RUC	7	Army	6
RUC/R	4	RUC/RUC/R	0
UDR/RIR	7	UDR/RIR	0
Army	15	Others	10
Republicans	31		
Loyalists	28		
Others	13		
TOTAL	267		
Bombs	635		
Shootings	1,830		
Incendiary bombs	56		

OPERATIONS

To be absolutely accurate in recording all the events that happened during those killing years, I would have to go through every newspaper covering that period to get everything in chronological order. It is impossible to remember every incident exactly in the order they happened. I have been able to establish the correct order of the major events through books and websites. (See Acknowledgements for further information.) In this chapter I will describe other deeds that took place, but not necessarily in strict chronological order.

In previous chapters, there have been accounts of certain MRF or USSF operations in which I might have taken part or known about, or been told about by Mike, or heard in Mike's car as they occurred.

This chapter contains descriptions of actual murders; in order to protect the families from further pain, I will not mention names or dates. I will relate the facts – the acts of torture inflicted on men who did not deserve that kind of justice.

Not all operations went according to plan. If the truth were known about how many went wrong or were aborted at the last minute due to unforeseen circumstances, despite OOBS being in place, there would be enough material for 100 books. As very few men knew their passage in and out of areas was safe, it kept them on edge; if they knew it was safe, they would have been less focused and thrown caution to the wind.

For every attack that was successful, there were about a dozen that weren't. Some examples of the kind of 'circumstances beyond our control' are detailed below.

• • •

A garage owner was in the process of locking the premises for the night when two men appeared, brandishing guns and wearing balaclavas. They told him to hand over the day's takings. As he prepared to hand over the money, a voice from beside them piped up, 'Would there be any chance of 20 cigarettes?'

This person had walked up from the road and crossed the 20 metres of forecourt. He must have seen what was taking place in front of him. The gunmen were preoccupied watching the owner, in case he tried any heroics, and hadn't paid attention to the door or the forecourt. One of them shouted, 'Are you fucking crazy? Get your fucking hands up now and stand beside him,' pointing towards the owner. The other man grabbed the bag of money and both disappeared through a gap in the fence round the garage. The sum reported as stolen to the papers didn't quite match the contents of the bag, not by a long shot. The owner had already put most of the money (in notes) in his pocket, but because of the interruption the men just grabbed the bag and made off. Of course, if that idiot hadn't showed up, the men would have noticed the bag was too light and searched him for the rest.

Another incident took place in the centre of Belfast. A team of men went to rob a company's payroll. They had a detailed map of the layout of the place and where the money was kept before it was distributed to other branches. They burst in and held the staff at gunpoint. What hadn't been explained to them was that a stairwell ran up the side of the building, which led to offices on the floors above. Worse than that, the wall between the stairs and the office they were in was made of Perspex, and they could see all these office workers walking up and down those stairs.

Basic logic took over and they concluded that if they could see the people outside, then the people outside could see them. With hoods. With guns. They just looked at each other and decided to cut their losses.

The report in the papers the following day was amusing. The office staff had been interviewed and gave this account: 'We were just standing about, preparing to get ready to start our day's work. Two gunmen burst in and told us to put our hands in the air. Then they just stood there looking at each other, and one of them asked the other one, "Where's the bomb?" The second man shrugged his shoulders and said, "Don't know." Then they both ran back outside.' The headline of the story read BOMBERS FORGET THEIR BOMB.

A couple of men intended to shoot a Republican at Glengormly. They arrived at the man's house and had just opened the gate, when this dog took a run at them, barking loudly. They just got the gate closed again in time, or one of them would have left a chunk of his arse behind in the dog's mouth. A shadow appeared at the window and the men fired a couple of shots at it before making good their escape.

Getting back to the safe house, he was asked how the job went. He replied as calmly as could be, 'I don't know. There was a fucking dog that decided it didn't fucking like the look of us and made a beeline towards the gate. We got out in the nick of time. A shadow appeared at the window, and I fired a couple of rounds at it. I don't know if I hit the bastard or not, but I'll tell you this, the fucking Venetian blind is dead. It definitely didn't make it.'

A couple of our lads from Glengormly knew the local UDA

commander very well and happened to be talking to him a couple of days later. He told them that the police were getting their knickers in a twist trying to get a lead on who carried out the attempted murder. The gun used, a 9mm Browning pistol given to us by the USSF, had been used in shootings and murders in a number of different places, including as far away as Portadown.

Another big operation was set up to clear a major electrical warehouse of its entire stock. It was to take place on a Saturday morning and it was planned to perfection. The drivers of the company's vans were allowed to take them home each night. On that Saturday, men called at the drivers' houses early in the morning and relieved them of the vans' keys. The vans were then driven off while others kept the men company for a while. Believe it or not, one of the drivers asked the two men with him if they'd like a cup of tea. They declined.

About a dozen men were waiting at the warehouse gates to load up the vans. They were hoping to do a number of runs using them so that everything would look normal and there would be no suspicion of any criminal activity. The vans arrived on cue, and everything was proceeding according to plan until one of the men's girlfriends who lived around the corner from the warehouse came running and told him she'd heard a police report about suspicious activity in the area. That was enough to make the guy in charge nervous enough to abandon the operation. As it turned out, the report had nothing to do with what was going on. No one could understand why the vans had been stolen then left neatly parked at the company's premises.

One of the men worked in a large store in South Belfast and was being given a hard time from one of the owners. He called us and asked for some of the chemicals to make a firebomb, saying he had a wee job to do. This guy was one of the most composed men you could ever meet. Nothing ever flustered him.

The next day, a huge blaze destroyed his workplace . . . The IRA was blamed.

• • •

In the early days, 90 per cent of clubs were run illegally by the paramilitaries so there was no such thing as 'closing time'. If you knew where to go, you could get a drink day or night. About half a dozen of our team were in a club one night when one of Billy's mates came over and whispered something to him.

Billy said to me, 'They've just done a taig downstairs and he's going to take us down and show us.'

We followed him down the stairs into a tiny room. A chair was in the middle of the room. A bare light bulb hung above it. The room smelled of stale sweat, piss and shit. And then I saw a body lying in a corner; naked, folded over itself, the face turned away as if in shame.

There were marks all over the man; his face was smashed almost to a pulp, and some of his teeth were lying on the floor. White, raised bubbles were burned into his skin, from a cigarette; puckers of pain. What kind of person could do this to another? And keep on doing it, because this must have taken a while. The man had emptied his bladder and bowels. He had been shot, but I couldn't see where, because he was covered in blood. The air was heavy and oppressive, and my stomach heaved. We went back upstairs. We were legless by the time we left to go home.

Drink and music were to become an essential part of our lives. Alcohol in sufficient quantities is Novocaine for the mind, but when it wears off, the throbbing pain returns and the only remedy is more alcohol. It came to a stage when I couldn't take the rubbish out without hearing the clink of bottles.

My first bad dreams came after that night. I shook awake, curled at the bottom of the bed in a puddle of sweat, dreaming of a body floating in a pool of blood. I felt as though I was drowning in the same pool. I lay awake for the rest of the night, too scared to go back to sleep.

During those years there were frequent occasions when people were punished for misbehaving or acting unprofessionally. This could take several forms: from a warning, a beating, a severe beating, kneecapping (one or both), shooting of elbows, to death, depending on the misdemeanour committed. There was a code of conduct that had to be followed, and woe betide anyone who didn't abide by it. These punishments were used throughout the Troubles and are still used today.

Up until the moment I wrote this, I had never given serious thought to how terrifying a experience it must have been for those young lads; seized, hooded, brought to a house, set down on a chair and then confronted by a number of men in black, faces covered by balaclavas, guns in shoulder holsters. Sometimes a gun was left on a table to create fear. I knew the idea was to scare the shit out of them, but I never considered the victim's point of view. Now, I can imagine the dread and terror they must have felt.

Stories were used to make sure the message got through. After dealing with the charge of their crime, whoever was in charge would stand in front of the captive, look directly into their eyes and tell them this story:

'Do you know how they killed Edward the fucking Second? You don't, do you? They shoved a red-hot poker straight up his arse. The reason they did that, there would be no marks on his body. They thought this was hilarious, because he was a homosexual and they thought it was a suitable way for him to die. Now, if your name is mentioned to us again, what happened to Edward the Second will look like a fucking holiday in fucking Portrush. Don't think I'm being fucking funny either, because I'm not.' The speaker would pause for a moment to let the warning sink in before finishing with, 'Get this fucking wanker out of my sight before I change my mind.'

The number of guys picked up a second time could be counted on one hand. Kneecapping was the most common form of punishment. It varied, depending on how serious your crime was or how much the person actually carrying out the punishment liked or disliked you. Men could be shot in the fleshy part of the leg and spend a few weeks on crutches, or they could be shot through the patella and joint, which caused the most agony and was very difficult to repair. In later years, I think it was the UDA who used a cordless Black and Decker to drill through the kneecap.

• • •

Although I have dealt with the death and destruction that was going on day in and day out, there were also many comical or unusual incidents. Black humour was a way of dealing with the fear and frustration, and paramilitaries needed a good laugh.

On one of those nights of confrontation between the Loyalists and the Security Forces, Tiger's Bay erupted. Riots were going on a number of different fronts. Vehicles were hijacked and set on fire to be used as burning barricades. A lamentable side-effect, no matter where the riots took place, was that shops were looted and buildings burned. Favoured targets of the mobs were bars. Catholics, even in Protestant districts, owned most public houses.

Late in the night, as the trouble started to die down, four bars in North Queen Street, all within 100 metres of each other – the Mount Bar, the Smoothing Iron, the Red Barn, the North Star Bar and its adjoining off-licence – were all ransacked by gangs roaming the area. Another bar about 150 metres away at the corner of Canning Street and York Street had been petrol-bombed by guys on motorbikes and was blazing.

A group of us were on our way up a small street towards North Queen Street, when a guy we knew, carrying a box, stopped and asked if we wanted some gear. Not knowing what sort of gear he was offering, we said yes out of curiosity. He opened the box and showed us bottles of spirits. Asking him where he got them from, he told us to follow him. He disappeared through the smashed window of the North Star Bar off-licence and began handing out more bottles. We left the scene with our arms full of drink and, after a session at Billy's house, we decided to go back and see what else could be had. By that time it had been completely emptied. A large crowd had gathered and there was a lot of shouting and singing coming from further up the street.

As we drew nearer, we could see lots of people sitting around tables in the middle of the street enjoying caseloads of drink stolen from the other bars. The Red Barn was ablaze and a fire engine was just arriving. As the firemen started unravelling their hoses, they were greeted with jeers from the now drunken crowd. They had just managed to get the water through the hoses when a young lad with a knife started to slice holes in them. After ten minutes, the firemen gave it up as a bad job and withdrew with the cheers of the mob ringing in their ears.

We could see the police down the road, inching their way up towards the crowd, which was still a fair size. They stopped about 50 metres away and just watched the party going on.

As there were only three Land-Rovers with six peelers apiece, they weren't going to take this crowd on. After half an hour of watching the proceedings from the corner, we called it a night.

The following morning, I was told what happened after we left. As daylight approached, the crowd started to dwindle and disperse. Three hours later, as they all slept off their hangovers, the police raided their homes and arrested the men known to them. I heard that most of them got six months for riotous behaviour.

I remember another incident during serious rioting on the Shankill. A bus had been hijacked and placed across the road, blocking it completely. A crowd of us decided to set it on fire. As we approached it, armed with petrol bombs and ready to light the cloth wicks, all of a sudden, about eight or nine soldiers popped up at the broken windows of the bus and opened fire with rubber bullets. I was hit on the shoulder and knocked to the ground, but I wasn't long getting to my feet and running back to the crowd. The crafty fuckers had sneaked up behind the bus and ambushed us.

Another night, we arrived when the rioting was well under-way. Billy asked a guy he knew how it was going, and the guy just turned and replied casually, 'Oh, we're winning. For every stone we throw at them, they're firing two rubber bullets.'

However, it was that night we got our first taste of CS gas. A canister landed a couple of feet from us and before we could react we were enveloped in a cloud, breathing in lungfuls of the obnoxious gas. It felt as if your throat had been rubbed with sand paper. It became difficult to swallow, then you coughed your guts up. I was temporarily blinded with tears streaming down my face, and I remember staggering down a side street. The women were all outside their houses with buckets and basins of water, and they helped to bathe my eyes and put water-soaked handkerchiefs over my mouth and nostrils to prevent my inhaling any more of the gas. When my eyes cleared, I could see my mates and others getting the same treatment. I felt a real sense of gratitude to those women. They didn't know us from Adam, but they were prepared to help us when we needed them. It was a momentary bonding of Loyalist people that I sensed many times over the years; with that spirit I knew in my heart the IRA could never defeat it.

Throughout the Troubles, some men became known as barroom Prods. They would sit around or prop up the bar speaking loudly about what they thought should happen. But, if you offered them a gun, and said, 'Right. Come on and we'll do it,' they would say, 'Does wind come in lumps? No. In that case, I've just shit myself.'

I met a number over the years. One sticks in my mind. We had only just begun our relationship with the USSF when a man we were familiar with, and knew from Friday night drinks in the Park Bar in Tiger's Bay, invited us to his house for a card school. He would spout about this, that and the next thing. One night, he dropped himself right in the shit. He began boasting that he could obtain weapons for the right price. A couple of us picked up on this and began to question him. We asked him if he was genuine. He kept on, becoming more adamant the more we interrogated him. We asked him if he would talk to some men we knew who would deal with him.

Being put on the spot like that, he said yes. We told him we would be in touch. Billy set up a meeting with his friends on the Shankill and we left it to them. His bluff was called and he almost died because of it. At the meeting, he promised the moon and stars, but when the time came to produce the weapons, it didn't happen. The men were not happy and threatened to blow the head off his shoulders for wasting their time. He never did any more spouting after that.

We recruited a member who owned a legal .22 rifle and a .357 Magnum pistol. He took four of us into the hills above Glengormly and we set up a firing range. After about half an hour's practice we heard a strange noise, which seemed to be getting louder all the time. We were in a small dip, firing across a field at targets pinned to a tree. Thinking a farmer on his tractor was coming to investigate, I told one of the men to have a look over the brow of the small hill behind us. He had just reached the top and was peeping over, when he yelled, 'Get the fuck down. It's an army helicopter.'

We dived under bushes and tried to make ourselves as small as possible. Although we were using legal weapons, getting caught would mean all sorts of tricky questions. Our names would have been put on the Security Forces list and we would be under close scrutiny. A few seconds later, the helicopter passed directly over our hiding place. If it had been ten metres either way, they would have spotted us.

. . .

Seven of our team arrived at a club one night for a couple of drinks before heading home. It was one they visited fairly regularly so they knew a lot of the men there. They ordered a drink and stood at the end of the bar nodding to a few of the guys. One of them came over and told them a taig was being interrogated in the basement and asked if they wanted to go down.

'Yeah, why not? We've nothing better to do,' Billy answered.

There were about a dozen men there and the victim was naked, spread-eagled and tied to a table. Someone had been working on him with a knife and he had been badly beaten.

His face betrayed his anguish, the frightened watchfulness of an abused child.

One of the men said, 'What about you, lads? You're just in time for the main event.'

The guy with the knife started to carve the initials IRA on the victim's chest. When he finished, he stood back and admired his handiwork. Then he reached down and cupped the man's scrotum, like someone weighing fruit. He slipped the blade under his testicles, and there was an ear-splitting scream from the victim as it was slowly brought upwards, severing his scrotum. Another blood-chilling scream cut through the hot, smoke-filled air and the man passed out. Somehow the silence was worse than the screaming. They said they had never seen so much blood; it poured like a waterfall over the edge of the table and splashed onto the floor. The guy with the knife held the man's penis and balls up in the air like a trophy.

Someone shouted, 'Sew them into his mouth like the IRA do.'

I had heard this rumour. It was a known torture carried out by Republicans on informers or soldiers.

A man then poured a handful of salt into a tumbler of water and stirred it, while shouting for someone to throw a bucket of water over the victim to revive him. For those who don't know, if you put salt in a wound, it causes excruciating pain.

Billy stared at the man disgustedly. He turned away, unwilling to meet his gaze. Then Billy spoke up to the commander, 'For fuck's sake, big lad, the guy will probably bleed to fucking death any minute. If you dump him anywhere, and he's found in that state, the press will have a field day and label us all as bad as the fucking Provos. We'll finish him off and bury him. What do you say?'

The commander thought for a minute and nodded his agreement. Billy walked over, put a 9mm Browning to the man's head and shot him. Thick black blood dribbled from his nose, mouth and ears as he died.

I arrived in the club at this point, asked if any of our lads had called in for a drink and was escorted to the basement. The horrific scene greeted me as I walked through the door. I do not believe in evil per se, only evil acts, but there are those for whom evil acts are second nature. The man who was still holding the knife looked like a normal person at first glance, although this impression was quickly dispelled when I noticed the seething intensity in his eyes. There was no sign of a basic humanity in them. Something was lacking.

Shock overwhelmed me. Afterwards, I could last for a few minutes without thinking about it, but at night, when I was alone, his ravaged face and broken body always intruded. I couldn't get my mind to rest, even for seconds. My mind would race so fast it felt as if it was going to burn out. Every night. It still does.

Over the years I met and watched men who took great pleasure in cruelty. There is really no human depravity that I have not seen. None. What I have seen human beings do to each other, would give the Marquis De Sade a serious feeling of inadequacy. Personally I gave up on a God existing during those years because if there is such a mythical being, He must be the cruellest, most hardhearted mass-murderer in history.

Many times throughout the troubles commentators referred to the killers as animals. I have never seen a wildlife programme showing animals kill and take premeditated pleasure in another's suffering. It was the lowest possible human behaviour, no, it wasn't human, more accurately inhuman, and in a way that only man could be. It was degrading to other creatures to bring them into this by calling the killers animals

I thought it was a humane thing that Billy had done – putting that poor man out of his misery. Some of the men voiced their disapproval, but thankfully their commander soon shut them up.

I have often wondered how many people vanished without trace throughout the Troubles. We know about some of the informers that the IRA killed and buried – known as 'The Disappeared' – as they eventually divulged the locations of bodies in the late 1990s. But I am convinced there are others. I suspect the number of deaths would increase dramatically.

I heard through the grapevine about a place in Newtownabbey where road works were taking place and, if you wanted to dispose of a body, you could dig into the side of the works, dump the body there, conceal it, and the following day a bulldozer would come along and cover it with more rubble, burying it completely.

• • •

It got to the stage that whenever you walked into a crowded club, you would look at people's faces and see the signs of depravity and corruption. Every stranger who entered a pub or club was immediately scrutinised and assessed as friend or foe. You rarely went to places you weren't known to somebody; it could mean ending up dead, or at the very least suffering a severe beating up some entry and left lying in a pool of your own blood.

I heard of a man who had a routine when someone was brought into a romper room for interrogation. He would sit down in front of the victim, who would be tied to a chair, and play a psychological game with him. He would start off with, 'Now, I want you to listen to what I've got to say to you so pay attention. You'll only get one chance. Do you understand what I mean by that?' He would wait for the man to answer and, if they didn't, he would lash out and punch him full in the face.

He would continue. 'Look, are you fucking deaf or stupid? I'm going to tell you what's going to happen to you. In an hour or so you're going to be dead, no matter what. That's the one thing you can be sure of. You're quite lucky in a way. The only thing any of us can be sure of in this life is that we're all going to die at some point in the future. You're going to get time to make peace with your God and friends with Jesus before you meet them. You should be thanking us because not many people get that luxury. It's normally here one minute, gone the next. The question is, how comfortable are you going to be during that hour? I'm going to ask you some questions and you will answer them immediately or I'll punish you. I can't be any fairer than that, can I?'

The usual questions were asked. Give us the names of your local IRA men. Who is their commander in your district? What are their addresses? Some would say they didn't know. Big mistake. He would walk over to a small table just out of sight of the captive, who would be craning his neck to see what was about to happen. But the table was positioned at just the right place. As he walked back past the victim, he would smash a hammer onto his knee.

After that, the victims would say anything; spill names and addresses of anyone who came into their head.

• • •

A gym workout was no substitute for the adrenaline-fuelled rush of combat. It drew you back; gave your life a sharp definition and stimulation due to the proximity of death. It felt like a hypodermic syringe had been plunged through your rib cage straight into your heart. Your blood sang with it.

Ulster descended ever deeper into a cycle of violence and dissolution that seemed unbreakable. It was a war situation.

Men got killed. No one had said they had to die in an honorable, Marquis of Queensbury-rules way.

During those killing years, murders were often classed as random killings. The truth is, a lot of them weren't. They were targeted. The gunmen could have shot indiscriminately at other Catholics, but usually they shot the target and left it at that.

On 18 February 1973, two postmen were shot and killed in Divis Street. While the gunmen were standing over them, continuing to shoot into the men's bodies, a witness ran towards the gunmen. Who knows what he intended to do, but the gunmen pointed their weapons at him and he had second thoughts. A brave man. The targets were dead; the operation was finished; time to go.

One time, a new guy was on his first operation. It had been drilled into him to fire a Sterling machine-gun in short bursts, to give you time to see where your shots were hitting and adjust your aim accordingly. He was told to lean out of the window as it reduced the noise inside the car and the hot shells would land outside the car. As his car approached the target, the windows were wound down ready for the attack. Nerves got the better of him and he opened up with the gun still inside the car. Empty cartilages were being ejected and flying all over his companions. Then his finger froze on the trigger and he emptied the magazine in one burst. Still, he had achieved the result, which is what it was all about. The target was dead. An OOB was in place at the time.

The Interrogator

On one occasion around the time of thse abductions, some men picked up a Catholic very early on a Saturday morning and took him to a romper room, tied him up and gagged him.

They left him there, as they didn't want to frighten anyone by banging on someone's door at that time in the morning, as it would have been thought a police raid was under way. They contacted a loyalist team around ten o'clock in the morning and took them to where he was imprisoned

He shambled, arms hung limply by his side, when he was brought in. There were dark hollow pockets under his eyes and his pupils looked like brittle crystals that would shatter at any minute. He appeared to be dying. The interrogator pointed at the chair in the middle of the room and asked him to sit. The victim slumped into it and stared blankly at the man. He was asked some simple questions to get him into the habit of answering automatically before the important questions came. His eyes wandered around the room listlessly, barely taking in the hooded men around him.

The interrogator tried to measure his subject's physical and mental breaking points, studying his gestures, any shifts in posture, changes in the tone of his voice, a certain look in this eyes.

His victim was at the farthest edge of whatever held him together and no longer had the strength to speak. He was lost in his own world, unconsciously trying to hide behind his silence. When questioned, a captive is required to answer, or face a painful lesson in the consequences of noncompliance.

Before the interrogator could resume his questions, one of the hooded men stepped in front of him and struck the victim; not one blow, so many blows the interrogator lost count. Other men picked him up each time he fell off the chair to hit him again. Then it stopped. The assailant's hand dropped, trembling slightly. He had worked out his frustrations and now stood back to see the damage he had inflicted.

Two men unsheathed their knives, preparing to practise their butchering skills. The interrogator didn't want this man to suffer any more. If he could have freed him, he would have. But he risked being cut himself.

The interrogator walked over to the victim and whispered, 'Bad luck, man. Better make friends with Jesus.'

As the two knife men approached, the interrogator grabbed the man's wrist and kicked him twice, causing him to fall, then planted his foot against the back of his neck, pinning him to the floor, and put two bullets in the back of his head.

The knife men looked angry; they had been robbed of their sadistic pleasure.

The interrogator ordered two men to dump the body later after dark.

Sometimes sleep did not come lightly to those who killed. They tried to fit all these little tiny pieces of things together and the best they could manufacture was a Frankenstein-like image. A gangly stitched together resemblance of a monstrous act. Only this Frankenstein monster was missing a few limbs and they couldn't bring it to life. They would wake from their strange disordered nightmares not understanding what they were about.

These men didn't think of the victim then but the victims faces came back with brief startling vividness later – then all at once a murdered man's face flashed into their mind as bright and complete as a high-resolution photograph. It came from nowhere it seemed. Perhaps, the product of a dormant memory circuit, which had gone momentarily hot, joggled by either a thump or smell.

From mid July 1972, the Shankill was the place to be. Many Catholics were picked up as they passed through the fringes of the district and brought to romper rooms for interrogation. Once they were caught, their lives were over. How easily or how cruelly they died, depended on which squad captured them. Some would be dead within an hour; others would die a slow and very painful death.

As we helped patrol the area with some men from the Shankill, word soon spread that a 'taig' had been picked up and where he was being held. Most of the time we would arrive after the man was killed and his body hadn't been dumped yet, so we could see what state it was in, whether he had died cleanly or slowly.

There was one time we arrived at a club where a guy had been tortured and was waiting for the final act to put him out of his suffering. He was in a bad way and I'm glad I wasn't there to witness it. It was like a game to some of these men. They counted the men present. I think it was about twenty. Matches were produced and one was broken and then they were held out for each man in the room. The one who drew the shortest got the job of dispatching him straight to the other side. The victim was semi-conscious, his breath coming in laboured gasps.

I looked around the room we were in. Other people had met the same fate as this guy had just experienced. I could see fresh blood that he had unwillingly donated to the décor. There were dark patches of dried blood on the floor and walls. Dark and ominous, not like blood at all, just dark red patches. A guy drew the short straw before it got to me. A gun was handed to him and everyone waited for the final act to happen.

The guy just walked over and fired. The bullet had entered through his cheek, wreaked havoc in the brain and exploded out the back, disgorging a cascade of brains, blood and bone onto the walls and floor. Nauseating how something so small could destroy a life so easily. The bullet's ugliness went much deeper, straight through the skin until it made its home inside or decides to leave the scene of destruction it had caused. Brains fucked by metal.

I stood there looking at the hole, at the gaping mouth of death. Bubbling internalized rasps came from the dying man. A flickering existence dissolving behind the eyes and draining into darkness. Exhalation, a bronchial sigh. The man sank into himself. Extinction. The act was incidental. The bullet always wins. A guy close to me just opened his mouth and out came a rope of vomit, hitting a couple of guys in front of him.

There is something about a pale body lying on the ground that gets your attention. It reminds you of the solemnity of your purpose. Somewhere connected to the body are a family and friends and they will miss the spirit that inhabited that flesh and bone.

The image of the body stayed with me. I couldn't wash it out of my brain. It always rose up to me tangled and bloody. I could not work for fear of it. In the small hours it woke me up, naked in a sweat-cold bed. A silent thing coated in darkness. I had to wash my hands and sit in the harsh light of the bathroom, shivering until the horror passed.

It was then a long and continuous whispering started. Moist lips against my ear, breath like a cold mist, trickling through. Words mixed and incoherent, broken at times, barely audible, yet suggestive, spoken in a child's voice that trembles slightly. Not soft and innocent, but cold and penetrating, a damaged voice. I was speechless, my mouth was dry, my head was whirling and it was like falling into a dark pit that had no bottom. Tears, loneliness and on a bad night, screams in the darkness, crying out unanswerable questions, into a long, empty and silent night. As I lay in my bed, I thought to myself, that the fires of hell would be a welcome relief.

The man had a ghost and my head was a haunted house he

ved in. Every now and then (usually without pain and always without warning) my brain would vomit the ghost out, where I had to look at him. He never changed. He never went bald. He never grew old.

It's one thing hearing about such things, but it's an entirely different matter when it's happening in full-blown emotional Technicolor in front of men carrying out an operation. An attack on a bar was one of those times. The men burst through the doors; it was strange there was no one on guard, as by this time most bars would have someone standing at the doorway watching in case of attack. It would usually be some old guy, depending where the bar was, who for the price of a few drinks would keep an eye out for the beginning of an attack and give a warning. Bars within a staunch Loyalist or Republican area, would have a couple of volunteers, with access to weapons hidden just inside the door, but in the case of a police raid, somewhere that any member of the public could have left them. With no fingerprint evidence, it couldn't be proven who had left them.

They opened fire with Sterling sub-machine guns; it was like a film in slow motion, every detail was vivid. Searing images imprinting themselves onto their brains, never to be erased, doomed to eternal memories of the sight unfolding in front of them.

The sight of a living, breathing human being being ripped apart like a stuffed doll did something to them. It was a vivid picture that burned in their brain at some primordial level, deeper than gut level. Beyond emotion. Over time, some actions, some acts of violence had been sorted out of the lexicon of human experience to the extent that there was no precedent, nothing to compare them to. No act of movie or T.V. violence, no act depicted in even the most graphic novel, served as a model.

Only in the primitive behaviour of the animal kingdom did such acts have significance, and even then the gory spectacle was only a foreshadowing of the level and efficiency of carnage that man was to perfect.

It was perhaps in that latent part of the animal brain, the unconscious, and the pre-self-conscious brain, which I saw in the cold and wet Belfast darkness, which made any sense at all

• • •

One Saturday night we had gone to a club we hadn't been to before. The guy at the door asked us who we were and for a name to vouch for us. Billy was able to give a name and the guy was duly brought out. He gave the OK and we were allowed in. It was like a lot of shebeens that had sprung up all over Belfast. We settled down for a good drinking session and enjoyed the music. I went to the toilet and was having a pee, when I heard the door opening.

I didn't think much about it – no one was walking towards the urinals – until I heard the click of a slide hammer as a bullet was snapped in line with a gun barrel. It is a truly terrifying noise. Sweat formed on my brow and the hairs on my neck rose.

He had moved so quietly I hadn't heard his footsteps. I'm sure he knew the effect it had on people because when I turned round there was a slightly sneering upward curl on his lips. As charming as a rattlesnake in heat. There was a Star .22 pistol pointing at my head.

'Who the fuck are you, and where do you come from?' he growled.

I gave him the name I had heard Billy mention and where we came from. He said he would ask the guy to be sure. I followed him out and watched as he approached the guy. By this time I was sweating like a pig. I saw him nodding a few times then he looked over and indicated that he was satisfied.

• • •

Sometimes, alone in my bedroom, I would wake from a night-mare, feeling regret, anguish, confusion, and I would ask God to explain why these things were happening. Then something would happen, something always happened. It might be an attack by the IRA, a senseless killing. A little voice in your head would tell you that it was OK; what Loyalists were doing was totally right. And everyone would carry on, elated again, as it provided the excuses needed to carry on.

One guy was responsible for making bombs. He loved it. They were like his babies. He didn't like anyone else touching them, in case they disturbed his handiwork. He had been trained by the MRF in a house in East Belfast One day, a pub was his target. He got out of the car, planted the device, made sure it was all correctly wired right, and walked calmly back to the car, saying, 'OK, just drive away normally. We don't want to draw attention to ourselves.'

They drove up to a hill overlooking the pub.

He said, 'Stop here a minute,' opened the door and got out, looking at his watch. You could almost hear him counting down the seconds.

The driver shouted, 'For fuck's sake. Will you get in here and lets get the fuck out of here.'

The guys felt their pulse quicken as the bomb maker stood and watched the moment the bomb detonated. They saw the fire, smoke and the dust as half the building slid away, and then smelled the odour of fire and death. They heard the clamour of destruction and the chaotic screams that followed it. They saw the ruined building with wires hanging like entrails.

The bomb-maker said, 'A masterpiece.'

The others thought, he's fucking crazy, and the driver slipped into first gear and drove off, wheels spinning.

The bomb-maker started laughing, 'Fucking magic, sheer fucking magic.'

The driver looked at him and grinned, but a cold chill traced a finger down his spine.

• • •

Sometimes the pressure got to them. They wouldn't give a fiddler's fuck about anything; hated the world and everything in it. They knew they were going crazy, but couldn't stop themselves. It was a sick kind of entertainment, really. People gave them a wide berth, treated them with velvet gloves. Might as well make the most of it, before sanity returned – if it ever would.

When men go like that, they are more dangerous, in their numbness. They would strike out at anything. It was just another wave in an ocean of hatred and they become convinced that there was nothing left to lose.

Information was passed onto Loyalists from the MRF that a room was being used as a meeting-place for known IRA men. An operation was set up and a gas cylinder device made, and a night confirmed as the republican's meeting night was picked for the mission. The men were picked for the operation and a time chosen. Safe houses were ready and they were set to go. The driver drove past the meeting place for a quick look to see if any security was present. As no one was spotted he swung the car round so it was facing the right direction for the escape route.

As two men carried the bomb to the meeting place, a couple of men, who must have heard the car idling, came out to see what was going on. They started yelling and the man standing at the car covering the men with the bomb opened fire, driving them back inside the building. As the fuse was lit and the men turned to make their escape another guy ran out of the place and kicked the bomb. One of the men fired along with the man at the car and the guy run back inside. He must have dislodged the fuse as the bomb failed to detonate. With an OOB in place the Loyalists made their escape.

During the Loyalist strike in 1974, we received a piece of information from the MRF, that the Andersontown News, which was a Republican newspaper, was being printed in a garage just of the Shore Road on the outskirts of North Belfast. An operation was set up quickly and two small gas cylinder bombs were brought from their hiding place. We were all set and ready to move, when someone shouted a warning that the peelers were coming, as it was heard through listening to the police radio waveband that suspicious activity was going on at our location. So bombs and guns were carried onto a mini-bus and we hightailed it out of there. It was strange as we drove the two bombs were rolling around our feet. We ended up at the UDA base in Rathcoole. The CO decided he would use them on an attack on a garage instead. It was just as well as they proved to be damp squibs and failed to detonate properly.

There are many instances where the justice system was proved corrupt. They are all recorded in the records of court trials and show a pattern that someone was indeed controlling the system. Who? Well it was either MRF, MI5, MI6, but it was definitely being manipulated by, if not one, then by them all.

Mike told us of one team who had got into difficulties. An operation had taken place by a very professional team and a number of men had been arrested. Never having anyone apprehended before, they were at a loss as to what went wrong.

Mike had called in a few favours and found it was loose talk at a club had been picked up by some informer and passed to the police.

He went on to say that he got a message to the men telling them not to admit to anything and to plead not guilty no matter what. There were four men involved. The first man was sitting in his cell when the screws came up to him and said, right get your gear ready you're going home the charges have been dropped.

The second man got two years suspended sentence, while the third got a small number of years, because he had to make a statement or his father would have been charged and convicted if he didn't. The sentence was very light for the offence.

The most remarkable case was the forth man. He had made a statement admitting serious charges, but had added a reason. The judge had used the reason at the trial and gave the police a rollicking over their failure to check whether the reason was true or untrue and found the man not guilty and released him.

I remember the words Mike had used to his men, 'Oh ye of little faith.' We found it hard to believe, but he gave us the different dates and the crimes. I took the time to look them up and it was exactly as he described them.

I thought these were unique cases, but many years later, as I was writing this book, I discovered it was only the tip of the iceberg.

In a later case the same judge, who was Lord Chief Justice at the time of both trials, did exactly the same with three policemen, who were charged with attempting to bomb a bar. In summing up he gave this statement, 'I recognise the motive for the attack on the bar and I feel the three policemen were misguided, wrong-headed and above all unfortunate. Their actions sprang from a feeling of frustration that ordinary police methods had proved relatively in-effective for combating terrorism in Armagh and elsewhere.' The three policemen received 2 years suspended sentences.

Yet another case in 1984, the same judge, as presiding judge in an appeal court, overturned a conviction of a former police-man, who had been sentenced to twenty years for robbery on the evidence given by an informer, dismissed the charge saying the evidence against him was inadequate. To highlight this con-nection between the Special Branch and Military Intelligence, the policeman knew about the informer having a relationship with the army and refused to talk about it. But a colleague did say that the informer worked for a special army unit and was trained by them. Point made.

In the same trial an Inspector admitted that the informer did work for Special Branch and an army intelligence officer. Defence council asked the Inspector if he had ever encour-aged persons other than policemen to shoot in unwarranted circumstances. Blair replied, he could not answer the question on the grounds it might incriminate himself. After a debate on the subject the judge ruled the policeman did not need to answer the question. This is further evidence that long after my involvement it was still continued and did in fact goes on right up to the present day.

Operatives

One operation was described to me vividly. A team was stand-ing waiting on a guy to arrive and he was running a bit late. It heightened their vigilance, put them on edge and gave them another drop of the adrenalin buzz. One of them glanced across to where one of the lads was stationed. A cigarette flared in a hidden doorway, exhalation tainting the night air, with harsh tobacco odour. Muted anticipation hung on the scene. Another operative moved and glanced over to where the first man was. Drawing deeply on his cigarette and then exhaling twin streams through his nose, he nodded over.

The IRA had murdered someone that day, but it was not revenge that led them to lie in wait for their prey. It was some primitive instinct that put them on the streets that night. Sweat was running down the shucks of his arse. His eyes were burning and staring straight ahead, with solitary purpose. He was operating on automatic. He couldn't have stopped himself even if he'd wanted to.

At those moments, during what always felt like a long wait, guy's would keep glancing at their watches, amazed that less than a minute had passed since they'd had last looked at it. That's when they would start thinking about the victims. What they were doing? Carrying on with normal days activities, working, eating, drinking, playing with their kids or maybe shopping. It didn't matter, because Death was lurking round the corner, watching and thinking, 'you'll soon be mine'.

The first operative was nervous. The things that men and women did to other human beings weren't right. He felt guilt and remorse on one side, but at that moment they couldn't touch him. He recognised them only as theoretical and hypothetical emotions. Evil, like depression, comes from nowhere, for no reason. It consumed him. He killed without thinking. Pain becomes bearable through other people's pain. Men had no soul in those moments.

He had always tried hard to justify the act with a rational excuse, so he came up with a perfectly good example. He and his colleagues were putting somebody to sleep the way they'd do with animals. Not death, not murder, just peaceful sleep.

His heart was beating way too fast. Not just from fear. But also from exhilaration. Paramilitaries killed without trial, without proof. They just knocked off whomever the MRF told them to take out. The sterile euphemism they used was 'sanctioned.' In other words, for what the MRF was doing, 'They were simply playing God.' They didn't knew the reason why someone was targeted. To be perfectly honest, operatives didn't give a fuck about a reason; this is what we had signed up for. They simply carried out orders, whether it was from the MRF or UVF Brigade Staff, was immaterial it had to be done.

A small whistle alerted the first operative to the fact that the victim was now approaching. His thoughts were slow and cumbersome, one still frame after another with no concept of plot or setting. This man had to die, no questions, take him out. As he turned towards his house, both operatives pounced, firing a number of shots into him, the second operative giving him the coup-de-grace with a single bullet to the back of his head, and they were gone. Mission accomplished.

The spilt second transfer from normality, life to death. The distance between life and death, heaven and hell, gunman and victim are very small. Right out of this life and straight into whatever was waiting for him on the other side, if there is such a place as the other side.

EPILOGUE

'The only way bad men triumph,
Is for good men to sit back and do nothing.'
Robert Burke

I WROTE THIS book to put the record straight, clarify some controversial incidents and fill in some gaps. Over the years, I have read many books about the Troubles, anticipating someone else, who was with the MRF during our training and operations, making public their experience. But no one has. It was up to me. Although many books concerning the activities of the FRU (another name for the first clandestine Military Intelligence actions started by the British Government in the early 1970s and then called MRF) have been published, when I look back on our secret war, I see a total waste of life; the absolute misery all paramilitaries caused to every person, no matter where they came from.

Protestants and Catholics in Ireland have been killing each other for centuries. Empires have risen and fallen, two World Wars have been fought, men have gone to the moon and back, but nothing much has changed in the gentle hills and glens of the Province of Ulster. If memory is our contribution to history, then history is the sum of our memories; memories, I confess, now in middle age, which have grown fainter with the passage of time. You must forgive me if I get a little carried away at times, but I'm an old man now and I have very little time left. I am compelled to write exactly what I think.

An important factor of the Troubles, at times overlooked, is the remarkable triumph, ultimately, of the human spirit over adversity. The people of Ulster, on both sides of the divide, endured hell and survived a holocaust forced upon them by events beyond their control. The hardship, poverty and suffering I witnessed throughout the years, of men, women and children, had a lasting effect on me. What was it all for? The Peace Process? That is all that has been achieved, and it has still not resolved anything. The Republicans have not achieved a full United Ireland and the Loyalists still have a sort of connection with the United Kingdom.

Why did Sinn Féin/IRA want to push for positions in a devolved government, in the running of the very state they have tried to destroy for centuries? It can't be done. I believe it's a contradiction in terms; in this campaign and in many others throughout history. Don't think for one second that Gerry Adams and the leadership of Sinn Féin/IRA have turned their backs on the philosophy of the Republican movement's objective of a United Ireland. They spout forth their words of peace while still in full operational capacity. They may be trying hard not to show it, but, to quote Gerry Adams' words many years ago, 'They haven't gone away, you know.'

The Provos issued a statement that was meant to placate the DUP and the Protestant population, declaring the war was over and their arsenal of weapons was decommissioned. If you believe that, you are living in cloud cuckoo land. Danny Morrison summed it up quite aptly on his website: the IRA was born out of the ashes of Bombay Street. (Bombay Street was burned out at the beginning of the conflict by a Protestant mob retaliating against a Catholic mob attacking Protestant homes.) My message to the Republican movement is: Don't piss down my back and tell me it's raining.

The IRA, supposed to be the protectors of the Catholic community, let them down when they failed to open their arms dumps to stop the attacks; so much so, that Catholics changed the meaning of IRA to I Ran Away. Are we supposed to believe they have done the same again? That they have put all their guns beyond use while the big bad Prods retain theirs? It is an insult to all rational people. They deserve to be locked away with other lunatics and the key kept in a UVF man's pocket.

Remember the words of Gerry Adams: 'We haven't given up our goal of a United Ireland, we're just going to achieve it by other means.' Beware of the enemy within.

Now he is telling young and not so young Republicans to join the Police Force of Northern Ireland. That should be treated with the contempt it deserves. Can you imagine one of these Republicans having to arrest another Republican? Does anyone actually believe this will happen? I am convinced it is another ploy concocted by Adams to wreck the Police Force; and now they are in a devolved government, they intend to destroy it from within.

The words of Sun Tzu, ancient China's foremost military strategist, come to mind: 'Know the enemy, know yourself; your victory will never be endangered.'

The question is, which of the two men in charge of the largest parties on either side, Ian Paisley or Gerry Adams, know their enemy best, in order to safeguard their victory?

I need someone to tell me what it's all been in aid of, because none of it makes sense to me any more. The people of Ulster have been let down, deceived and betrayed by governments throughout the centuries. By politicians, by paramilitaries, in fact, by just about anyone you can think of. Does anybody care?

The spectacle of the British Army and police blocking the paths of Loyalists walking their traditional routes is too much for me. I believed that Protestants had the right to march along the Queen's highway, wherever and whenever they choose. I believed that any infringement of that right to march was another concession to the Taigs, IRA, Sinn Féin and the Pan Nationalist Front.

The stand-off at Drumcree revealed something much more ominous about the political landscape of Northern Ireland. The Protestant ascendancy in Ulster has crumbled and Sinn Féin/Catholics/Pan National Front/IRA are winning. There is no longer the will to resist in Protestant districts, as we had back in those killing years.

For 30 years we watched the British make concession after concession to the Catholics and the IRA, but the Good Friday Accords were more than I could bear. It would only lead to one thing, British withdrawal from Northern Ireland and union with the Irish Republic. Two previous attempts at peace – The Sunningdale Agreement and the Anglo-Irish Agreement – had been torpedoed by Protestant intransigence. We could be stuck with the present Peace Accord for ever, and not only will this generation pay the price, our children and our grandchildren will. I find that hard to live with.

The damage done to everyone's minds, especially children's, will never be erased. Everyone who became involved with a paramilitary organisation is to blame for the physical and mental torture inflicted on ordinary innocent people. Yet, I believe no one has the right to condemn any Protestant who took up the call to arms. We were forced to take drastic measures to safeguard our future, our religious freedom and a free country for our children. I can't imagine what would have happened if the Protestant people hadn't stood up to be counted.

Terrorism is a form of war. It's a psychological war, the intent of which is to demoralise. Terrorism is a form of theatre, committed by actors for an audience. The desired outcome is not destruction itself, but the publicity caused by the destruction. Terrorism is cheap and it only takes a handful of dedicated individuals: the World Trade Center's twin towers (3,000 killed), the Bali bombing (200 killed), the Madrid train bombing (200 killed), the Oklahoma bombing (168 killed), London bombing (52 killed) and countless dead in Iraq. Anarchy has been let loose upon the world, and everywhere innocence is drowning.

Muslim fanatics have introduced the suicide bomber into their repertoire of weapons, and there is no way they can be beaten, when men and women are prepared to give up their lives for a cause. The first suicide killer was mentioned in the Old Testament, when Samson pushed the pillars apart causing the building to collapse, killing himself as well as his enemies.

When you finally acknowledge that everything you ever fought for, everything you ever believed in, your country, your flag, has been taken away, it is devastating. I feel as if my entire life has been flushed down some toilet while I wasn't looking. For years, I've been marching forward with my head in the air and my pants round my ankles.

When a young man has seen other young men die, he knows death is not a glorious thing. It is a loathsome thing. As for the rest – the details, what may or may not have occurred – they belong to the imagination. To take real events and expose them to the public is a task I did not undertake lightly. Whether such an undertaking is meaningful, or even moral, readers can judge for themselves, but such questions must be asked about any account of the past. Whether this story can be understood without knowing who is telling it and to what precise end he is telling it, is a matter for the individual reader to wrestle with.

Questions, questions, questions. When I get some answers, I'll keep you posted. I'm only a man, not an oracle.

Love and freedom are such repugnant words to me. So much cruelty has been done in their names. Some call it patriotism, others call it love, but murder is murder, no matter what the translation.

All the lies we spout about dying for one's country; that's all they are, lies. Religion itself is a kind of lie. Friendship is a promise of future loyalty; loyalty no matter what comes. Promises are the bricks of life and trust is the mortar. But fate returns no dividend on loyalty.

Marriage evolved to solve the problem of how society could control the human urge to reproduce – the strongest urge humans possess, except for the urge among the weak-minded to invent supernatural beings to worship, because they're afraid of dying. Let others worry why God spoke to Moses from a burning bush, instead of a sycamore tree or a Tesco's aisle or a TV set. They say the bad sleep easy, because they have no conscience about what they have done. That easy sleep only lasts for a lifetime. Devine retribution begins after death. The need to make amends grows into a compulsion. The Lord , we all know, has ways of confounding proud mortals who swear oaths too lightly. Back before Christ, men sacrificed those around them to placate Gods who knew no mercy and whose natures they imitated in their actions. Blood sacrifices, pigeons with their throats cut falling like rain unto the high alter, the blood of slaves who were whipped into submission by brutal overlords, the blood of rebels on high crosses. Jesus was a rebel.

I never quite trusted religion; I always felt that a man's destiny lay in his own hands. I have become agnostic. I don't give mental assent to the abstractions of Paul. When I die, I'm going straight to heaven, because I've spent my time in hell.

When I was a young man, I did believe in God; a conventional enough belief, even banal, but sufficient at a certain age to sustain a life of self-denial. I was a believer, though I am not sure what it was I believed in. Does that make sense? Young men are such strange creatures, especially to their older selves.

When you look at different religions in the world, what a mess. I have studied many of them, in the hope of trying to understand why people who believe in a god, sometimes the same god, have to kill and murder in his name. Three of the main religions all stem from the same man, Abraham; the father of Judaism, Christianity and Islam. Yet in all these religions there are different sects. You have Orthodox Jews and Zionist Jews, Protestant and Catholic Christians, Sunni and Shi'ite Muslims.

The men who created these religions seem to have spent a considerable time alone in deserts, where their gods appeared to them, giving them their books, rules and commandments on how their people should behave. I suppose, if you spend that length of time in the desert you will eventually see and hear almost anything.

Each day, I felt myself closing down to the Jesus of history, the forgotten, mythologised, emasculated firebrand, whose face would not fit in any modern church, or for that matter, most synagogues. I have my own doubts, but they don't matter; the churches will make their own Jesus, a whole tribe of Jesuses, to suit their own prejudices. They'll find ways of twisting everything.

I used to ask myself who's in charge. I had to stop asking myself such unanswerable questions. They were not good for the head. Either you had faith or you had not? And if you did not, then you did not believe in God, or that there was a balance to the madness. A balance to the violence, a balance to the acts of people like Lenny Murphy. And if you had no faith, if you no longer believed in God, then you were not bound by the old sanctions that warned against violence. And if there was a God, then I believed that He would understand.

An absent Godhead is not enough. Hume's pendulum swings very heavily, I believed in so many things: in my country, in peace, in purification, in something I called mankind. Some of these I even believed in at the same time, if you can credit it.

My true love had slipped away. It started with a genuine love for my country and what I thought it stood for. But the Ulster I loved was changing fast, becoming a whore to activists and gut-less politicians. I'm not talking about some kind of nonsensical, flag-waving, Twelfth of July kind of patriotism. I'm not a guy who goes to church one day a week in order to absolve myself of the sins I committed on the other six. I loved my country. I lived it. I breathed it. Always did. That is why, when other guys my age were farting about, I joined the UVF. I wanted in.

I know some people will think I'm a psychopath, who want-ed any excuse to kill people. I grew up believing that there was some kind of absolute right and wrong. I grew up believing that principles and a man's word meant something. That's all gone now, filed under BULLSHIT.

The justice system has so profoundly betrayed this nation, there are only two choices left: watch the country go down in flames or fight back. But sitting by, waiting for politicians and lawyers to do the right thing, is not going to achieve it. Someone's got to stand up and say enough is enough.

Both sides have been portrayed as a bunch of illiterate, re-ligious fuck-ups, but that's not true; good people always out-number the bad, ten to one.

Face it, wherever Italians and Irish gather, both domineered by the Catholic Church, whether in Hell's Kitchen or Heaven's Basement, there is corruption and murder. It comes in finance, in politics, in flesh, black, white, scarlet, purple, beneath the coloured robes of office. My view is that the Catholic Church makes it easy to get away with all types of sin, by taking the power of God away from Him and giving it to Man.

A short verse written by John Milton in *Paradise Lost* (1667) sums it up:

> Here we may reign secure, and in my choice
> To reign is worth ambition, though in hell
> Better to reign in hell, than to serve in heaven.

• • •

The people of Ulster are left with two choices: 1) to turn to the Irish and their perennial obsessions with parochialism and bigotry, their antiquated laws on abortion, contraception and divorce, along with their deep hatred of women; 2) stay with the English and their obsessive secrecy, their institutionalised racism, their politics of greed and self-interest, their deep groundswell of intolerance, of populist chant, of naked, tabloid-driven, aggressive man-in the-street culture.

My time spent training and operating with MRF backing was one of the most challenging and exciting periods of my life, but it changed me forever. I went beyond being a person trying to defend my country. They taught me to kill. It was part of the training, part of the dehumanisation programme. It left me with a cold hard place where my conscience used to be. Something numb now lay in the place where my heart had been. The hearts of the old are hard, a mass of scars. Nothing could make it soft or supple again. Not prayer, not daily attendance at a church. I had caught expressions in my own eyes that said more than words: determination, conviction, a sort of weary holiness that served well enough for the day-to-day business of making sense of things. Rarely did I feel free to own up to the sheer thrill of it all.

It was only when I finished with active service that I realised what I had lost, what they had taken away from me. I would get it back eventually. Only now I suffer when anything with the slightest hint of the hand of human kindness reaches out its tentative fingers; whenever I see or hear anything remotely poignant, I am reduced to a quivering, tearful wreck. The hardness has gone, to be replaced with a remorse so deep I don't think it has a bottom to it.

I remember getting pissed out of my head one night after an operation and listening to Pink Floyd's *Dark Side of the Moon*. I thought they had discovered a map to the cosmos and the mind. Like some kind of treasure hunt, the meaning of life could be discovered from the lyrics, if you listened long enough, got pissed enough. Lying in bed, finding it hard to sleep (as usual) that night, I thought: what a useless, senseless waste this whole dirty scene is. I felt my throat back up. I couldn't stop thinking about the terrifying crimes, the conscienceless murders, I had seen.

I'm now a 50-odd-year-old-man; I have no wife, no children of my own. Why? Because, during those years when young men should be out enjoying themselves, looking for someone to settle down with, have a family and live in harmony with the world, I was engaged in a war of hatred. I gave almost ten years to the cause and know men who gave a lot longer. After my release from Long Kesh, I drifted with the wind. I couldn't be bothered with anything or anyone.

A kind of wilful inertia settled over me. Hours and days seemed to flash by while I did nothing but walk the streets and look at the sky. Sometimes, I simply lay on my bed and watched the light change as the sun moved slowly round me. One night, as I sat staring at the moon, it seemed as though it was an opening to another, better world. Better, because it would lead me somewhere other than the world in which I now felt myself something of a stranger – disorientated and adrift, physically and morally. This was not the world I had signed up for.

Nothing worked any more, the rules I had grown up with, abided by, no longer applied. Order and justice seemed to be quaint notions from another time and place.

I considered myself lucky to have been caught for a stupid crime and not something more serious. I couldn't get the young men out of my head who were still inside serving life sentences. Jesus, at 30 I was positively ancient compared to those young lads. Routine was a thing of the past. In the shadows behind our eyes hid the past we ran from, or pursued. Ordinary life had changed. I wasn't the same person I used to be. I never will be again.

They say time seems to pass more quickly as you grow older. They also say there's a good reason for that, that the brain measures time by how much of it there is to remember, so each year is a smaller proportion than the one before, of life to date. It's a sour little trick to be a victim of, because it means pleasure, however intense, grows ever more fleeting. There's a flip side to the trick: pain obeys the same rule.

If a man tramples all over his image of himself, something dies inside. They were rotting away from the centre, because they had compromised nearly every principle in which they believed. They should never have done that. They were doing the right thing for all the right reasons, with all the wrong consequences. Particularly when the man is afflicted with gangrene of the soul. There's a stench to gangrene and it gets into your nostrils.

Once violence laid its ugly hand on you, innocence was lost forever. It changed all of us. Politicians at every level of government have sent a clear message: hostility works. Mean is in. It's cool. The media give most airtime to whoever shouts the loudest. If you kill enough people, burn enough buildings, rob enough banks or threaten enough people, they'll give you what you want. Real violence is ugly. Real murder is a tragedy that family and friends never get over.

People sat in their living rooms watching the violence spill into their lives through their TV screens. Night after night, day after day, the bodies piled up. The ranting and raving got more and more intense. Volume. Impact. What you said mattered less than how loudly you said it. It seemed that the planet was spinning out of control. It seems to me there is no difference these days in what's right and what's wrong. Besides, no one cares any more.

I have dug into my subconscious, to bring back memories I had suppressed in the deepest recesses of my mind. But now that I have invoked them, in order to write this book, I'm not sure I can handle them a second time around. Music still makes things a little bit better. I'm in my mid fifties now, and music still helps. But only for a while; when it stops, it carries on in my brain. It never stops in there, one song after the other. I suspect I am slowly losing my marbles.

I think of events in the past very often, sometimes with tears in my eyes. In such a situation, you can become one of two things, a criminal or an insane person. Bad or mad. Mike once told us it would be hard to pull the trigger when someone is crying and pleading for his life, calling to his god to save him. Yet, it didn't really arise, as many poor victims were barely conscious when it was time for them to meet their god. Those that were, were probably praying for death to relieve their pain.

I am very tired; those who have to struggle will always have to pay the price. As the army saying goes, 'Sympathy is to be found in the dictionary, between shit and syphilis'. At the beginning, I walked the walk of the righteous, courage that came from the knowledge that God was with me, that I was doing the right thing.

Over the period I cover in my book, I met a lot of men whose minds appeared to work normally, but which were wired wrongly. Somewhere in the labyrinth of circuitry, wires were crossed that created a mental short circuit, which spluttered and flared in the darkest part of the human soul. It was a black place where logic could not survive. What kind of society creates men like that, where sanity was sucked into madness. A place where a rational mind entered at its own peril?

I think, like most of us who took part in the violence, we are now looking for a life in which we can escape our past. My past is attached to me like a mooring rope, the further I travel, the stronger I feel its pull. It is a shifting and elusive presence, but a palpable one. You are who you are and there's nothing you can do to change it. A lot of my memories are gone, but the worst ones and I sit together, sleep together. I spend my days with the ghosts of innocent people.

The thing most people don't understand, especially Americans, is that there will never be complete peace in Northern Ireland. The day of the gun and the bomb and the balaclava are over for the moment. We may stop slaughtering each other for a while, but nothing is going to change. In the Westminster elections in May 2005, the two extremist parties, the DUP and Sinn Féin, were in the ascendancy. The people are starting to polarise once again and the moderates are being squeezed out.

Isn't there only one truth? Yes, but if you look through someone else's glasses, the scene will be distorted. Everyone sees things in different ways. So who's right? Depends on how you see it. The only time a man really understands the reality of death, of the final pain, is the moment of his own.

The IRA produced a book, *Titghra*, to honour their dead; in it, there are more lies, contradictions and cover-ups regarding Republicans killed by Loyalists. They include Danny Cassidy, a 40-yearold Sinn Féin election worker, assassinated in April 1992 (in the book they call him an 'oglach', the Irish word for soldier, hence a PIRA volunteer); in 1991, Padraig O'Seanachain, another member of Sinn Féin and described as an 'oglach'; and Alan Lundy, another 'oglach', assassinated in West Belfast in May 1993.

This suggests two things: 1) that Loyalist paramilitaries had highly accurate information on their targets from whatever the MRF was calling itself at that time; 2) there was a policy to distance some victims of Loyalist terrorism from the IRA. There is a tribute to the Shankill bomber, Thomas 'Bootsy' Begley, who died along with nine Protestants, including two children, in an explosion in a fish shop, when his bomb went off prematurely.

Nothing is what it seems and the dirty tricks continue, 30 years on.

Winston Churchill described the country of Russia as 'an enigma inside a mystery, wrapped up inside a puzzle'. What we had been up against was a cornucopia of conspiracies, a jumble of conspiracies, wrapped up in more conspiracies. There were too many layers of collusion and connivance. Young men were sent to fight for their country and then betrayed, erased. They would say it was to protect them. What a joke. It was to protect the Government and the Army; to conceal what the Army had asked them to do in the name of patriotism.

When you go out on an operation your senses become razor-sharp. Why do you think all those World War II veterans can still sit round a table telling war stories from 60-odd years ago so vividly, when most of them can't remember a thing their wives said to them over the breakfast table that morning? I can recall almost every waking hour I was planning or carrying out an operation.

The exhaustion, strain and fear don't dull your senses; your brain has to work in overdrive to function.

Sometimes I would laugh out loud at the bleeding-heart commentators who said we were out of control. What the fuck did they know about it? We had lived through it, seen the death and destruction going on around us? But I am not marching any more and I am listening to some obscure song that says war isn't worth it, war is never worth it, and, even when it is worth it, it isn't worth it. In the end even war has to run up the white flag, surrender.

Remember, what is, isn't, and what isn't, is. The MRF never existed. There were no Loyalist death squads. The Army buried them for ever. It might enable you to understand the complex facts surrounding the secret, dirty, little war of Military Intelligence units.

Although at time the MRF appeared very amateurish – for example, sitting over drinks with a Fred and confiding in him about secret operations taking place, say The Four Square laundry service which resulted in a member of their group being shot dead – in our unit it was highly professional in all aspects, from training to operational capabilities. A lot of murders committed by MRF squads, protected by them, have never been solved. This is why a new team of retired detectives has been gathered to try and solve over 2,000 unsolved murders. It is doomed from the start. They will never find what has been deliberately erased. They might be able to discover who carried out murders that weren't done by MRF-protected squads, but in all probability they won't, as each killing could be ascribed to any number of squads.

The Provisionals found out how good the MRF was when a couple of operations almost destroyed the IRA with a subsequent loss of manpower and morale.

After a few drinks one evening in the Times Bar, Mike, Billy and I went to Billy's house with a couple of bottles of whiskey. Mike began to tell us about two operations that had taken place some time ago and had had the IRA running around like headless chickens. He said those operations had almost destroyed the Provos.

It involved a sting within the ranks of the Provos although Mike wouldn't divulge much more.

Apparently, agents working for them made public that top IRA men were fleecing the IRA's funds and lining their own pockets, to the tune of around £100,000. The IRA were forced to investigate the allegation, and a witch-hunt ensued with a lot of press coverage.

The second operation involved the placement of men in Crumlin Road Prison on a bogus charge where they started to spread the word that a lot of Provos were British informers. This caused a stink within the IRA's ranks, with men who were not informers subjected to rigorous interrogation about their activities. We were fascinated by all this covert activity and realised the MRF was up to its neck in virtually everything that was happening, as we had suspected. (The book, *The Dirty War*, proves these operations took place and goes into great detail.)

The Army has always been evasive when questioned about MRF activities. When the press asked a senior Army officer about the use of civilians, he refused to comment, describing it as 'getting into deep matters'. Deniability, as I outlined at the beginning, was paramount at all stages, and even if you could prove it, it would still be denied. That is why I'm trying to set the record straight now. I hope this book will give some people answers and information regarding some of these events, which occured when Loyalists had reached breaking point. From 1970 the IRA was on the offensive while we sat back and allowed the security forces to get on with imposing the rule of law on the IRA The important fact that must be taken into account is that Loyalists, in my view, only went on the offensive after two and a half years of taking whatever the IRA threw at us and when Stormont was abolished and Direct Rule was imposed. Enough was enough, was our feeling

• • •

There are bad people out there, doing bad things. The time has come to snap out of your numbness and recognise what's happening in this country. The killer is at the door. Are you going to open that door and let him in to murder your family and say there is nothing inherently bad about that action? No. You know it's right to defend your family against violence, against evil. Can we afford to let these men in to help govern our country? The truth is, they are already in and it's going to be very hard to remove them.

Each side had its share of brutal acts. Each side tried to outdo its counterpart's cruelty. At some stage, it had to reach the bottom and it eventually did. We reached that point in the 1990s; when Johnny Adair's C Company, UFF, was killing more Catholics than the Provos, killing Protestants was the turning-point. We enjoyed seeing the bad guys scared of the good guys. This was the way it was supposed to be. Or should it be the *really* bad guys scared of the other bad guys. I'll leave you to work that out.

But the whole damned world is fucked up these days, isn't it? No one cares what you see when you turn out the light, or what you see when you leave it on. For that matter, they don't care if you dress in ladies' underwear or beat the wife or hump the pet Labrador. Everyone deserves privacy, except citizens who get laid out on steel tables, with some white-coat peeling off their face. No privacy there.

A man once told me that one of the keys to life is appreciating things when they happen, because they never come again. I had a great time at war, in fact I nearly cried when it was over. But, I had developed a phobia that I would fall in love with combat, which I did, glued to the television screen whenever violence broke out all over the world. Death and destruction appeal to me. When I watch it, I become another version of me; I am a stranger to myself.

They say to be careful of the bullet that has your name on it, as it will always get you in the end. It wasn't the named bullet I worried about, it was the one marked, TO WHOM IT MAY CONCERN. As for old operators, many have died. And the ones who don't have a terminal illness are raving alcoholics, and the ones that have kicked the booze are on Prozac. If you ask me, was it all worth it? the resounding answer is NO.

Why can't all the people on this planet realise that religions, colour, creed and money shouldn't matter? We should all consider ourselves earthlings, tear down the borders, and stop pouring billions and billions into wars, especially when we see so much suffering, and fellow earthlings dying from starvation or drinking polluted water.

I remember sitting one night in a club waiting for the word to go. There were a couple of men from another team with us. One of them kept cocking and uncocking his gun. The noise was infuriating; I wanted to concentrate on the operation and my role. The CO came in and shouted, 'Right, lads, who has the balls? Let's get this fucking show on the road.'

Was he crazy? Of course he was crazy; anyone who has men sitting beside him with guns is crazy. We were all mad, we had to be, madness got you through it. Some words by Pink Floyd sum it up, I think, 'I've been mad for fucking years.'

I could not ignore the madness. It broke against my mind. Some people have said that nothing can make you feel more alive than having death at your elbow. A gun has one purpose and one purpose only, to kill. Anything else is bullshit. Damaged lives aren't easily rebuilt, although many have laughter lines still there in spite of the troubles, and worry lines because of them.

I will close with the words I ended the prologue with as I feel the words are relevant to both sides of the conflict

FOR GOD AND ULSTER, IF THERE IS SUCH A PERSON AS GOD MAY HE FORGIVE US ALL
FOR WHAT WE DID IN HIS NAME.
AMEN.

THIS BOOK IS A WARNING TO THE BRITISH GOVERNMENT.

YOUR TREACHERY IN FORCING THE PEOPLE OF ULSTER TO ACCEPT SINN FEIN/IRA INTO GOVERNING THE COUNTRY, WHICH THEY HAVE TRIED TO DESTROY FOR DECADES IS SUMMED UP
IN THE WORDS OF NUMBERS 32: VERSE 23 FROM THE BIBLE

BUT IF YE WILL NOT DO SO, BEHOLD,
YE HAVE SINNED

AGAINST THE LORD:
AND BE SURE YOUR SINS
WILL FIND YOU OUT

COME CLEAN PRIME MINISTER AND TELL THE
PEOPLE THAT WHAT IS CONTAINED IN THIS
BOOK IS THE TRUTH, WHICH THE BRITISH
GOVERNMENT HAS REFUSED TO DO SINCE THE
QUESTION WAS FIRST ASKED. WHAT ACTIVE ROLE
DID BRITISH MILITARY INTELLIGENCE PLAY IN
THE CONFLICT AND HOW DID THEY COLLUDE
WITH LOYALISTS?